CHILDREN'S ACCESS TO JUSTICE

CHILDREN'S ACCESS TO JUSTICE

A Critical Assessment

Edited by
Mona Paré
Mariëlle Bruning
Thierry Moreau
Caroline Siffrein-Blanc

INTERSENTIA
Cambridge – Antwerp – Chicago

Intersentia Ltd
8 Wellington Mews
Wellington Street | Cambridge
CB1 1HW | United Kingdom
Tel: +44 1223 736 170
Email: mail@intersentia.co.uk
www.intersentia.com | www.intersentia.co.uk

Distribution for the UK and
Rest of the World (incl. Eastern Europe)
NBN International
1 Deltic Avenue, Rooksley
Milton Keynes MK13 8LD
United Kingdom
Tel: +44 1752 202 301 | Fax: +44 1752 202 331
Email: orders@nbninternational.com

Distribution for Europe
Lefebvre Sarrut Belgium NV
Hoogstraat 139/6
1000 Brussels
Belgium
Tel: +32 (0)800 39 067
Email: mail@intersentia.be

Distribution for the USA and Canada
Independent Publishers Group
Order Department
814 North Franklin Street
Chicago, IL 60610
USA
Tel: +1 800 888 4741 (toll free) | Fax: +1 312 337 5985
Email: orders@ipgbook.com

Children's Access to Justice. A Critical Assessment

This book is also made available in French as *L'accès des enfants à la justice : bilan critique*, published by Dalloz in 2022.

Artwork on cover: Tanor / Shutterstock

ISBN 978-1-83970-197-9
D/2022/7849/13
NUR 820

British Library Cataloguing in Publication Data. A catalogue record for this book is available from the British Library.

ACKNOWLEDGEMENTS

This volume results from a partnership entitled *Children's Access to Justice and Vulnerability* involving researchers and institutions across four countries, including the University of Ottawa, Leiden University, Université catholique de Louvain, Aix-Marseille University and the University of Bordeaux. It could not have happened without the active collaboration of all partners involved. We are grateful to the Social Sciences and Humanities Research Council of Canada (SSHRC) for funding this partnership development project.

In particular, this book is a product of the conference organized by the University of Ottawa's Interdisciplinary Research Laboratory on the Rights of the Child (IRLRC) entitled *Children's Access to and Participation in Justice*, held online on 21 and 22 May 2021, with the help of the partnership's researchers and collaborators.

We thank all those who contributed to the conference's very rich exchanges, and especially the authors who wrote contributions for this volume. We acknowledge the following for their financial or logistical support, contributing to the success of the conference and the ensuing publication: SSHRC, *Accès au droit et à la justice* (ADAJ), the University of Ottawa and the Civil Law Section and Human Rights Research and Education Centre, the Embassy of France, Canada, whose contribution helped to ensure that the contributions written in French could be translated into English. We are grateful for the collaboration between Intersentia and Dalloz, allowing for the publication of all the contributions in English and in French. We also thank all students who helped along the way, with a special thanks to Myrto Giannakopoulou, LL.L. candidate at the University of Ottawa, who helped us to finalize the contributions for publication.

Finally, thank you to Ann-Christin Maak-Scherpe from Intersentia for taking on this project, and Rebecca Moffat for overseeing the production of the book.

CONTENTS

LIST OF CONTRIBUTORS

Nicholas (Nick) Bala has been a professor of law at Queen's University in Kingston, Canada since 1980, focussing his work on issues related to children and families involved in the justice system. Much of his research is interdisciplinary, and he has undertaken collaborative projects with psychologists, social workers, criminologists, and health professionals. He has published extensively, and his work is often quoted by all levels of court in Canada, including the Supreme Court of Canada, and has also been cited by courts in the United States, Britain, New Zealand, Singapore, and Australia. Professor Bala was elected a Fellow of the Royal Society of Canada in 2013, and in 2019 became a Distinguished University Professor at Queen's University.

Rachel Birnbaum Ph.D., RSW, LL.M., is a professor at King's University College at Western University in London, Ontario. Her primary areas of teaching and research focus on children and families, social work ethics and the law, and research methods. She has presented nationally and internationally on parenting assessments, child legal representation, children's participation in family disputes, and on the intersection between law and social work. She is a member of The Royal Society of Canada, College of New Scholars, Artists, and Scientists, and recipient of several research awards.

Apollonia Bolscher is a lecturer and researcher at the Child Law Department of Leiden Law School. She teaches Children's Rights and Family Law in the Dutch LL.B. program and the LL.M. Child Law program. She publishes on child participation in legal proceedings and children's rights issues. She recently completed a multi-disciplinary research project commissioned by the Dutch Ministry of Justice and Safety about the procedural position – including the right to be heard – in family and child protection proceedings.

Philippe Bonfils is a professor at Aix-Marseille University, where he is Honorary Dean of the Faculty of Law and Political Science, and a member of the Private Law and Criminal Sciences Laboratory. He is a lawyer at the

Bar of Marseille. His law practice, teaching, and research focus on criminal law and minors in criminal justice – as victims and as young offenders. He is co-author, with Adeline Gouttenoire, of *Droit des mineurs* (2021, 3rd edition), published by Dalloz.

Marine Braun is an independent expert on access to justice and juvenile justice issues. Formerly a lawyer at the Brussels Bar (Belgium), and project manager for civil society organisations (Defence for Children International) and international organisations (United Nations – UNDP, IOM), over the past 10 years she has contributed to reforming and improving justice models by promoting access to and quality of justice systems for children in several European and African countries. Her current initiative consists of the development of a unique practical tool that identifies language and attitude techniques for professionals in the justice system.

Mariëlle Bruning is a full professor of Child Law at Leiden Law School. She is the founder of the Leiden Child Law Department and the program director of the Dutch LL.M. Child Law and teaches Child Protection in the LL.M. Advanced Studies in International Children's Rights program. Her research focuses on youth care, child protection, children in alternative care, violence against children, child participation in legal proceedings, and children's rights. Bruning is an honorary deputy (juvenile) judge at the Amsterdam District Court.

Adeline Gouttenoire is a professor at the University of Bordeaux. She is the director of CERFAPS (European Research Centre for Family, Insurance, Personal, and Health Law) and of the Institute of Minors. She is president of the Gironde Departmental Observatory for Child Protection. She publishes on family law, child protection, and children's human rights. She is co-author with Philippe Bonfils of *Droit des mineurs* (2021, 3rd edition), published by Dalloz.

Jean-Frédéric (J-F) Hübsch is a Ph.D. student at the University of Ottawa's Faculty of Law and a member of the University's Interdisciplinary Research Laboratory on the Rights of the Child. His research focuses on integrating children's rights into education law, with a particular focus on how rights-respecting pedagogies can inform education law and policy. He is a licensee of the Law Society of Ontario and from 2015 to 2020 was counsel with the Office of the Ontario Ombudsman, where his work focused on education law, municipal law, administrative tribunals, and French-language services. He is an active member of the Ontario Bar Association's Education Law and Child and Youth Law sections.

Fanny Jolicoeur is a doctoral candidate in law at the Université du Québec à Montréal. She holds a certificate in journalism as well as a bachelor's and master's degree in social work. Her current research interests focus on issues related to Aboriginal governance of youth protection and more specifically on the point of view of the Innu children of Uashat mak Mani Utenam on the concept of the child's interest. She is the research co-ordinator of project 14 *Accès au Droit et à la Justice* (ADAJ). Finally, she has worked as a social worker for over 15 years.

Kamel Khiari has a doctorate in law (LL.D.). He is a lawyer and associate professor of law and economy at Sainte-Anne University (Nova Scotia, Canada).

Ursula Kilkelly (Ph.D.) is a professor of law at University College Cork in Ireland, where she is Head of the College of Business and Law. Her expertise is in international children's rights law and youth justice. She has published several monographs, edited collections, and over 60 journal articles in these areas. She is co-editor, with Professor Stefaan Pleysier of KU Leuven, of *Youth Justice*, the Sage journal. In 2010, she founded the Child Law Clinic, which provides research services to those litigating children's rights. She is chairperson of the Board of Management of Ireland's national facility for the detention of children referred by the courts.

Blandine Mallevaey is a professor at the Faculty of Law of the Catholic University of Lille (France). She is holder of the Chair 'Childhood and Families', at the Centre for Research on the Relationship between Risks and Law. She specializes in civil and criminal law concerning persons, family, and children. She created and directs the Master 2 in Child and Family Law as well as the University Diploma in the Rights and Best Interests of the Child. Since 2020, she has been a member of the Council of Europe's working group on the protection and best interests of children whose parents are separating. She co-authored the report *Feasibility study of the protection of the best interest of the child in parental separations proceedings* (2021) with Nuala Mole.

Deborah McMillan is Commissioner for Children and Young People in Jersey. She is a former Director for Children's Services in Wales and worked for the Welsh Government as a professional advisor working with ministers to develop expertise around Adverse Childhood Experiences, and supported a cross-government policy agenda around well-being and poverty. Throughout her career, Deborah has been involved in developing early intervention and prevention, and shaping the way services are delivered for children, young people, and their families. As the first commissioner in Jersey, Deborah is putting in place the building blocks to make long-lasting change and to make life better for the island's children and young people.

Coline Moreau has a master's degree in law from the UCLouvain in Belgium. She is currently a full time Ph.D candidate in Criminology at the Social Sciences Faculty of the University of Ottawa. She is member of the Canada Research Chair in Legal Traditions and Penal Rationality directed by Professor A. Pires. She conducts her research in the areas of criminal law, criminology and human rights. She is particularly interested in the topics of sentencing and enforcement as well as innovation and obstacles to innovation in criminal law reform. In addition, she conducts research into children's law concerning the effectiveness of children's rights. She is also invested in the discovery of leadership and has been assistant for a leadership course at the University of Ottawa.

Thierry Moreau has a doctorate in law, is an extraordinary professor at the UCLouvain, and has been a lawyer in Belgium for more than 30 years. He teaches at the university and practises at the bar in the fields of children's rights, youth welfare and protection law, criminal law, prison law and ethics. He is the director of the *Centre interdisciplinaire des droits de l'enfant* (Interdisciplinary Centre for the Rights of the Child). After having been a member and then president for more than 20 years of the Commission of deontology of youth assistance of the *Communauté française* of Belgium, he is currently president of the Advisory Committee relating to the detention centre for minors of this same Community. He is regularly consulted as an expert in his fields of specialization by political bodies. He has written several books and articles on these subjects.

Eléazar Michel Nkoué holds a doctorate in international law from the University of Grenoble Alpes. He is an assistant lecturer at the University of Yaoundé II, Faculty of Legal and Political Sciences in Cameroon. He is a member of the Center for studies and research in international and community law. His research focuses on environmental law, the rights of Indigenous peoples, human rights, and international law.

Mona Paré is a full professor at the University of Ottawa, Faculty of Law, Civil Law Section, and Vice-Dean for Graduate Studies. She holds a Ph.D. in Law from Queen Mary College, University of London. She is a founding member and director of the Interdisciplinary Research Laboratory of the

Rights of the Child. Her research and teaching concentrate on children's rights and international human rights. She is leading a partnership project on children's access to justice, funded by the Social Sciences and Humanities Research Council of Canada (SSHCR), which has led to the publication of this book.

Malika Saher is a lawyer-mediator at the Hochelaga and Garage à musique community social pediatrics centres, which are administered by the Fondation Dr Julien. The mission of the latter is to make community-based social pediatrics care and services accessible to the greatest number of children in vulnerable situations. She is also currently an LL.M. candidate.

Caroline Siffrein-Blanc is *maître de conferences* in private law and criminal sciences at the University of Aix-Marseille, Faculty of Law and Political Science. She is a member of the Private Law and Criminal Sciences Laboratory. She specializes in family and children's law, and her teaching and research focus on filiation, the evolution of families, the place of the child in the separation of his or her parents, the voice of the child in court and the protection of the child in educational assistance. She publishes widely in these areas.

Daisy Smeets is an assistant professor of Forensic Family Science at the Institute of Education and Child Studies at Leiden University. Her focus is on pedagogical insights regarding legal and forensic procedures, such as the well-being of foster children after out-of-home placements, or how the police talk to children in sexual abuse cases. Recently, she collaborated on a multi-disciplinary research project about the procedural position – including the right to be heard – in family and child protection proceedings.

Caterina Tempesta, B.A., LL.B., LL.M., is senior counsel at the Office of the Children's Lawyer (OCL) of the Ontario Ministry of the Attorney General where she provides legal representation to children and youth at all levels of court in Canada. She has frequently written and presented on issues relating to children and the law and contributed to the development of the Canadian Bar Association's Child Rights Toolkit, a resource for legal professionals to better understand and implement a child's rights-based approach in practice. In 2019, she obtained her LL.M. in Advanced Studies in International Children's Rights from Leiden University.

INTRODUCTION

A Critical Review of Access to Justice for Children

Mona PARÉ, Mariëlle BRUNING, Thierry MOREAU
and Caroline SIFFREIN-BLANC

Following the adoption of the Convention on the Rights of the Child (CRC) in 1989, it is no longer possible to exclude children from addressing the justice issues that affect them. They are recognized as having the right to express themselves on matters that concern them, in all proceedings in which they have an interest. Thirty years on, how far have we come? Are the rights that are recognized effective? How are they implemented? What purposes do they serve? Is justice child-friendly? Are children to be found in the justice system? Now is the time for a critical review.

Children's access to justice suffers from the ailments affecting access to justice for all, such as involving a lack of information, cost, the shortcomings of legal aid, the complexity of the steps and formalities, the slow pace of proceedings, etc. In addition, children encounter difficulties linked to their specificities. In thinking about justice, no priority is given to adapting it to them. Conceived for adults, applied by adults, the judicial system does not primarily offer justice adapted to the differences that distinguish children from adults.

Over the last decade we nevertheless see initiatives emerging at the international level that question this situation. Prominent among these have been the Guidelines of the Committee of Ministers of the Council of Europe on child-friendly justice (2010),[1] the Report of the United Nations High Commissioner for Human Rights (2013),[2] and General Comment No. 12

1 Council of Europe, Guidelines of the Committee of Ministers of the Council of Europe on child-friendly justice (2010), <https://rm.coe.int/16804b92f6>.

2 UN High Commissioner for Human Rights, (2013), Access to justice for children: report of the United Nations High Commissioner for Human Rights, [16.12.2013], Doc. UN A/HRC/25/35.

of the Committee on the Rights of the Child, on the right of the child to be heard (2009).[3] These texts highlight the paths to be followed to improve the effectiveness of children's right to access the justice system. However, it is also necessary that States decide to make this a concrete priority.

An inter-university partnership was formed in 2017 to reflect on those issues. It brings together researchers from the University of Ottawa in Canada, the University of Leiden in the Netherlands, the Catholic University of Louvain in Belgium, and the Universities of Bordeaux and Aix-Marseille in France. The partnership was possible thanks to a grant from the Social Sciences and Humanities Research Council of Canada (SSHRC).[4] Within a networked logic of collaborative effort, the research teams decided to emphasize children's access to and participation in justice, within the proceedings that fall under 'child protection'.[5] The choice of this research field is explained in particular by the limited number of works addressing access to justice for children in this field. The research on access to justice has, until now, chiefly concentrated on children within the criminal justice system. Nevertheless, every day many more children are confronted with child protection proceedings.

The common feature of the research conducted in each country is Article 12 of the CRC, which provides as follows:

1. States Parties shall assure to the child who is capable of forming his or her own views the right to express those views freely in all matters affecting the child, the views of the child being given due weight in accordance with the age and maturity of the child.
2. For this purpose the child shall in particular be provided the opportunity to be heard in any judicial and administrative proceedings affecting the child, either directly, or through a representative or an appropriate body, in a manner consistent with the procedural rules of national law.[6]

---

3 Committee on the Rights of the Child, General Comment No. 12 [2009]: The right of the child to be heard, [20.07.2009], UN Doc. CRC/C/GC/12.

4 In addition to the grant from SSHRC, we acknowledge a contribution by the Embassy of France in Canada towards the translation of contributions from French to English.

5 This term will be used in the contributions for uniformity, while recognizing that different terminology may be used in different countries.

6 Convention on the Rights of the Child, General Assembly Resolution 44/25 of 20.11.1989, entry into force 02.09.1990, Article 12.

The objective of the research was twofold: first, to discover the concrete mechanisms used in each State to implement children's right to be heard and to participate in the justice system. Subsequently, to take an interest in the viewpoint and experience of the concerned parties on listening to and participation of children in the field of child protection, including those of professionals and children.

To this end, in each of the four countries the teams undertook qualitative research studies, primarily using interview techniques or the administration of questionnaires. The respondents included – depending on the teams – magistrates, social workers, lawyers specialized in defending minors, and young adults and/or children. While the legislative and judicial mechanisms may at times be very different, and while the research methods and the target population were not identical in the work of each team, it is interesting to note that generally speaking, the results converge with regard to the obstacles to full effectiveness of children's rights to express themselves freely on issues that concern them in the field of child protection, as highlighted below.

The research findings were presented during a conference organized by the Interdisciplinary Research Laboratory on the Rights of the Child (IRLRC) of the University of Ottawa. Faced with the restrictions imposed by the COVID-19 pandemic, it was planned for May 2020 but postponed to 20 and 27 May 2021, and held by videoconference.

This conference was also an opportunity to compare the research results with the work of other researchers from eight different countries working on questions in connection with children's access to and participation in the justice system, in areas other than child protection, and/or on specific thematic areas. Divided into four sessions, with each introduced by a plenary presentation, the conference took the form of discussions between researchers. The plenary presentations addressed: the risks of perverse effects from the participation of children in the justice system (Thierry Moreau); examination of the growing international effort for child-friendly justice (Ursula Kilkelly); access to justice for children in Canada (Nicholas Bala); and the paths to overcome hurdles and become more inclusive (Ton Liefaard). The topics addressed during the panel discussions bore on: the parties involved in the justice system; international justice; civil and criminal proceedings; the institutions that have a role in justice for children; particular attention to specific groups of children; as well as systemic barriers to children's access to justice. The conference conclusions, presented by Adeline Gouttenoire, offered concrete suggestions for the effective implementation of Article 12 of the CRC.

This book reflects many topics that were discussed during the conference. It is divided into four parts. The first part offers a synopsis of the results of the research carried out in the context of the partnership. The two following parts contain the contributions of the other researchers who contributed during the conference: the second examines the voice and place of children within various proceedings, and the third addresses obstacles to access to justice, and methods, and projects facilitating it. The fourth part offers thoughts and conclusions that open the way to future research efforts and to action for the benefit of children.

Part I begins with the contribution of *Adeline Gouttenoire* and *Caroline Siffrein-Blanc*. Through a questionnaire and individual meetings, the research team collected the opinions of various professionals (magistrates, lawyers, children's aid staff) with regard to the application of Article 12 of the Convention on the Rights of the Child in the area of child protection. The responses obtained and the interviews held made it possible to bring to light different professional practices and visions on the issue of hearing the child in child protection. The contribution aims to put into perspective the theoretical statements and practical viewpoints of the professionals on the implementation and effective enjoyment of children's right to be heard. The professionals' disagreements, which are sometimes very pronounced, illustrate the extent to which the subject is both stirring and complex. *Mariëlle Bruning* and her colleagues *Daisy Smeets* and *Apollonia Bolscher* undertook a similar research project in the Netherlands. After setting out the state of the law, this multidisciplinary research team shares with us the experiences and opinions of the professionals, collected through questionnaires and interviews with judges, lawyers, social workers, guardians *ad litem*, and staff of the child and youth law centres. The experiences of the youth and their parents are likewise included, based on questionnaires. This setting in context of numerous opinions emphasizes the contrasts that cut across the practice of the hearing of the child, and especially how the various actors experience this. One of the main conclusions is the importance of direct hearing by the judge, as underlined by the young people. The authors conclude with a series of suggestions aimed at improving implementation of the right of the child to participate in family and protection proceedings. In Belgium, *Coline Moreau* and *Thierry Moreau* conducted semi-structured interviews with young people who have had experience in child protection proceedings. The research objective was to spotlight realities present but unnoticed in application of Article 12 of the CRC. The research findings question the methods implemented for the hearing of young people. Just like in the research undertaken in the Netherlands, young people have a view of their hearing that is different from that of the professionals and of their parents. Even though the adults recognize the importance of hearing children as a way of taking in their views, the young people do not feel listened to, and indicate that the presence of the parents is inhibiting. The research of *Mona Paré* in Quebec, Canada, was undertaken with judges of the juvenile court, social workers representing the Director of Youth Protection, and children who have had experience in court. The research aimed to set out on the one hand the scope and form of children's participation in the proceedings, and on the other hand to assess the risks and benefits of children's presence in court. She also questions the pertinence of formal testimony as a means of hearing children. This research highlights that practice is not always clearly framed by the law, and that professionals' attitudes are very diverse with regard to the participation of children in judicial proceedings. She concludes with suggestions to improve current practices, for children to have greater opportunities for participation and to be more respectful of their rights.

Despite the differences in terms of methods, these research efforts allow us to draw useful comparisons between the various legal systems regarding children's place within the justice system. The research highlights in particular differences in relation to the conditions under which children get access to justice (as a full-fledged party, through hearing or giving testimony), the age from which the child may enter the courtroom in their own right, the place and duties of the child's lawyer, etc. A comparison of legislation alone is insufficient, as is demonstrated by this research. Listening to the professionals is an absolutely necessary complement, as is listening to the children, especially as it makes it possible to bring to the fore a different approach to the aims of hearing children and the implementation methods to be promoted.

Part II is devoted to research efforts that have to do with the participation of children in other kinds of proceedings, beyond child protection. The contribution of *Blandine Mallevaey* deals with French family law, emphasizing the differences between whether proceedings concerning the child have or have not been brought before a family court judge. The author demonstrates the difference between access to justice and the right to participate. Since the child is not a party to the family proceedings, they are deprived of all access to the family court judge, in the absence of a proceeding already brought before them.[7] On the other

[7] They/them are used instead of he and she throughout this book as gender inclusive pronouns.

hand, if an action is initiated, the right to participate in the proceedings is recognized via the mechanism of hearing them in court. Nevertheless, the author criticizes the various obstacles to such access to the judge. *Rachel Birnbaum* and *Nicholas Bala* present the results of their research over the course of several years, bearing on children's participation in family proceedings in the various provinces of Canada, which have laws and practices that vary in this area. The authors assess the advantages and disadvantages of the various methods for children's participation in these proceedings. They likewise note the obstacles that children encounter, in a quasi-systematic way, in the various systems. Their research demonstrates that children want to be involved in decision-making that concerns them.

The contribution of *Philippe Bonfils* addresses the place of children's views in criminal proceedings in France. The author explains that access to criminal justice for minors appears different depending on whether we consider minors as perpetrators of offences or as victims. Regarding child offenders, the issue is that of knowing how criminal justice will take account of their specificity – in particular with the adoption of a Minors' Code. In the case of minors who are victims, the issue is that of allowing minors to have their voices heard, notwithstanding their age, their legal incapacity, and the trauma resulting from the infraction. Whether involving juvenile offenders or victims, the author describes improvements in French law that allow for adaptation and better access to children. With a more critical stance, *Deborah McMillan*, the Commissioner for Children and Young People for the Bailiwick of Jersey, examines the legislative provisions and attitudes of the professionals on this Channel Island in relation to youth criminal justice. The author's professional experience and research lead her to conclude that the legislation, as well as structural and cultural elements, prevent the application of a justice adapted to minors who are in conflict with the law. There is thus a lack of compliance with the CRC.

The contribution of *Jean-Frédéric Hübsch* is interesting in that it deals with the participation of children in a conflict resolution process outside judicial proceedings, examining the place of children in administrative procedures involving school discipline in the province of Ontario in Canada. He shows the lack of procedural guarantees recognized for children in the disciplinary proceedings and then addresses alternative processes that could replace these disciplinary proceedings, looking to improve respect for the child's right to equity and to promote discipline of a new kind.

Ursula Kilkelly examines children's access to international justice. She demonstrates that, even though the Guidelines adopted by the Council of Europe constitute a tool that was conceived in the first instance to be implemented in domestic law, they are also very useful at the international level. Nevertheless, she finds that international justice is still not widely accessible to children. Among the numerous barriers to overcome are children's lack of knowledge of their rights, a shortfall in training of law professionals, and the rule of the exhaustion of domestic remedies for international complaints about children's rights. In this context, the author regrets the lack of effectiveness and the mismatch between international remedies and the specificities of children.

Part III invites a more specific examination of obstacles to children's access to justice and of certain avenues for solution. Two contributions deal with particular challenges that children encounter in countries in transition in access to justice. *Kamel Khiari* questions the official national statements and positions that proclaim children's right to access to justice in these States. He underlines the formal character of these texts, and their ineffectiveness. He points out a series of difficulties for developing countries that may prevent or hinder children's access to and participation in justice, and researches avenues for a solution that might be brought to bear on them. In turn, *Eléazar Michel Nkoué* offers a concrete example of this type of difficulty by depicting the situation for children's access to justice in Cameroon, where several legal instruments have been adopted providing measures for access to the justice system for minors. He nevertheless demonstrates that the effectiveness of these instruments is lacking, at least for part of the population – namely indigenous people. They are marginalized and face great challenges in accessing justice. According to the author, the problems are not so much of a legal and technical nature, but of an anthropological, socio-political, and economic nature.

Several contributions examine methods and projects that could advance or improve children's access to justice and their participation in the process. *Marine Braun* demonstrates that a variety of communication techniques may be conducive to taking children's opinions into consideration. As she sees it, it behooves the professionals to challenge themselves and to get training in these new techniques, insomuch as the children teach us that they are dissatisfied with communication with the adults in the judicial arena. These various techniques are about more than verbal exchange between the child and the adult, bearing also on the attitude of the adult towards the child, which includes respect, empathy, and trust in the child's opinions. *Caterina Tempesta* looks particularly at the role played by the child's lawyer, which, she argues, is crucial. Lawyers appear as an interface between the child and the adult world. At the end of a critical analysis of the legal methods through which children's opinions gain access to the court (guardian *ad litem*, *amicus curiae*, advocate) the author considers that legal representation by a lawyer is the most appropriate model for fostering the effective participation of children in family court proceedings, and is the most respectful of the rights of the child. The contribution of *Malika Saher* bears on a particular population category made up of children who attend a Community Social Pediatrics Centre. She collected the accounts by the latter of their experiences in connection with the courts, in the context of youth protection proceedings. One of the strong points of social pediatrics lies in the working method, which is centred on the needs, interests and fundamental rights of children from vulnerable backgrounds. The children are considered experts in their situations, and bearers of solutions guiding the doctors, social workers, lawyer mediators, and therapists in their work. It is noted that they are equipped with their rights, and realize their capacity to have a positive effect on their situation and their environment. The collaborative authoring of the contribution – together with children – provides a perfect example of this. The contribution of *Fanny Jolicoeur* presents a new way of giving children a voice. Her research focuses on children who are seldom heard: indigenous children. She presents a participatory research method for questioning indigenous youth on their views of the child's best interests: *Photovoice*. By asking the children to express their vision of the best interests of the child – by means of taking photos and making comments on them – the researcher brings to the fore aspects of reality to which verbal exchange gains access only with great difficulty. The method would thus make it possible to implement participatory research that looks to provide a route to access to justice for indigenous children.

Lastly, in Part IV, the contribution of *Thierry Moreau* appears as a counterpoint. It cautions to the risks of abuses and of negative effects of children's access to the justice system. If taking children's opinions into consideration is unquestionably an advance, one also has to wonder about the aims that it serves. There is a next stage beyond the rights of the child that translates into demands and responsibilities weighing on the adult in the way they act when they allow the child to become an actor in the judicial arena. Finally, the conclusion presented by *Adeline Gouttenoire* recognizes the diversity of implementation of children's participatory rights, which is necessary given the different types of procedures. Yet, she recognizes certain constant features that allow for general recommendations, and concludes with a call for harmonization of practices.

Whether involving investigations undertaken by the researchers from the network, or contributions from the other participants, all highlight that there is still a long way to go to make the child a full-fledged subject of justice. Indeed, one cannot focus solely on the legal instruments. How they are implemented is at least as decisive. And yet, it needs to be well noted that while numerous legal instruments today guarantee the rights of the child, the justice systems – judicial or otherwise – have been designed and implemented with an adult logic. Legal instruments have properly introduced some adaptations to children, but they remain designed and built in accordance with a justice system meant for adults. Law systems have not yet made the Copernican Revolution breakthrough that would consist in thinking and applying justice starting from children, who – let us recall – are at the only life stage that all human beings experience. This book demonstrates that a movement is nevertheless taking shape in this sense, even though it is very far from having been completed. Increasingly, professionals working in the justice system sense the interest in putting children at the heart of the justice process, and adapting the latter to the differences that distinguish them from adults – whether the distinguishing factors are common to all children, or particular to certain categories of them. Many contributions have underscored the responsibility of the adult world in this regard, particularly in its manner of applying the legal instruments, which represent merely a doorway that opens onto a field to invest with new practices. The challenge is before us, since, as the adage reminds us, actions speak louder than words. Let us hope that this publication may contribute to keeping the fire burning in the boiler of the train travelling towards a truly child-friendly justice. We owe it to children. In the time of the pandemic and of the many ecological, social, and economic challenges, it is necessary to support our children in a new approach. Ignoring this necessity will leave children with a wasted legacy that will hardly serve as a basis for a more respectful world for everyone.

PART I

CHILDREN'S ACCESS TO JUSTICE IN CHILD PROTECTION PROCEEDINGS

THE PRACTICE OF HEARING THE CHILD IN CHILD PROTECTION PROCEEDINGS IN FRANCE

Caroline SIFFREIN-BLANC and Adeline GOUTTENOIRE

1. INTRODUCTION

Since the beginning of child protection in France, created by Order No. 58/1301 of 23 December 1958, the children's judge (JE) has an obligation to hear the minor prior to ordering protection measures. The objective was to consider the minor as a concerned party in the proceedings, not only by acknowledging their status as a party, but also by eliciting their perspective on the difficulties they were going through within their family, by observing their behaviour in the presence of their parents, or by seeking their buy-in, as much as that of their parents, to the protection measure.[1] Stated unambiguously right from the start, the principle of hearing the child in protection proceedings ensures adherence by French legislation in this area with the requirements of the Convention on the Rights of the Child (CRC).[2]

---

1 M. CREBASSA, 'L'audition de l'enfant par le juge aux affaires familiales et le juge des enfants' (2009) *AJF*, p. 328. E. DURAND, 'Parole de l'enfant: Brèves réflexions d'un juge des enfants sur l'audition en assistance éducative' (2014) *AJF*, p. 27.

2 Articles 9 and 12 of the CRC. Under the influence of the CRC, the Decree of 15.03.2020 replaced the age criterion with the notion of 'discernment'.

The general principle of hearing the child has been recognized within the Civil Code and by the Law of 8 January 1993.[3] A true right of the child to be heard in proceedings concerning them was later enshrined in Article 388(1) of the Civil Code[4] by the Law of 5 March 2007.[5] Under French law, the hearing of the child in judicial proceedings rests on two separate arrangements: one under ordinary law, grounded in Article 388(1) of the Civil Code, and the other by special instruments, in particular those on child protection,[6] but also with regard to emancipation[7] or adoption.[8]

In the context of taking the child into care prior to or following a court order for child protection, Article L. 223(4) of the Code of Social Welfare and Families provides that, generally speaking, the child social welfare department (ASE) examines with the minor any decision concerning them and obtains their opinion. In addition, Article L. 223(1)(1)(5) of the Code of Social Welfare and Families provides that the minor must participate in the preparation of their 'plan for the child', in line with mechanisms adapted to their age and degree of maturity.

Concerning the legal proceedings for child protection, the mechanisms for hearing the child are set out by Article 1182(2) of the Code of Civil Procedure (CCP).[9] Implementation of this legislation is the subject of case law of the Court of Cassation, which gives us an idea of its reach. Nevertheless, until our research no study had addressed the practice of hearing minors in child protection, while such research efforts have been carried out regarding the hearing of the child by the family court judge (JAF).[10]

Qualitative research was thus conducted in 2019 regarding the hearing of the child by the JE. Using a questionnaire with 44 questions,

---

3 Law No. 93-22 of 08.01.1993, amending the Civil Code regarding civil status, the family and children's rights, and instituting the family court judge, Official Gazette, 09.01.1993.

4 Article 388-1 of the Civil Code.

5 Law No. 2007-293 of 05.03.2007, reforming child protection, JO, 06.03.2007. Decree No. 2009 572, 20.05.2009, pursuant to the hearing of the child in judicial proceedings, JO, 24.05.2009, p. 8649.

6 See Articles 1182 and 1189 of the Code of Civil Procedure (CCP).

7 Article 413-2 of the Civil Code.

8 Law No. 2016-297, JO No. 0063 of 15.03.2016.

9 Article 1182, as amended by the decree of 15.03.2002.

10 B. Mallevaey, 'Audition et discernement de l'enfant devant le juge aux affaires familiales: 55 recommandations pour améliorer la participation de l'enfant aux décisions judiciaires le concernant au sein de sa famille' (2018) *Mission de recherche Droit et Justice*, p. 32 <http://www.gip-recherche-justice.fr/publication/audition-et-discernement-de-lenfant-devant-le-juge-aux-affaires-familiales-2/>; G. Barbier, 'La pratique bordelaise de l'audition d'enfant' (2012) *AJ fam.*, p. 498.

the opinions of various professionals were collected concerning the application of Article 12 of the CRC, within the area of child protection. The mixed questions were distributed over five broad thematic clusters: (1) capacity of discernment (or capacity to form their own views); (2) the child's choice to be heard; (3) the conduct of the hearing; (4) assistance to the child by a lawyer at the hearing; (5) and the impact of the child being heard on the judicial decision and on the child. The 98 responses obtained (29 from children's judges, 28 from lawyers, and 41 from professionals from the ASE), along with individual meetings, made it possible to bring to light differing practices and visions on the issue of hearing the child in child protection. Interestingly, the responses to certain questions vary considerably depending on the category of professionals queried, which makes the subject both fascinating and complex.

Both theoretical and practical clarifications on the place of the child's statements in child protection may be divided into four major issues: (1) the very existence of the hearing, which is theoretically mandatory; (2) the conditions for such a hearing, and in particular the criterion of 'discernment'; (3) the conduct of the hearing; and (4) the impact of the child's statements on the decision.

2. THE EXISTENCE OF THE HEARING OF THE CHILD

Unlike the arrangements under the ordinary rules of law, in the special procedures it is required that the judge hear the child, without it having to be requested by the minor or their parents. In child protection, two legal provisions provide for hearing the minor: First, Article 1182 of the CCP, according to which,

> the judge shall notify the Public Prosecutor as to the opening of proceedings; when they are not litigants, the judge shall also notify each one of the parents, guardian, and the person or representative of the agency to which the child has been entrusted. The judge hears each of the parents, the guardian, the person or representative of the agency to which the child has been entrusted, and the minor when capable of forming their own views …

Secondly, Article 1189 of the CCP provides that,

> at the court hearing, the judge hears the minor, their parents, guardian or person or representative of the agency to which the child has been entrusted,

as well as any other person the hearing of whom would seem pertinent to them. They may excuse the minor from appearing, or order that they withdraw during all or part of the rest of the proceedings.

The mandatory wording of these provisions warrants us to consider that hearing the child constitutes an obligation for the judge.[11]

The Court of Cassation has reiterated on many occasions that hearing a minor in child protection proceedings constitutes a right, classifying it as a public order measure.[12] However, in a judgment of 14 February 2006,[13] it indicated that hearing the child was mandatory in the proceedings, provided the child is capable of forming their own views, but not at the hearing in court. This mandatory requirement that the child be heard may be set aside in the event of an emergency, since according to Article 1184 of the CCP, the children's judge may take interim measures without granting the minor a hearing.

The obligation of the JE to hear the minor in the context of child protection proceedings has a much broader scope than that weighing on a JAF. In ordinary law proceedings, Article 388(1) of the Civil Code does not require the judge to hear the minor on the sole basis of the latter requesting to be heard by them. Conversely, Article 1182 of the CCP compels the judge to systematically prompt the hearing of the minor, without the latter needing to request it. In this regard, judicial review is triggered when it is not mentioned in the file, or in the ruling, that the child has been heard by the trial court, or there is no mention of the existence of circumstances rendering such hearing inappropriate.[14]

In proceedings under the ordinary rules of law, when a minor refuses to be heard, the judge assesses the merit of this refusal.[15] The wording may lead to confusion and suggest the child must justify their refusal. Yet, according to the Committee on the Rights of the Child, Article 12 of the CRC must be interpreted as a right and not a duty.[16] There is no comparable wording with regard to child protection. The judge is not asked to review the merit

---

11 Civ. 1re, 03.10.2000, JCP 2000. IV. 2709.

12 Civ. 1re, 30.06.1981, Gaz. Pal. 1982, 1, 391, note J. Massip; Civ. 1re, 25.06.1991, No. 90 05006 and No. 90 05015, Bull. civ. I, No. 210; D. 1992. 51.

13 Cass. 1re, 14.02.2006, Appeal No. 05-13.627.

14 Civ. 1re, 08.06.1999, RJPF 1999, No. 7, p. 23.

15 Article 388(1) of the Civil Code.

16 Committee on the Rights of the Child, General Comment No. 12 (2009): The right of the child to be heard, 20.07.2009, para. 71(v), CRC/GC/12 <https://www.refworld.org/docid/4ae562c52.html>; above n. 10, Annex no. 9, see the proposed amendment of Article 388-1.

of the child's refusal, but in practice the professionals – and predominantly the ASE staff and the lawyers – seek the causes of this refusal on the part of the minor, in order to be certain this is really a choice on their part. The professionals queried are unanimous: the refusal to speak is a right, in the same way as is the right to be heard. Nevertheless, some of them indicate that because of the child's position, at times exercising the right of refusal can be very difficult for them. Refusal therefore becomes indirect, taking the form of short answers or non-response. In practice, 90% of the judges queried believe this right is seldom exercised, and 10% are of the view that it never is. The lawyers' answers are more qualified, with only 22% believing that this right is often exercised.

This difference in perspective among professionals could perhaps be explained by the fact that in the presence of their lawyer, the child would be in a better position to voice a refusal – reinforcing the idea that lawyers are particularly necessary in child protection proceedings.

3. CONDITIONS TO BE HEARD: THE NOTION OF DISCERNMENT

Within the framework of the general right of the child to be heard, the hearing – which occurs only in the inquiry phase and not during the hearing in court – necessarily turns on a demand from the child or from a parent,[17] and on two paramount criteria: (1) capacity of discernment, and (2) that the proceedings concern them. Decree No. 2002/361 of 15 March 2002[18] made hearing the child in protection proceedings conditional on their capacity to form their own views and removed the possibility for the judge to dismiss the hearing of the minor based on their age or of their condition.

Capacity to form their own views is a condition for hearing of the minor in the two arrangements – common and specific – for protecting 'the right of the child to be heard'. This notion was introduced into French law so as to avoid the threshold effects resulting in a reference to a particular age. The report produced under the direction of Blandine Mallevaey starkly highlights the lack of common aspects in proceedings under the ordinary rules of law before a JAF for assessment of capacity

---

[17] Article 338(2) of the CCP.

[18] Decree No. 2002 361 of 15.03.2002, D. 2002. 1433, comm. M. Huyette; *Dr. fam.* 2002, chron. 14, comm. A. Gouttenoire.

of discernment, patchy practices, and thus, the sources of inequality of treatment.[19] The Court of Cassation precludes capacity to form their own views from being confounded with the child's age,[20] and requires trial courts to justify lack of discernment, other than solely in reference to the age of the minor.[21] In particular, it establishes a link between the child's dependence in relation to their parent, and their capacity to form their own views.[22] In a judgment from 14 February 2006,[23] the Court of Cassation considered that the court of appeal cannot be reproached for not having expressly explained why the minor had not been heard in the course of the proceedings, provided that it stands out that the trial judges clearly articulated that the child in question was not endowed with the capacity to form their own views as needed to be heard.

In the context of child protection, only Article 1182 of the CCP requires children to have the capacity of discernment, and such is not the case with Article 1189, pursuant to the hearing of the child in the courtroom. As it appeared from responses to our questionnaire that the majority of children's judges carry out only one single hearing, at the time of the courtroom session, it is no surprise that they state that they hear the views of the children, even though the latter are not endowed with the capacity to form their own views.[24] The answers given to the question of 'is there an age threshold below which you deem there is no capacity to form their own views?' are revelatory: Only 17% of the magistrates answered no, with the others in their large majority setting this threshold at between five and six years of age. While professionals from the ASE and the lawyers more generally refer to the age of six or seven years, they specify and underline the considerable diversity of practices.

In parallel, some of the professionals surveyed refer most often to the child's age in order to determine whether they are capable of forming their own views – despite this being contrary to the Court of Cassation

19 Above n. 10, p. 42 ff. See Recommendation No. 3.

20 Civ. 1re, No. 11 20357, D. 2012, Panor. 2267, obs. P. Bonfils and A. Gouttenoire; Civ. 1re, 05.03.2014, No. 13 13.530, D. 2014. Panor. 1787, obs. P. Bonfils and A. Gouttenoire.

21 Civ. 1re, 18.03.2015, No. 14–11583, *AJ fam.* 2015, 282 obs. S. Thouret.

22 Civ. 1re, 15.05.2013, No. 12 12.224; along the same lines, Civ. 1re, 12.04.2012, Panorama droit des mineurs, D., 2012, 2267, obs. A. Gouttenoire and P. Bonfils; CEDH, *Sophia Gudrun Hansen v. Turkey*, 23.09.2003, Req. 36141/97, F. Sudre, *Les grands arrêts de la Cour européenne des droits de l'Homme*, PUF, 2011, p. 578; above n. 20, Civ. 1re, 05.03.2014.

23 Above n. 13, *Dr. fam.* 2006, comm. No. 162, obs. P. Murat.

24 See also E. Durand, 'Parole de l'enfant: Brèves réflexions d'un juge des enfants sur l'audition en assistance éducative' (2014) *AJ fam.*, p. 27.

case law[25] and the recommendations of the Committee on the Rights of the Child.[26] While 52% of the judges queried deem age to be one among several criteria, and 48% of them a decisive criterion, they nearly unanimously acknowledged the absence of any prior assessment of the child's capacity to form their own views. They stated that at times they rely on the assessments carried out by the social or child protection services to make a determination as to the appropriateness of hearing a minor or not.

If the hearing of the child appears to be more systematic in child protection than in the context of the ordinary law, it is no less true that this criterion continues to be assessed differently depending on the courts and the law firms, thus leading to unequal treatment in the exercise of the child's right to be heard.

4. THE CONDUCT OF THE HEARING

In contrast to proceedings before the family court,[27] the child is a party to child protection proceedings and must be able to be heard just like the other parties in the court hearing. Hearing the child in a child protection matter serves several different objectives. It is essential to allow the child to express their needs, fears, and what they consider to be their interests. But it is likewise envisaged by the judges as a means of collecting information useful for a ruling. This is also the occasion for the child to hear what is said concerning them, their interests, the dangers identified, and the measures envisaged to ensure their protection. It allows the child to hear what the judge and the others present have to say, and thus to follow the child protection efforts that will follow the ruling, while situating the responsibilities of each. Looking to respond to these objectives as a whole, in child protection matters it is envisaged in theory that the child be heard by the judge[28] at the inquiry phase if they are able to form their

---

25 Civ. 1re, 18.03.2015, No. 14 11.392, Bull. civ. I, 2015, No. 58, RJPF No. 5, 05.2015, p. 28, note I. Corpart; *AJ fam.* 2015, p. 282, obs. S. Thouret; Proc. No. 5, 05.2015, comm. 161, note M. Douchy-Oudot; *Dr. fam.* No. 6, 06.2015, comm. 123, obs. A.-C. Reglier; RTD civ. 2015, p. 352, obs. J. Hauser; RLDC 05.2015, No. 126, p. 49, obs. M. Desolneux.

26 UN Committee, above n. 16, para. 20.

27 Before the JAF, the child is largely heard prior to the hearing, alone or with their lawyer or the person of their choice. In more exceptional cases, the JAFs agree to hear the child after the parents have been heard.

28 Unlike the arrangements under the ordinary rules of law, in which the JAF may delegate a designated person to that purpose (Article 388-1 of the Civil Code), in child

own views, and then during the court hearing, regardless of their level of maturity.

The study shows there is in practice a great confounding of these two phases of listening to what the child has to say. According to a majority of the professionals surveyed, the child is only heard one single time, during the court hearing, which contravenes the distinction that is nevertheless well established in the CCP, between court hearing and hearing the child. In addition, hearing the child during the court session generally leads to the child being heard in the presence of all the parties. The answers given by the judges show highly variable practices, with some systematically listening to the child in the absence of the parents, immediately prior to the court hearing, and others doing so solely if the child so requests, and still others depending on their age and level of maturity. The lawyers and ASE staff attest to these highly variable practices from one judge to another, and to the difficulties this generates: insecurity; impossibility of preparing the child; stress on the child due to finding themselves in the presence of their parents; and difficulty for the child in speaking freely, which leads them at times to remain silent. These practices had already been criticized in earlier reports[29] and the study confirms this. It would be necessary to revive the discussion on the requirement to systematize the hearing of the child alone (or in the presence of their lawyer) prior to hearing their parents,[30] unless there are convincing reasons to do otherwise.

Regardless of the mechanism, be it ordinary or special law, the assistance of a lawyer for the child is not a legal obligation but merely an option. Within the framework of child protection proceedings, Article 1186 of the CCP provides that a minor capable of discernment[31] may choose their counsel or request of the judge that the Bar Association president appoint one for them ex officio, and the judge must inform the minor of this right

protection cases the hearing of the child is undertaken solely by the JE (Article 1182 of the CCP).

29 See in particular Ombudsman for Children, *Annual Report*, 2005, <https://juridique.defenseurdesdroits.fr/doc_num.php?explnum_id=18363>; A. Gouttenoire and I. Corpart, '40 propositions pour adapter la protection de l'enfance et l'adoption aux réalités d'aujourd'hui' (2014) *Documentation française*.

30 Ombudsman for Children, above n. 29, Proposal No. 14; A. Gouttenoire and I. Corpart, above n. 29.

31 Above n. 18, Decree No. 2002 361, amending the CCP and in relation to child protection – which looked to improve the exercise by minors of some of their procedural rights – subordinates the exercise of children's rights to their capacity to form their own views, whether in regard to being heard, the consulting of their file, or the appointment of a lawyer. Civ. 1re, 23.11.2011, No. 10-16.367, *Dr. fam.* 2012, comm. 30, obs. C. Neirinck, rtd civ. 2012, p. 109, Obs. J. Hauser.

from the time they are first heard[32] and not in the summons to the court hearing.[33] Since the assistance of the lawyer is not mandatory, even in the case of placement in care,[34] it was interesting to gather the views of the professionals on the effective exercise of this optional right for the child to be assisted. According to 79% of the judges and 82% of the ASE staff, the child is assisted seldom or never. As such, to the crucial question of 'Do you think children should be routinely assisted by a lawyer?', both the judges and the ASE staff answer overwhelmingly in the negative (93% of the JEs and 71% of the ASE staff), while the lawyers are nearly unanimous (96%) in answering in the affirmative. Various grounds are cited for rejecting such mandatory assistance: the lack of training of the lawyers; the cumbersome nature of the proceedings, notably for AEMO (Child Protection in an Open Setting) measures; a systematic presence not always protective of the interests of the child; and at times its irrelevance. As systematicity does not meet with unanimous approval – even though the position of the lawyer is nevertheless recognized as insufficient – a compromise solution might be found by giving the judge the power to have a lawyer appointed ex officio in all cases where they deem it useful.[35] With respect to the selection of the lawyer, 50% of the JEs and 54% of the lawyers believe the child's lawyer is requested mainly by the parents, even though 70% of the ASE professionals believe they are the source of the request for counsel for the child. If in principle there is freedom of choice of counsel, the appointment of the latter in matters of child protection puts into question the principle of independence when they are appointed by the parents or by child social welfare. We may however think that the frequent recourse to specialized lawyers in the defence of children limits the scope of this criticism.

5. THE IMPACT OF CHILDREN'S OPINIONS ON THE RULING

When the child expresses their needs, their fears, their demands, or their refusals of protection, the judge is sovereign to assess the scope of their

32 The interested parties are reminded of this right at the time of their initial hearing, upon pain of it rendered void (civ. 1re, 15.01.1991, Bull. civ, i, No. 18, gaz. Pal. 1992, 1, pan., p. 138).

33 In the arrangements under the ordinary rules of law, informing of this right must be undertaken at the time of the summons to be heard (Article 338(6) of the CCP).

34 See Ombudsman for Children, above n. 29, p. 108, Proposal No. 14; A. Gouttenoire and I. Corpart, above n. 29; M. Picot, 'L'avocat de l'enfant', *Droit de la famille* No. 7/8, 07.2006, Study 37. Above n. 10, Proposal No. 29 ff., and in particular No. 38.

35 A. Gouttenoire and I. Corpart, above n. 29.

remarks as a function of the circumstances of the case. Even if the judge must always strive to gain buy-in by the child to the measures envisaged, their ruling might be quite contrary to the wishes expressed by the child. Hearing the minor ought to remain advisory. More generally, it appears that the impact of what children have to say on rulings is perceived in a highly variable manner among the professionals. A large proportion of them (40% of the JEs, 44% of the lawyers, and 55% of the ASE staff) believe this impact is moderate, while for a not insignificant part of them the impact is substantial (32% of the JEs, 40% of the lawyers and 29% of the ASE staff). A small proportion of those queried believe this impact is considerable (3.6% of the JEs, 3.7% of the lawyers, and 0% among the ASE staff), or conversely, very low for very few of them (3.6% of the JEs, 0% for the lawyers, and 7.9% for the ASE staff). Note that certain professionals believe that this impact is impossible to determine (4.6% of the JEs, 11.1% of the lawyers, and 7.9% of the ASE staff), which may raise questions pertaining to the way the judge communicates with the child and the other intervenors in the proceedings.

In addition, to the question 'Does the judge feel bound by the child's opinion as of a certain age?', while the judges are nearly unanimous in answering in the negative (89%), the lawyers and the professionals from the ASE appear to have a more qualified opinion on the issue (55.6% of the lawyers and only 34% of the ASE staff answered 'no'). Moreover, even if all of the professionals recognize the principle of the independence of the judge in relation to children's opinions, they acknowledge that the impact of what children say has greater weight as they approach the age of majority.[36] Thus, the will expressed by an adolescent (from 14–15 years of age, or even from 12 years of age for the ASE staff) becomes a key criterion for the ruling.

6. CONCLUSION: THE ESSENTIAL NATURE OF HEARING THE CHILD

Concerning the perception of children's opinions, 40% of judges believe the children speak freely, but the lawyers – and even more so the ASE staff – seem less optimistic (28.5% of the lawyers and 15.8% of the ASE staff

[36] See also by way of comparison. C. Siffrein-Blanc, 'Les critères de la mise en place de la résidence alternée: étude de décisions de cours d'appel (Bordeaux, Lyon, Aix-en-provence and Versailles)', *Dr. fam.*, 07–08.2019, Special report, p. 15, No. 28.

believe the children speak freely) and a larger majority of them believe the children speak with fear and suspicion (48% of the lawyers and 65.7% of the ASE staff). On the other hand, the professionals converge when they are questioned on the way in which the children perceive their hearing. For 53.6% of the children's judges, the minor considers their hearing as a fundamental right (the same for 29% of the lawyers and 10% of the professionals from the ASE) or as a chance, according to 32.2% of the judges, 48.1% of the lawyers, and 36.7% of the professionals from the ASE. These positive conceptions of how the children see their hearing do not exclude acknowledging that the hearing is also a source of stress for the minor. But only 3.6% of the children's judges, 18.5% of the lawyers, and 21.1% of the professionals from the ASE believe the hearing is solely a source of stress; 3.6% of the children's judges, 3.7% of the lawyers, and 10.5% of the professionals from the ASE believe children envisage their hearing as simply an obligation. Thus, according to the professionals, the hearing continues to be perceived by the majority as positive for the children, even if everyone agrees in recognizing its stressful character for the child – in particular when they are in the presence of their parents. If the professionals acknowledge that the hearing may constitute a risk of increasing the child's vulnerability, in that it is always an ordeal that re-opens wounds and touches on the deep intimacy of private and family life, they all converge in concluding that the participation of the children in the judicial proceedings is essential in regard to child protection, both for the child and in order to produce sound justice.

CHILD PARTICIPATION IN DUTCH FAMILY LAW AND CHILD PROTECTION PROCEEDINGS

Mariëlle BRUNING, Daisy SMEETS and Apollonia BOLSCHER

1. INTRODUCTION

According to Article 12 of the Convention on the Rights of the Child (CRC) children have a right to participate in legal proceedings and the child must be given the opportunity to be heard in any legal proceedings affecting them. Age limits can be used, but according to the Committee on the Rights of the Child, they cannot be absolute and they should leave space for younger children to have the opportunity to be heard by the judge.[1]

[1] Committee on the Rights of the Child, General Comment No. 12 (2009): The right of the child to be heard, [20.07.2009], CRC/C/GC/12, pp. 70–74, paras. 20–21, 52 and Committee on the Rights of the Child [2006], *Day of General Discussion on the Right of the Child to be Heard* (Forty-third session, 11-29.09.2006), para. 51.

It also follows from international standards that children should be heard directly (by a judge) or indirectly (by an expert outside the courtroom), and they should be able to choose this themselves.[2] The CRC remains silent about the child's right to (independently) initiate proceedings. But from other international standards it can be deduced that children who are confronted with legal proceedings are entitled to child-friendly proceedings and also have the right of access to justice and the possibility to challenge court decisions that are relevant to them.[3] Furthermore, according to international standards children must be provided with a legal representative or a guardian *ad litem* (GAL) when there is a potential conflict between children and their parents.[4]

In Dutch civil law, other than in exceptional cases, children are not competent to participate autonomously as litigants. Even though children lack competence to participate autonomously in civil law proceedings, they do have the right to be involved in family and child protection proceedings. For children from the age of 12 years or older, this is embodied in the right to be heard in court. In 2016 the Government Committee of the Reassessment of Parenthood recommended to the Dutch government that special attention should be paid to the procedural position of children in family law and the question whether improvements were necessary from an international children's rights and a psychological and pedagogical perspective.[5]

This contribution discusses the legal position of children and forms of child participation in Dutch family and child protection proceedings. In family and child protection proceedings, in particular, children are confronted with court proceedings in which decision-making takes place

---

2 For example: above n. 1, General Comment No. 12, para. 35. According to Mol, States cannot simply decide to provide children with only one manner in which to be heard; children should be provided with a choice between forms of participation; C. Mol, 'Children's Representation in Family Law Proceedings' (2019) 27(1) *The International Journal of Children's Rights*, p. 70.

3 *Guidelines of the Committee of Ministers of the Council of Europe on Child-friendly Justice*, 17.11.2010, IV, paras. 34–35; Article 5 of the European Convention on the Exercise of Children's Rights, <http://www.worldlii.org/int/other/treaties/COETSER/1996/1.html>.

4 Committee on the Rights of the Child, General Comment No. 14 (2013) on the right of the child to have his or her best interests taken as a primary consideration (Art. 3, para. 1), CRC/C/GC/14 (2013), para. 90. See also above n. 3, *Guidelines of the Committee of Ministers of the Council of Europe on Child-friendly Justice*, para. 3.3.1.

5 Government Committee on the Reassessment of Parenthood, *Child and Parents in the 21st Century*, Den Haag: Government Committee on the Reassessment of Parenthood 2016, recommendation 14.

that can have an enormous impact on their lives. In this contribution, implementation of the child's right to participate is analyzed from both a legal and pedagogical perspective to show how legislation and policy are implemented in the daily practice of Dutch family and child protection proceedings.

This contribution discusses two aspects of the right to participation in legal proceedings: children's right to be heard and the procedural position of children. First, the current legal position of minors in Dutch family and child law proceedings is discussed. Thereafter, the contribution discusses how children's procedural position and their right to be heard is implemented in policy and current practice.[6] Finally, the contribution analyzes whether in Dutch family and child law proceedings the child's right to participation in legal proceedings as enshrined in Article 12 of the CRC is effectively implemented in Dutch legislation, policy, and daily practice, and whether any changes are necessary.

2. THE CURRENT POSITION OF MINORS IN DUTCH FAMILY LAW AND CHILD PROTECTION PROCEEDINGS

2.1. THE CHILD'S RIGHT TO BE HEARD

The Dutch Code of Civil Procedure provides that the judge will give children aged 12 years and older the opportunity to present their views in family and child protection proceedings regarding them.[7] Children aged 12 years and older have the right to choose whether to be heard in court or not: the court invitation to be heard is an option, not a duty. There are a few exceptions to invite every child aged 12 years and older for a child hearing, for example, when the case is of minimal relevance to the child.[8]

---

6 This chapter is based on our research commissioned by the Dutch Ministry of Justice in response to the Government Committee's recommendations, conducted by a multidisciplinary research team (the Child Law Department of Leiden Law School and the Departments of Forensic Family and Youth Care Studies and Developmental and Educational Psychology of the Faculty of Social and Behavioural Sciences); M.R. Bruning, et al., *Children in proceedings: from communication towards effective participation ('Kind in proces: van communicatie naar effectieve participatie')*, Meijers-reeks nr. 335, Wolf Legal Publishers, Nijmegen 2020.

7 Article 809 of the Dutch Code of Civil Procedure.

8 Article 809 section 1 of the Dutch Code of Civil Procedure. Other exceptions are: when it is plausible that the child does not want to be heard, when a child is unable to

Children younger than 12 years may also be given the opportunity to be heard; they are not invited by default by the court, but the judge has a discretionary power to decide on hearing the child on his or her request when the child is sufficiently mature. In other words, this group of children does not have the *right* to be heard.[9] There is no guidance from statutory provisions on the modalities and methods on the child hearing. In 2015, the Courts of Appeal developed a professional standard of how the child should be heard in appeal.[10]

In current practice, initiatives have been taken in recent years, opting for a lower age limit to hear children. The District Court of The Hague, competent in all Dutch child abduction cases, invites all children six years of age and older for a child hearing. The Amsterdam District Court invites all children eight years of age and older in family law and child protection cases for a child hearing.

2.2. CHILDREN AS INDEPENDENT PARTIES

Children are in principle incapable of autonomously participating in legal proceedings and lack locus standi. Children are represented by their parents or guardians. In the event of a conflict of interests between parents as the legal representatives and a child about matters relating to the upbringing of the child or the child's property, a GAL can be appointed to act on behalf of the child instead of the child's parents or guardians.[11] Courts have a discretionary power to appoint a GAL in such situations; a request can be rejected by the court. In proceedings on legal parentage, courts are obliged to always appoint a GAL.[12] In some situations, children have the right to initiate legal proceedings and be a party to them. Such exceptions are fragmented in the Dutch Civil Code and have 12 years, and sometimes 16 years, as the lower age limit. In child protection proceedings, children aged 12 or older who are confronted with a child protection order have several opportunities to file requests to the court.

---

be heard due to physical or mental health problems, or when the judge fears that the child hearing will negatively influence the child's health and development.

9 M.R. Bruning and J. Peper, 'Giving Children a Voice in Court?' [2020] *Erasmus Law Review*, online (in English) at <http://www.erasmuslawreview.nl/tijdschrift/ELR/2020/1%20(incomplete)/ELR-D-19-00030.pdf>.

10 *Professionele standaard* kindgesprekken 09.12.2016, <http://www.rechtspraak.nl>.

11 Article 1:250 of the Dutch Civil Code.

12 Article 1:212 of the Dutch Civil Code. See also, W. Schrama, et al., *International Handbook on Child Participation in Family Law*, Intersentia, Cambridge 2021.

Children have no legal representation in child protection proceedings. Only those who are confronted with a (request to) out-of-home placement in a secure treatment setting – constituting a deprivation of liberty – are represented by a lawyer. Children's parents or care givers usually have no legal representation in child protection proceedings. In family law proceedings, parents are usually represented by a lawyer, but the child has no independent legal representation.

In some family law matters Dutch law provides children aged 12 or older with the possibility of approaching the court informally and asking for a specific decision. Informal access to court is available in matters related to parental responsibilities after divorce, separation, care, and contact arrangements between a child and a parent.[13] This option can also be used when the child has not yet reached the age of 12 years but may be regarded as capable of making a reasonable evaluation of their interests in the matter.

3. CHILDREN'S PROCEDURAL RIGHTS IN PRACTICE

To investigate current practices regarding children's procedural rights in Dutch civil law, we carried out an empirical study to examine the experiences and opinions of professionals in legal practice, children, and parents. A total of 272 professionals filled out an online questionnaire and 21 of these participated in an additional interview. First, questionnaires were sent to judges, family and child lawyers, social workers, GALs, and employees of the Child Protection Board and of Children and Youth Law Advice Centres. Further, questionnaires were sent to 136 young adults aged 16 to 24 years old, of whom 43 had experienced family law or child protection proceedings as a child. Finally, we collected data from 131 parents of children who had experienced family law or child protection proceedings. Research questions of this study included the extent to which children use their right to participate in family and child protection proceedings, current practices regarding the right to be heard and the procedural position of children, and aspects that could be improved.

---

13 Article 1:251a section 4, Article 1:253a section 4, Article 1:377g of the Dutch Civil Code.

3.1. CHILDREN'S ACCESS TO JUSTICE

All children have the right to express their opinion on matters concerning them, but the age limit used in the Netherlands narrows down the group provided with this opportunity. Our study showed judges rarely invite children younger than 12 years old for a child hearing, which confirms previous research regarding the strict interpretation of the Dutch age limit of 12 years old.[14] In our study, the majority of judges who have interviewed children under the age of 12 state children requested this themselves, which means children's rights are taken seriously. But why are judges so hesitant to initiate a child hearing with children younger than 12 years old?

Extensive research has been conducted on barriers regarding child participation. Professionals seem to have a general image that participation is stressful for children and that children should be protected against it.[15] For young children in particular, the degree to which children may be influenced by their parents also plays an important role. Due to loyalty conflicts, children could be scared to express a contradicting opinion. Consequently, professionals fear that this may restrict children from providing their own authentic opinion.[16] In our study, we asked all professionals for reasons not to invite children under the age of 12 for a child hearing. Results confirmed the previously mentioned findings: loyalty conflicts and parental influence. The assumption that participation would

---

14 K.A.M. van der Zon and M.P. de Jong-de Kruijf, 'Hoger beroep tegen een uithuisplaatsingsbeslissing en de rol van de minderjarige' (2015) *Trema* afl. 3, pp. 298–307. H.C.M. Aalders, 'De rechtspraktijk inzake gezagsbeëindiging vanuit kinderrechtelijk perspectief', *FJR* 2018/63, afl. 11, pp. 61–66. A. van Triest, 'Het kinderverhoor in het ressort Den Bosch onder de loep', *FJR* 2004, afl. 26, pp. 16–26.

15 B. Arad-Davidzon and R. Benbenishty, 'The role of workers' attitudes and parent and child wishes in child protection workers' assessments and recommendation regarding removal and reunification' (2008) 30(1) *Children and Youth Services Review*, pp. 107–21; M.D. ten Brummelaar, et al., 'Participation of youth in decision-making procedures during residential care: A narrative review' (2018) 23(1) *Child & Family Social Work*, pp. 33–44; G.G. van Bijleveld, C.W.M. Dedding and J.G.F. Bunders-Aelen, 'Children's and young people's participation within child welfare and child protection services: a state-of-the-art review' (2015) 20(2) *Child and Family Social Work*, pp. 129–38.

16 S.A. Vis, A. Holtan and N. Thomas, 'Obstacles for child participation in care and protection cases – why Norwegian social workers find it difficult' (2012) 21 *Child Abuse Review*, afl. 1, pp. 7–23; J. Cashmore, 'Children's participation in family law decision-making: Theoretical approaches to understanding children's views' (2011) 33(4) *Children and Youth Services Review*, pp. 515–20; F. Bell, 'Barriers to empowering children in private family law proceedings' (2016) 30(3) *International Journal of Law, Policy and the Family*, pp. 225–47.

be stressful for children was mentioned most often by over half of the participants. Participants were hesitant about the cognitive development of children under the age of 12, as they worried these children may not be able to verbalize their opinion and oversee the consequences of their wishes. However, research on child development shows children are capable of having a meaningful conversation with an adult when they are in kindergarten (age four to six).[17] Talking to a judge might be too far-fetched at this age because complex instructions or questions can be difficult for these children. At the age of eight, though, children's communication[18] and reasoning skills have developed so much[19] that a child hearing should be possible from that age.

In contrast to children under the age of 12, older children in principle are invited for a child hearing. Although our study showed that most of these children accept this invitation to talk with the judge, it also shows not all children seem to make use of this opportunity. Almost half of the judges who participated in our study mentioned children often do not respond to this invitation letter. Also, about a third of children indicated they did not respond to the court's invitation letter. These findings were surprising in light of other studies demonstrating that children want to participate in these cases.[20] In line with this assumption, children confirmed they experience stress in anticipation of a child hearing, mainly caused by a lack of information and not knowing what to expect. However, this was mentioned by children who had participated in a child hearing, so this factor was no reason *not* to participate. According to literature, loyalty conflicts could also form a barrier to participate.[21] In line with this, some children in our study felt as if they had to choose between parents or feared giving a response that contradicted one of the parents' views. Given that children who did not participate in child hearings were more

---

17 N.E. Hall, S.A. Wagovich, and N. Bernstein Ratner, 'Language considerations in developmental stuttering', in E. Conture and R. Curlee (Eds.), *Stuttering and related disorders of fluency*, 3, Thieme, New York 2007, pp. 153–67.

18 D.A. Brown, et al., 'Developmental differences in children's learning and use of forensic ground rules during an interview about an experienced event' (2019) 8 *Developmental Psychology*, pp. 1626–39.

19 A. Diamond, 'Biological and social influences on cognitive control processes dependent on pre-frontal cortex' (2011) 189 *Progression in Brain Research*, pp. 319–39.

20 J. Cashmore, 'Promoting the participation of children and young people in care' (2002) 26 *Child Abuse & Neglect*, afl.8, pp. 837–47; J. Cashmore and P. Parkinson, 'Children's participation in family law disputes: The views of children, parents, lawyers and counsellors' (2009) 82 *Family Matters*, pp. 15–21.

21 F. Bell, 'Barriers to empowering children in private family law proceedings' (2016) 30(3) *International Journal of Law, Policy and the Family*, pp. 225–47.

often involved in a divorce or custody rather than a child protection case, this factor could have been a barrier to participate. However, some of the young people in our study also mentioned that they simply did not feel the need to talk to the judge. In previous research this has been reported by children who are satisfied with post-divorce arrangements.[22] Thus, it is also possible that cases in which there is no child hearing involve low levels of conflict. Finally, the professionals in our study stressed that children might not have responded to the court's invitation due to practical reasons, such as travelling or requesting the day off at school. Also, the procedure of receiving a letter from the court which children must answer and send back may not be very encouraging and is outdated: children nowadays are not used to sending letters in an envelope through a mailbox.

Regarding children's access to justice, we examined the extent to which children initiate proceedings. Our study showed this rarely happens, which confirms previous research.[23] When it occurred, it concerned the possibility to write an informal letter to the court in custody and divorce cases; however, judges rarely experienced children initiating formal proceedings. In line with previous studies,[24] our study showed children and parents had little knowledge of such possibilities.

3.2. CURRENT PRACTICES

In the Netherlands, children are directly heard via a child hearing with a judge talking to a child, which differs from countries in which other professionals may speak to children and report the child's voice to the judge, in other words: an indirect mode of child participation.[25] In our

---

22 V.M. Smits, *Participatie van het kind bij het ouderschapsplan*, Maklu Uitgevers, Apeldoorn/Antwerpen 2015.

23 M.H.L. van den Hoogen and P.J. Montanus, 'Hoe staat het anno 2017 met de informele rechtsingang?', *FJR* 2017/62, afl. 11, pp. 286–89.

24 S.D. Block, et al., 'Abused and neglected children in court: Knowledge and Attitudes' (2010) 34 *Child Abuse and Neglect*, No. 9, pp. 659–70; H. Bouma, et al., 'Meaningful participation for children in the Dutch child protection system: A critical analysis of relevant provisions in policy documents' (2018) 79 *Child Abuse & Neglect*, pp. 279–92; U. Kilkelly, *Listening to children about justice: Report of the Council of Europe consultation with children on child-friendly justice*, Council of Europe, Strasbourg (2010); K. van Hoorde, et al., *Bouncing Back. The wellbeing of children in international child abduction cases*, European Union-funded research project Enhancing the Well-being of Children in Cases of International Child Abduction (eWELL) 2018.

25 Indirect modes of participation are used for example in Australia, Canada, Scotland, England and Wales: C. Mol, Comparative analysis, above n. 12.

study, almost all professionals preferred judges talking to the children directly. Similarly, children want to see the judge who makes the decision with a great impact on their lives. In our study, only GALs felt judges could be more equipped to talk to children. This is not because they have doubts regarding judges' communication skills, which are positively evaluated by both professionals and children. For instance, almost all children felt taken seriously and agreed that judges made them feel comfortable and asked clear questions. Rather, the reason why GALs would prefer to talk with children themselves and report the child's voice to the judge concerns contextual factors. These professionals can schedule multiple appointments with children and take more time to talk with them than a judge, which can be beneficial in cases where children struggle with loyalty conflicts, for instance.

Children indeed confirmed child hearings are rather short. According to the judges in our study, the conversations last about 15 minutes, which is consistent with other studies,[26] just as the finding that the location can differ between cases.[27] About 40% of the judges in our study stated the conversation usually takes place in the courtroom. Although this is a very formal environment and therefore not the best choice to talk to children, judges explained there is not enough time to visit a separate room in between court proceedings. To save time, judges stay in the courtroom and often keep on their robe as well. This is especially true for child protection cases in which the child hearing immediately precedes the court hearing, which also decreases the available time for interviewing a child (sometimes not even more than five minutes as opposed to 15 minutes in family law proceedings).

It has been shown before that a formal setting can make children feel uncomfortable and cause stress.[28] About 60% of the judges in our study mentioned they *do* use a separate room to talk to children. This could be the council chamber, or an office reserved for child hearings. The latter is often considered a child-friendly location; however it must be noted children found the room 'boring'. Because the definition of a 'child-friendly location' can be quite subjective, we asked judges to describe the room reserved for child hearings. Of the judges who reported that the child hearing took place in a separate room, 70% indicated this room

---

26 Above n. 14.

27 Ibid.; A. van Triest, 'Het kinderverhoor in het ressort Den Bosch onder de loep' (2004) *FJR*, afl. 26, pp. 16–26.

28 A. van Teijlingen-Pover, 'De gerechtelijke procedure in jeugd- en familiezaken door de ogen van de kinderen' (2019) 2 *Trema*.

had colourful walls and posters, or other pictures. Only 30% indicated the room also included child-oriented attributes such as games, pencils, or stuffed animals. These judges were all from one specific court in the Netherlands, which also experimented with talking to children under the age of 12 and reported that this room made children feel at ease.[29] Not only do the participants in our study confirm such a child-friendly room makes it easier to talk to children, but so does the relevant literature on talking to children.[30] Children who feel safe are more inclined to speak their mind. Participants in our study mentioned that being able to bring a trusted third person to the hearing could also help children feel comfortable; however, their influence may have negative effects. In current practice, children are not supported by any third person during a child hearing.

3.3. ASPECTS FOR IMPROVEMENT

Both the duration and location of the child hearing are mentioned as aspects that could be improved, and the lack of information was also mentioned repeatedly. As reported before, some children experienced stress because they did not know what to expect. Proper age-related information seems to be lacking, and most of the parents mentioned children need help understanding the invitation letter for a child hearing. Furthermore, children rarely receive information about the judge's decision. In some cases, it is possible for judges to talk directly to children and explain the decision. However, in family law cases the court's ruling does not immediately follow the child hearing. In these cases, judges rely on parents to inform children, yet children would prefer to receive information directly from the court. In this light, some courts in the Netherlands have experimented with child-friendly judgments and with writing a separate recital in the judgment specifically addressed to the child.[31] However it has been suggested that 'simplifying' a court judgment could be challenging for the precision of the decision and that it could also be wise to inform children through a third party who 'translates' the decision.[32] Our study

---

29 These judges were all from the Amsterdam District Court.

30 M.F. Delfos, *Luister je wel naar mij? Gespreksvoering met kinderen tussen vier en twaalf jaar oud*, SWP Uitgeverij, Amsterdam 2009; above n. 28.

31 Above n. 23; T. Liefaard and S.E. Rap, 'Hoezo kindvriendelijk? Over "child-friendly justice" ter bevordering van effectieve participatie van kinderen in juridische procedures en besluitvorming' (2018) 41(6) *FJR*, pp. 180–86.

32 J.H. Lieber, 'De rechter en de taal van het kind' (2018) 41(6) *FJR*, pp. 172–79.

showed such an alternative finds support among judges. Also, other research has demonstrated children support this as well.[33]

Importantly, participants in our study also suggested to lower the age limit regarding child hearings. About half of the professionals in our study favoured such a change because they felt children under the age of 12 should also be given the opportunity to express their opinion on the matter. As a new age limit, the age of eight was preferred by a majority of professionals and children. Thus, children between eight and 12 years of age would then be given the opportunity to be heard.

4. CONCLUDING OBSERVATIONS AND RECOMMENDATIONS

The findings of our study lead to the conclusion that the right to be heard, the formal procedural position, and context factors for effective participation in Dutch family and child protection proceedings need adjustment.[34] Young people should be taken more seriously in family and child protection proceedings and their possibilities to effectively participate need to be improved, and age limits should leave space for younger children to have the opportunity to be heard.

4.1. THE RIGHT TO BE HEARD

In the Netherlands, an age limit of 12 years is used in legislation for children to be invited to be heard in court. Still, according to the Dutch Code of Civil Procedure, children younger than 12 years could be invited for a child hearing by the discretionary power of the judge. In practice, the age limit of 12 years is not very flexible and younger children are hardly heard in court. This conclusion does not align with the child's right to be

---

33 R. Fitzgerald and A. Graham, 'Something Amazing I Guess: Children's Views on Having a Say About Supervised Contact' (2011) 64 *Australian Social Work*, pp. 487–501.

34 This contribution presents some findings of our research report in which we also analyzed relevant international human rights standards. A literature study was conducted with insights from pedagogical sciences and neuropsychology in order to answer to what extent children are able to participate in family and child protection proceedings. The recommendations that are presented here stem partly from this research report (above n. 6).

heard and the interpretative statements of the Committee on the Rights of the Child. Furthermore, this conclusion does not match with current pedagogical and psychological insights underscoring younger children's communication and reasoning skills and ability to talk to a judge.

Based on our research findings, we recommend the age limit is lowered and that children from the age of eight are invited for a child hearing. In addition, the possibility for children between four to eight years to talk to a judge in family and child protection proceedings is worth exploring. This young group of children should be given the opportunity to be heard both indirectly and directly with the support of a GAL who is responsible for the provision of information before and during the child hearing. After the hearing the GAL should explain the court decision to the child.

Furthermore, the importance of a supporter for the child before, during, and after the child hearing has become clear. The possibility for a child of taking a GAL or other third party to the child hearing should become standard practice, or at least this possibility should be offered in advance.

4.2. LOCUS STANDI

With regard to the formal procedural position, we recommend Dutch children from the age of 12 should receive party status and should have independent legal access in issues related to parentage, adoption, divorce, custody, access rights, and child protection. This recommendation implies that they should be able to initiate such proceedings independently and should also be authorized to autonomously appeal a judgment. Children from 12 to 18 years of age should be competent in litigation with regard to the aforementioned subjects and should have locus standi. Children aged 12 years and older competent to express their views and who want to initiate proceedings should be represented by a lawyer. This lawyer represents the child's wishes and opinions, and also has the task of carefully informing the child about the legal proceedings.

4.3. CONTEXT FACTORS FOR EFFECTIVE PARTICIPATION

Over the last decade, important steps have been made in the Netherlands to improve children's participation in family and child protection proceedings. Child hearings have been developed and children appreciate how judges talk to them and take them seriously. In order to guarantee effective participation of children in family and child protection proceedings it is not only important that children younger than 12 years of age be taken more seriously, but it is also necessary to further improve context factors.

First, we recommend further research into what exactly is meant by 'child-friendly', partly from the point of view of different stages of development of children and youngsters with corresponding different needs with regard to child-friendly proceedings. A 'child-friendly' environment for a 16-year-old, for example, can differ from a 'child-friendly' environment for four-year-olds or for eight-year-olds. Continuous attention should also be paid to effectively inform children of their rights with regard to family and child protection proceedings. Children must also be better informed prior to the hearing about the content of the proceedings and the general course of affairs at the court.

We propose the court summons children in a child-friendly manner; further investigation would be desirable for more modern alternatives to the invitation letter from the court. We suggest introducing child-friendly waiting rooms and meeting rooms in court. More attention should be paid in this context to avoid unwelcome encounters between children and other involved parties in court proceedings.

Furthermore, sufficient time should be available for a conversation between a child and a judge; this means that investments are necessary to further improve child hearings. Continuous attention is also needed for permanent professional training for judges who hear children in court. In every court ruling concerning family or child protection decisions, it must be made transparent how the opinion of the child has influenced the court decision. Finally, child-friendly case-law – for example, by way of writing a separate recital in the judgment or the writing of an entire judgment in child-friendly language – should be encouraged.

CHILDREN'S VOICES ON THEIR RIGHT TO BE HEARD IN THE FIELD OF CHILD PROTECTION IN BELGIUM (*COMMUNAUTÉ FRANÇAISE*)

Highlighting of Blind Spots Regarding the Place and Role of the Parents

Coline Moreau and Thierry Moreau

1. INTRODUCTION

Article 12 of the Convention on the Rights of the Child (CRC) guarantees the right of discerning minors to be heard on all matters affecting them, and to have their opinion taken into consideration. The Committee on the

Rights of the Child notes this demonstrates the particularities of the legal and social status of children. On the one hand, they lack full autonomy from adults, but on the other they are subjects of rights.[1] Children are simultaneously the same as and different from adults. They are human beings whom we must take seriously, while taking into account the factual differences distinguishing them from adults, without considering them as mini-adults, which they are not.[2]

For both the Committee on the Rights of the Child and for the European Court of Human Rights (ECtHR), the child's view is not considered as one element of appreciation among others to determine his or her interests, but rather as the determining element.[3] Yet it took several decades to recognize the interest of – and even the need for – taking a child's view into consideration in the legal field. Since the 1990s, recognition has followed demand. Provisions have thus been adopted in various areas of law concerning young people (family, child protection, juvenile delinquency, education, etc.) to gather the opinions and/or obtain their participation in the decision-making process. Two legal mechanisms were mainly used. The first is the hearing of the minor during the administrative or judicial procedure without him or her being a party to the case. Conversely, the second consists of making the child a party to the proceedings in the same way as the adults concerned.

While children may now make their opinions known, neither the mechanisms for youth assistance and protection, nor the nature of the judgments have changed significantly. Is it enough to insert mechanisms allowing minors to make their voice heard for these procedures to become truly child friendly? To answer this question, it seemed relevant to turn to the young people themselves and interview them. By taking the word of young people as the cornerstone, our research fundamentally questions the capacity of the youth assistance and protection system to achieve its objective. In other words, is it enough to obtain a minor's opinion or to allow them to be present at the hearing to institute an appropriate and complete participation on their part in the decision-making process?

---

1 Committee on the Rights of the Child, General Comment No. 12 (2009): The right of the child to be heard, 20.07.2009, s. 1, CRC/C/GC/12.

2 Th. Moreau, 'Intérêt et droits de l'enfant ou les deux éléments constitutifs du droit de l'enfant au respect', in Th. Moreau, A. Rasson Roland and M. Verdussen (Eds.), *Le droit de l'enfant au respect*, Anthemis, 2013, pp. 145 ff.

3 Committee on the Rights of the Child, General Comment No. 14 (2013) on the right of the child to have his or her best interests taken as a primary consideration, 29.05.2013, §43; ECtHR, *Hokkanen v. Finland*, No. 19823/92 §61. ECtHR, *Bronda v. Italy*, No. 40/1997/824/1030, §62; ECtHR, 19.09.2000, *Gnahoré v. France*, No. 40031/98, §§61 and 6.

We confined ourselves to the field of child assistance and protection. This choice is based on two grounds. On the one hand, the hearing of the child in family law has already been the subject of several evaluations in Belgium.[4] It therefore seemed appropriate to focus on this other aspect of children's justice which deals with the care of minors in difficulty and at risk, or minors in contravention with the law.[5] On the other hand, these procedures impact the lives of the young people concerned in a very significant way. It is therefore interesting to understand how they feel once taken into consideration.

After placing the interviews within a cross-cutting perspective, we noted that two points stood out in particular. We have limited ourselves to those in this contribution, given the limited space that has been assigned to us. This is, on the one hand, the perception of young people about the place given to their parents and, on the other hand, their feelings about the impact of their words.

Given the method and the limited sample, the present contribution cannot claim to be exhaustive. It seeks only to add to the debate concerning the impact of taking the opinion of minors into consideration in the proceedings concerning them.

2. THE LEGAL FRAMEWORK FOR CHILD ASSISTANCE AND PROTECTION PROCEDURES

In order to allow the (international) reader to grasp the scope of the concerns of young people in their full extent, it seemed necessary to present the context of intervention to which our research participants refer to.

---

4 See L. Jacobs, 'La parole de l'enfant face à la séparation parentale: regards croisés sur les pratiques d'audition' (2017) *Rev. trim. dr. fam.*, pp. 649 ff.; M. Mallien, 'L'autorité parentale, l'hébergement et la prise en considération de l'opinion de l'enfant par le juge: les apports des droits fondamentaux et la pratique des juridictions familiales', in *L'hébergement de l'enfant: réflexions pluridisciplinaires*, Limal, Anthemis, pp. 6 ff.; Youth Rights Department of Namur, *L'audition civile du mineur: la voix des jeunes*, Report issued by the SDJ, 2017; J. Marquet and L. Merla, *L'intérêt de l'enfant dans la mosaïque familiale: ce que cela signifie pour les enfants*, Observatoire de l'Enfance, de la Jeunesse et de l'Aide à la Jeunesse, 2015; Th. Moreau, et al., 'La parole de l'enfant … (mal)entendus?' Proceedings of the conference organized by the Youth Rights Department, 01.06.2005 in Charleroi, SDJ, 2006, pp. 21 ff.

5 Although they are also affected by these procedures, we did not interview minors who have been victims of criminal acts committed by other minors.

2.1. THE BELGIAN INSTITUTIONAL FRAMEWORK

Since the 1980s, Belgium has been a federal State.[6] Alongside the federal government, there are federated bodies exercising exclusive powers over a delimited territory as assigned to them by the Constitution or by laws passed by qualified majorities. There are two types of federated bodies: the Regions (powers aimed at a certain economic autonomy) and the Communities (powers founded on language, culture, and matters relating to the person).

Figure 1. Regions and Communities in Belgium[7]

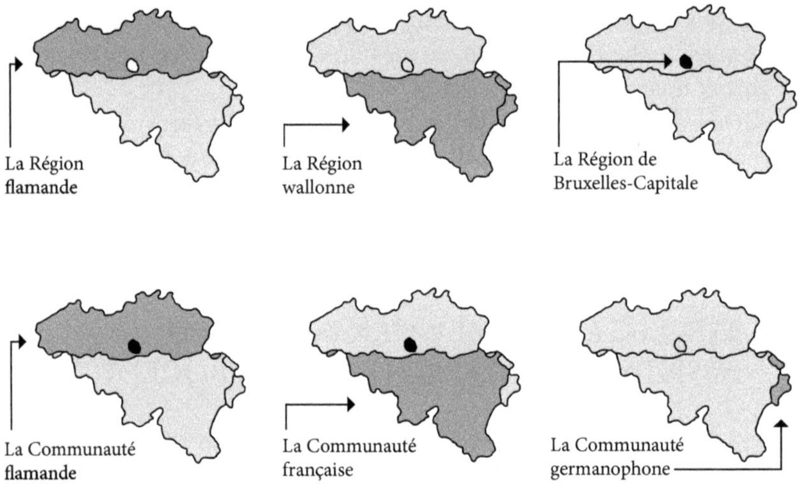

Each body has its own institutions and each exercises powers over a defined territory. At present, the judiciary only exists at the federal level. There are no jurisdictions under the federated entities. Several services in charge of investigative missions on behalf of the courts or the enforcement of their decisions come under the federated entities.

Since the sixth Reform of the State in 2014, child assistance and protection is entirely entrusted to the Communities.[8] Consequently, in

---

6 Constitution of Belgium, 1896, Article 1, <https://www.dekamer.be/kvvcr/pdf_sections/publications/constitution/GrondwetUK.pdf>.

7 Former website of the Belgian Government, <http://belgium.fgov.be/fr_index.htm>.

8 Article 5, Section 1 of the Special Institutional Reform Law of 08.08.1980, as amended by the Special Law of 08.08.1988 and by the Special Law of 06.01.2014. Previously, only one part of this matter was under Community jurisdiction.

Belgium, this matter is the subject of four sets of legislation, namely one for each Community, plus Brussels.[9] The criterion for the distribution of cases is the residence of the parent at whose house the minor has the primary residence. Each Community creates the institutions for child assistance and protection.

2.2. CHILD ASSISTANCE AND PROTECTION IN THE *COMMUNAUTÉ FRANÇAISE* (FRENCH COMMUNITY)

The young people who participated in the research reside in the territory of the *Communauté française*. In order to properly grasp the significance of their comments, it seemed important to give a brief presentation of the rules that apply in that Community.[10]

According to the *Code de la prévention, de l'aide à la jeunesse et de la protection de la jeunesse* (hereafter, the *Code de la jeunesse*), the granting of aid (youth assistance) is a priority for minors in difficulty or at risk. The *conseiller de l'aide à la jeunesse* (youth assistance counselor) directs the *service d'aide à la jeunesse* (Youth Assistance Service (SAJ)). At the request of the young person, the family, a third party or the public prosecutor, the *conseiller de l'aide à la jeunesse* seeks solutions to problematic situations which must be approved in writing by the young person aged 12 years or over and by his or her parents.

If the aid granted turns out to be impossible and if the *conseiller de l'aide à la jeunesse* considers that the minor is in danger, he or she must inform the *procureur du Roi* (public prosecutor) of the situation. The latter may submit the case to the *tribunal de la jeunesse* (juvenile court), so that it may deliver a binding youth protection measure. The difference between Brussels and the territory of the *Communauté française* lies at the level of enforcement of the measures ordered by the juvenile court.

---

9 The territory of Brussels is part of two communities. Prescriptive measures may thus not be imposed on a Brussels inhabitant through legislation of the *Communauté francaise* or of the *Communaué flamande* (Flamish Community). They are determined by the *Commission commmunautaire commune*, a specific body composed of an equal number of members of the Parliaments of the two communities.

10 For more details, see M. Preumont, Th. Moreau, P. Rans, and D. De Fraene, in *Le Code de la prévention, de l'aide à la jeunesse et de la protection de la jeunesse*, Brussels, Bruylant, 2019; A. De Terwangne, B. Marique, and N. Nounkele, *Le Code de la prévention, de l'aide à la jeunesse et de la protection de la jeunesse. Changements et perspectives*, Brussels, Bruylant, 2019; M. Preumont, *Mémento du droit de la jeunesse*, Brussels, Kluwer, 2019; F. Tulkens and Th. Moreau, *Le droit de la jeunesse en Belgique. Aide, assistance et protection*, Brussels, Larcier, 2000.

In Brussels, the Ordonnance (Order) of 29 April 2004 provides that the *tribunal de la jeunesse* has jurisdiction for the handling of the whole file, including monitoring the enforcement of its measures. Conversely, in the unilingual territory of the *Communauté française*, judgments of the *tribunal de la jeunesse* are limited to general guidance of the intervention: maintenance in the living environment or placement. The implementation of the measures is entrusted to the *directeur de la protection de la jeunesse* (Director of Youth Protection), who directs the *service de protection de la jeunesse* (Youth Protection Service (SPJ)). They undertake the necessary investigations, provide concrete content to the guidance adopted by the judiciary, mandate the services, review the measures and each year report to the Public Prosecutor's Office if they consider that a renewal of the binding measures is necessary. Their decisions may be reviewed before the *tribunal de la jeunesse*.

For minors in conflict with the law, the sets of legislation are different in Brussels and in the territory of the *Communauté française*: the Law of 8 April 1965 in Brussels; the *Code de la jeunesse* on the rest of the territory. Nevertheless, the two systems have closely related philosophies. The model is one of protective guidance, with a consequent openness towards restorative justice.

2.3. THE HEARING OF THE CHILD AND THEIR PARTICIPATION IN THE DECISION-MAKING PROCESS

Young people subject to an intervention by the youth assistance and protection system may, depending on their age, be heard and/or participate in the decision-making process. This can be done in various ways.

At the SAJ, a young person old enough to express themselves must be summoned to be heard, on the one hand, during the preparatory enquiries undertaken by the SAJ representatives or the mandated services, and on the other hand, during the formal meetings where the assistance agreement is negotiated with the youth assistance counselor.[11] If they so wish, the young person may be assisted by a lawyer and/or by a trusted individual. Furthermore, if they are over 12 years old, they must give their written consent to the chosen measure.[12] For minors from 12 to 14 years of age, such agreement is only valid if the minor is assisted by a lawyer.

---

11 Article 22 of the *Code la jeunesse*.

12 Article 23 of the *Code la jeunesse*.

The child's word will also be collected during the implementation of the measure, both by the SAJ representatives and by the mandated services.

In the case of legal proceedings, a minor at risk who is 12 years of age or older is legally a party to the case. They have the right to express themselves, as part of the exercise of their rights to defence, at each court hearing to which they are summoned, under the same conditions as adults, namely, depending on the case by summons or by cautionary statement.[13] Young people must necessarily be represented by a lawyer.[14] A minor under the age of 12 also has the right to appear and to express themselves, but, paradoxically, there is no obligation to summon them.

When the SPJ is responsible for implementing the decisions of the juvenile court, the gathering of the minor's view is carried out in the same way as during the intervention of the SAJ, with the difference that the agreement of the young person and of their parents is not necessary in order to decide on the measure.[15] The minor may be heard both during the inquiries and during the meetings with the director, or during the implementation of the latter's decisions.

A minor prosecuted for an offence is always a party to the proceedings. They are summoned to all of the court hearings if they are 12 years of age or older.[16] During the handling of the file, the magistrate is assisted by representatives from child protection belonging to the SPJ. These representatives meet with the minor both during the inquiry phase and during the phase of implementation of the measures. The minor is also heard by the intervening parties belonging to the services which carry out the measures ordered by the juvenile court.

3. THE RESEARCH METHODOLOGY

Our qualitative research is based on semi-directed interviews with 10 young people.[17] This type of interview is neither entirely open, nor directed by a large number of precise questions. The researcher invites the interviewee

---

13 Article 46 of the Law of 08.04.1965.

14 Article 54bis of the Law of 08.04.1965.

15 Article 40 of the Youth Code.

16 Article 52 of the Law of 08.04.1965 for hearings in chambers, when the juvenile judge rules on the interim measures. Article 46 of the Law of 08.04.1965 for public hearings.

17 On this type of interview, see D. Ruquoy, 'Situation d'entretien et stratégie de l'interviewer', in *Pratiques et méthodes de recherche en sciences sociales*, Armand Collin, Paris, 1995.

to speak openly, in the words of their choosing and in the order that suits them. The researcher simply seeks to bring the interview back to the objectives of the research and to ask the questions the interviewee does not arrive at on their own, at the most appropriate moment and as naturally as possible.[18]

Among the young people interviewed, five were still in the child assistance and protection system, while the other five had left it. This distribution made it possible to have different points of view from young people 'still concerned' and young people observing the situation *a posteriori*. The sample was composed of six boys and four girls.

The purpose of the research was to hear from young people on how their opinions are taken into account in the resolution of a situation. To fully respect what they said, we decided to quote them as is, in their own words, rather than interpreting their statements. Many of them expressed astonishment at the idea that we could be interested in their opinions. In return, they placed a great deal of confidence in us, and for this reason we regarded it as essential to remain faithful to their words.

Analysis of the empirical data enabled us to bring to light certain blind spots with regard to the position and role of the parents within the context of the child hearing.

4. THE RELATIONSHIP BETWEEN THE YOUNG PEOPLE'S RIGHT TO BE HEARD AND THEIR PARENTS

The procedures for child assistance and protection are often activated either because of the behavior of the minor him- or herself, or because of the behavior of his or her parents or environment. In these various procedures, the minors have the right to speak.

4.1. THE PLACE OF PARENTS IN THE HEARING PROCESS

The child's hearing may sometimes take place without the presence of parents, and sometimes in their presence, which can be a problem for young people. The majority of young people confided they have had

---

18 R. Quivy and L. van Campenhoudt, *Manuel de recherche en sciences sociales*, 3rd ed., Paris, Dunod, 2006, p. 171.

difficulties expressing themselves in the presence of their parents. Some of them explained that they were unable to speak freely:

> While I knew for a week that I was going to have an appointment, I was wary and stressed out, because I didn't know what was going to happen with my parents … I wasn't in good shape … The problem is that when you're young, you are easily frightened of things … especially when you have a 'hard time' with your parents or whatever (I4).

Some indicated they had been afraid of hurting their parents:

> But we're talking about my mom. With her psychological issues, there are highs and lows and I have no desire to incur her wrath either … Well I'm not against my mom, but there are times when I say things … For example, when the judge asks me whether I am enjoying myself at school, etc. – well I say yes, whereas my mom would prefer that I were close to her and that I were at the school close to the house, and that she were the one to help me do my homework, etc. (I6)

Another one indicated, 'I don't know how to talk to my parents, so … well I do, but not about things that hurt … so to take this on in front of everyone – well no' (I9).

Many indicated they feared an aggressive response from at least one of their parents. One young person told us, 'Well, the thing is that my dad is not aware that I remember what happened to me, what he did to me up to when I turned six. Even now. So I have always been on the defensive, not daring to express myself with him' (I7). Another young person added, 'Well, in my opinion I'm still a little reserved because, to this day my father still scares me a little. So errr … I think that basically I didn't say everything because I was still afraid that afterwards I would face reprisals' (I9). Another stated that, 'being heard at the court hearing in the presence of your parents is still traumatic. Well I mean you find yourself in situations where it just isn't pleasant for a child.' (I5).

Sometimes the reason behind the difficulty of speaking in front of one's parents is less clear: 'Well, sometimes I wouldn't dare to speak very much because, well, in front of both your parents sometimes you're a little uncomfortable' (I5).

Speaking appears to be simpler when not in the presence of one's parents: 'In fact, I didn't end up expressing myself orally when everybody was there, when my parents were there. But when it was just with the judge etc. there, generally I ended up speaking' (I9). One participant thus suggested that for the young people themselves, 'in the end it would almost be necessary to have the meeting without the parents. This will be easier for them, for them to express themselves and try to find better alternatives' (I4).

For the young people interviewed, the time allotted to the parents and to the child should be even. Otherwise, this translates into, in their opinion, a kind of bias towards the parent who is listened to longer or, at the very least, it shows a lack of consideration and interest in the child's opinions. Thus, one participant explained:

> I waited thirty minutes in the waiting room so I could have thirty seconds in the office, eh (…) Yes, it was very quick. The court clerk and all that talked and then they said 'well, that's fine, we'll extend the contract to next year' (I10).

Another young person explained:

> We were told to arrive at 1 pm and at 5 pm we still had not been heard. It was our parents' lawyers with our respective lawyers who spoke with our father and our mother … Yes, they talked about us, but not with us. And so we waited something like four hours in that waiting room doing nothing, eh. Because the goal was that we be heard as well. (I5)

The participant indicated they were heard for 20 minutes, 'but in fact the decision had already been made among the adults'. By contrast, recounting the unfolding of an interactive public hearing, the same young person said that, 'I find that the time there is very free. I was always able to take the time with the words that I wanted, so I think that's good' (I5). Another young person stated further, in regard to the SPJ:

> So my father had already started the interview all by himself, but he's a big manipulator, he babbles and babbles. And then my mother had an interview of exactly 20 minutes, while my father had an hour and a half. And then I was interviewed. That seemed to me like 15 minutes. Perhaps it was more, but the representatives didn't take any notes. And in any case, when I returned, they clearly told me that 'we already have our opinion on the issue', even though I hadn't even been heard … I was like 'Oh, OK, I wasn't able to explain myself.'… There it is – we no longer have any confidence …, it's the child protection service, not the service for protection of mom and dad (I2).

For some, the rule according to which a minor gets the floor at the end of the process constitutes a real difficulty:

> Whenever I spoke, they would say to me to 'wait your turn', all of that sort of thing. As a result, I waited and at the end of the meeting, I had my turn to

> speak for 10 minutes … Each time it was at the end of the meeting that I was able to truly express myself freely, eh. And in the end I didn't even manage to do that, because I was too flustered with my parents, who were shouting, and everything that they were saying that had nothing to do with me (I4).

4.2. THE IMPACT OF YOUNG PEOPLE'S VOICES ON THE INTERVENTION

Generally speaking, young people sense that what they say is not an element that has a decisive impact on their care. Many feel what they say does not carry the same weight as what the adults say. The words of one young person summarized this feeling quite well, 'I think that, today in society, children are considered to be inferior beings to adults, who are not particularly mature or who do not have the right to say what they think etc. and who must do as they are told' (I5). They carry on, showing their disappointment:

> I find it unfortunate that the judgments and the ways of seeing young people are still confined to 'we are the grown-ups and you are the little ones, so listen to us'. I mean, there is a change that has been made, everyone lives what they live, there is an experience behind each person, there is a family situation and there is a coming to maturity, there is a school setting. I mean, one cannot judge someone simply because they are under 18 … So I find it a shame and sad, whether it is the judge or the SPJ or anyone in today's world, that they see young people as something inferior to them in terms of everything that is legal, or in speaking and taking decisions, etc. (I5).

They add that knowing how to express oneself well is an asset: 'If someone of my age or even younger, or older, goes and doesn't know how to express themselves, what they have to say will have less impact than someone who knows how to speak well' (I5).

This feeling of injustice mixed with disappointment is also evoked in connection with the place occupied by the view of each participant in the reports or judgments. 'When you read the reports, what we explained, what we children explained – that took up three lines, and then three pages for mom and three pages for dad. So the children didn't have a great deal of impact' (I2).

A similar feeling was also expressed when the judgment does not contain a response to the young person's requests:

> Pfff, yeah, when I received the judgment there was no response to what I had said, to what I managed to express. So it is true that it is often a disappointment.

> And it is often the opposite of what I in fact asked for. So it's true that I would say that it's quite sad ... to see that. It's true that there are many points that are focused more on the adults and less on me, in fact. So it is always in relation to my parents: my parents, who got custody, their rights, etc. – and less with respect to what I asked for. So I think that it's really sad in fact, that ... I have the impression of being a circus animal performing before the judge, one who speaks and who says things – and less of being someone who has an impact and who is credible from their perspective. (I5)

Conversely, being heard can sometimes be a turning point in their care:

> There I think there was a turning point. I felt much more comfortable with all of those people like that who were there more within the justice system and so forth ... Because I felt, I suppose, because I felt listened to, and they did something because I wasn't doing well ... They finally did something for us. And so I told myself 'it's good, they are there for us' and so in my opinion I was much closer and much more comfortable then. (I7)

By contrast, the majority consider the right to be heard formalistic and that their opinion is not a determinant criterion for decision-making. One participant explained:

> Well, broadly speaking they theoretically respected our rights, I guess, but from a point of view that is really ... well, in reality, in fact not so much. In the end I get the feeling that they listened to us, but actually it was much more based on our parents as well. In the end they took far more account of the opinions of our parents than of ours, eh. (I2)

Along the same lines, a young person explained, 'Yeah, you really feel disoriented because they tell you that it's for you, but from the very beginning you have the feeling that in the end it's simply because your parents are like cat and dog' (I4). Another one added:

> For me, personally, I do not believe that a young person who is placed in care by the justice system really has their opinions taken into account. (...) I have had the impression somewhat that this is the fact ... in the end, I speak just to hear myself speaking, eh. (I6)

From their experience, this participant realized that taking what they have to say into consideration depends less on its content than on the consistency of their requests with the perspective of the social actors who are responsible for them. 'They support my requests, so that helps. But if they shot me down, if they weren't with me, what I have to say would be worth nothing, eh' (I6).

5. SOME BLIND SPOTS BROUGHT TO LIGHT

We carried out a cross-cutting re-reading of the interviews, during which we looked into the problems raised by the participants. As a result, blind spots appeared – namely, elements that are present but in relation to which the system remains blind.

Analysis of the participants' concerns makes it possible to discover that, although they do not fundamentally question the priorities assigned by the system, the young people do not encounter these priorities when they are subjected to being taken into care. They thus highlight a discrepancy between the formal and the concrete which, from their perspective, discredits the system.

The right to be heard is recognized and guaranteed. Nevertheless, it appears that within the framework of the current system, young people experience difficulties in freely and fully expressing their opinions. On several occasions, young people have told us that they perceive their parents as speech inhibitors. They do not want their parents to be informed of the things they say in confidence to the social workers – to the point of preferring to remain silent, should there be a possibility of their report being accessed by their parents. Neither do they wish to speak in front of their parents at the hearing. It emerged from the participants' discourse that the presence of their lawyer somewhat allays the unease they experience in relation to their parents.

Some young people see in their lawyer a veritable ally:

> And so, since the parents are there … it's above all the fact that the parents are there. You explain [to the care worker] things that your parents do not necessarily know. As a result, you're afraid that they will say it to the judge or whatever, and again you're afraid of the consequences. Whereas when it's the lawyer, I don't know … What differentiates them is that the care worker works with the SPJ and all. The lawyer too, but she's independent of that mess. (I4)

Young people's attitudes leading to self-censoring are explained by a fear of letting their parent down, a fear of reprisals, or a fear of hurting. For these reasons, they argued for direct contact with the judge. One participant underlined that being heard may only be favourable for them if it takes place away from the parents:

> Yes, because with the pressure of the parents being beside you, you don't know what you might say, you don't know … there are too many things that come back … it's really necessary that the young person be alone, and that the judge say to them that there is no problem, that they can speak to them, that nothing will get out, that nothing bounces back, eh. (I4)

The interviewees illustrated a pernicious effect of the adversarial principle that legal practitioners hold as an essential and incontrovertible guarantee, but that does not appear to be very compatible with child-friendly proceedings. In this regard, the ECtHR ruled that it is sometimes necessary in the case of minors to drop the mechanisms that in general protect the rights of adults who are on trial, if that is what is necessary in order to respect the child's specificities, so as to allow them to be fully involved in the process.[19] Respecting the child as a person, as defined in the CRC, implies respect for the differences linked to their status as a child, which may lead to a transformation in the requirements of a safeguard that is just as fundamental as the right to a fair trial.[20] Not accounting for these differences would provoke a disaster, since formal respect for the rights guaranteed by the CRC would undermine the values that it is intended to protect.[21]

The participants highlighted that the parents are those regularly perceived by the professionals as the principal beneficiaries of the intervention. The young people asked themselves whether they matter to the professionals:

> I get the feeling that they listened to us, but actually it was based much more on our parents as well. In the end, they took much more notice of the opinions of our parents than of ours, eh … We constituted collateral damage who ought to wait nicely. As a result, you never feel that you have been heard there. (I2)

---

19 ECtHR, judgment *V. and T. v. United Kingdom*, 16.12.1999, Sections 85–91, <https://archive.crin.org/en/library/legal-database/t-and-v-v-united-kingdom.html>.

20 Ibid.

21 Such a situation leads us to the concept of disaster threshold, on which we are working with the Canada Research Chair in Legal Traditions and Penal Rationality, led by Professor Alvaro. P. Pires. The disaster threshold is crossed when the system undermines the values that it has a duty to defend.

'Before I had my care workers, that seemed to me totally skewed, because it was just my parents that they listened to. Even if I said something, it's borderline if they listened to me' (I4). This finding could perhaps be explained by the fact that the intervention methods are developed based on approaches that hold the parents as being the cause of the intervention, and thus the problem to address – rather than as collaborators in seeking a solution.[22]

6. CONCLUSION

We were struck by the participants' maturity and their capacity to make their feelings understood. They have an irreplaceable expertise in the field of child assistance and protection. Their point of view sheds a new light on their place and their standing in matters concerning them.

In highlighting blind spots, they bring to the fore what they are lacking: 'the conditions in which they put us to speak, … I think that's one of the most important' (I7), as 'they give us the opportunity to speak, but not in an ideal setting' (I2). Young people refer us to the method applied in the system. The willingness to hear them is there and seen by them, but the encounter does not happen on the best terms. They provide leads to better meet their need to be actors: connect with young people where they are, create the conditions for free expression, take them seriously, and understand the complexity of their parents' position. More than technique, these avenues for reflection are first and foremost the personal responsibility of the actors. In the eyes of the young people, the way things are done appears to be more important than the doing itself.

22 See in particular G. Ausloos, *La compétence des familles*, Eres, 1995; G. Hardy, *S'il te plaît, ne m'aide pas! L'aide sous injonction administrative ou judiciaire*, Eres, 2012; Th. Moreau, 'Les enjeux de la réforme de la protection de la jeunesse', (2001) 207 *JDJ*, pp. 37 ff.

THE SIGNIFICANCE AND EFFECTIVENESS OF CHILDREN'S PARTICIPATION IN JUDICIAL CHILD PROTECTION PROCEDURES IN QUEBEC, CANADA

Mona Paré

1. INTRODUCTION

Access to justice has many facets, with one of them involving giving the child an opportunity to voice their opinion and hearing those opinions. This is particularly important in child protection proceedings which can have a major impact on the lives of children whose security and development are at risk. In the province of Quebec, Canada, the law on child protection guarantees the right for the child to be heard. However, how the child should be heard lacks clarity. The only specific provisions in the law that apply to judicial proceedings concern the child's right to be represented by counsel and child testimony in court. While the law focuses on voluntary measures that are decided in collaboration with the parents, the majority of child protection cases end up in court, where an adversarial procedure is followed. Since children's right to be heard has been recognized as a general principle applying to all children's rights,[1] it is crucial to understand how this right is implemented in the context of child protection, including how children are really heard in judicial proceedings, and how child representation and testimony work in practice.

The analysis in this contribution is based on empirical research conducted in four judicial districts in Quebec between 2017 and 2020.[2] Its aim was to understand when and how children participate in judicial court proceedings, and how professionals (judges and caseworkers) and children, who have had an experience in youth court,[3] perceive children's participation in judicial proceedings and their right to be heard. Based on interviews conducted with 12 judges, 17 caseworkers, and 10 children, as well as an analysis of the law and observation of practice, this contribution first examines the significance and importance given to children's participation in judicial proceedings as represented in the law and as perceived by the research participants. It then critically examines the effectiveness of current practice, and finally suggests measures to improve practice so that it may be more respectful of children and their rights.

2. SIGNIFICANCE AND IMPORTANCE OF CHILDREN'S PARTICIPATION IN CHILD PROTECTION PROCEEDINGS

2.1. AS RECOGNIZED IN THE LAW

Quebec law is particularly clear on the fact that children have the right to be heard in court proceedings that concern them. The Quebec Civil Code

1 Committee on the Rights of the Child, *General Guidelines Regarding the Form and Content of Initial Reports*, [1991] UN Doc. CRC/C/5, <https://digitallibrary.un.org/record/137523?ln=en>. On the contents and importance of this right, see Committee on the Rights of the Child, General Comment No. 12 (2009): The right of the child to be heard, (20.07.2009), CRC/C/GC/12, pp. 70–74 <https://www.refworld.org/docid/4ae562c52.html>.

2 Research findings and methodology have been exposed more thoroughly in M. Paré and D. Bé, 'La participation des enfants aux procédures de protection de la jeunesse à travers le prisme de la vulnérabilité' (2020) 61(1) *Les Cahiers de Droit*, p. 22, and M. Paré and E. De Bellefueille, 'Children's place and voice in Quebec's child protection proceedings' (2021) 34(1) *Canadian J. Family Law*.

states: 'The court shall, in every application brought before it affecting the interest of a child, give the child an opportunity to be heard if his age and power of discernment permit it'.[4] The Quebec Youth Protection Act (YPA) is even more respectful of children's rights, since it does not tie child participation to age or discernment. For example, Article 6 states: 'The persons and courts called upon to take decisions respecting a child under this Act must give this child (…) an opportunity to be heard'.

Adopted in 1977, it is the first law in Canada that is expressly based on child rights, clearly stating that all decisions 'must be in the interest of the child and respect his rights'.[5]

What is also particular to the child protection proceedings in Quebec, compared to other Canadian jurisdictions and most other proceedings concerning children in Canada, is children's status as parties. This gives them similar rights to other parties, who, in child protection proceedings, are the governmental child protection entity: Director of Youth Protection (DYP), and the child's parents.[6] For example, party status gives children the right to appeal youth court decisions.

While there are many rights granted to children in Quebec's child protection legislation, including many provisions specifically concerning children's right to participate and to be heard in non-judicial and judicial proceedings, most of these are stated in a general way. For example, children are to be treated with courtesy, fairness, and understanding[7] and child participation must be encouraged by all those with responsibilities under the Act.[8] However, some rights are more detailed. In the context of judicial proceedings, these include the child's right to counsel and child testimony. The court must inform the child of their right to be represented by a lawyer and ensure the child is represented by an advocate independently from their parents.[9] Relating to testimony, all children are presumed competent to testify. Those under 14 years of age will promise to say the truth instead of taking the oath, and this has no impact on the value of their testimony. It is up to a party to prove to the court that a child is not able to understand and

---

3 In Quebec, a specialized court (Cour du Québec, chambre de la jeunesse) hears both child protection and juvenile justice cases.

4 Civil Code of Quebec, CQLR c. CCQ-1991. Interestingly, the terminology of 'age and power of discernment' has not been discussed in case law or amongst researchers. The article is mostly used to allow child representation by a lawyer in a family law case.

5 Youth Protection Act, CQLR, c. P -34.1 [YPA], Article 3.

6 In some cases, the Quebec Human Rights Commission is also a party.

7 Article 2.4(1) of the YPA.

8 Article 2.3 of the YPA.

9 Articles 78 and 80 of the YPA.

answer the questions; if this is the case, the court may declare that the child is not competent to testify.[10] The court may also exceptionally dispense a child from testifying if testimony could be prejudicial to the child.[11] It is important to note, however, that a declaration made by a child who does not testify for either reason stated above is admissible as evidence.[12] Furthermore, given that children are vulnerable and impressionable, the law allows the court to hear a child without the presence of other parties. However, their lawyers will remain present to ensure procedural rights of all parties are respected.[13]

In sum, children's participation and their voice are given much importance in legislation. Yet, the law does not provide for ways in which children should participate or be heard. Recognizing that children have the right to a lawyer and that all children should be able to testify, unless considered prejudicial to the child, is not inclusive of all methods of participation, which may range from an expert report on the views of the child to a judicial interview of the child.[14] Moreover, the YPA's formulation around testimony and legal representation can lead to varied interpretation and practice by professionals.

2.2. AS UNDERSTOOD BY PROFESSIONALS AND CHILDREN

Research participants recognized that children have rights, and that participation has important benefits for children. However, participants also had reservations about children's participation in court proceedings. It should also be noted that the concept of participation was generally understood as child testimony and/or children's presence in court. There was thus limited understanding of the scope of child participation and children's right to be heard, which can be through various means.[15]

---

[10] Article 85.1 of the YPA.

[11] Article 85.2 of the YPA.

[12] Article 85.5 of the YPA.

[13] Article 85.4 of the YPA.

[14] See R. Birnbaum and N. Bala, 'Child Participation in Family Dispute Resolution in Canada', in this volume, describing Canadian research on children's participation in family law cases.

[15] See the explanation given in: above n. 1, General Comment No. 12. See also: L. Lundy, 'Voice is not enough: conceptualizing Article 12 of the United Nations Convention on the Rights of the Child' (2007) 33(6) *British Educational Research Journal*, p. 927; K. Tisdall, 'Children and Young People's Participation: A critical consideration of Article 12', in W. Vandenhole, E. Desmet, D. Reynaert, and S. Lembrechts (Eds.),

Most importantly, participation cannot be simple presence in court; it must involve the child giving their opinion to the decision-maker or to someone who will relay it to the decision-maker.

The main reservation about child participation was made based on age. It was commonly agreed by judges and caseworkers that adolescents should be active participants in proceedings, while young children should be sheltered from the court. There was no agreement on the age under which children should not participate. Judges seemed to identify a higher age (around 13 or 14 years), while some caseworkers mentioned children under seven or eight years of age. Children participating in the study also recognized that younger children (under 10 or 12 years of age) should not come to court because of their lack of understanding and because the courthouse is an intimidating place. In practice, only adolescents come to their court hearings, while younger children come only if they need to testify. Sometimes, children are brought to court to meet with their lawyer and leave after their meeting.

Some specific situations concerning the child and their family were also noted as indications that a child should not come to court. These included the child's mental health and disabilities, parents' mental health and behaviour, as well as high-conflict separation cases. It was felt that children diagnosed with mental health problems should not be present in hearings, as this could be detrimental to them. Judges were also of the opinion that the presence of children caught in parental conflict was not advisable. While these children will most likely want to testify, they may suffer from parental alienation and their testimony may be instrumentalized by parents. Caseworkers also noted the difficulty of asking a child to testify when they live at home. Some parents place the blame of the decision on the child, especially if the child sides with the DYP or testifies against a parent. The consequences of testimony may be hard for the child, and they can feel regretful, scared, and responsible for the entire situation.

Thus, there is some contradiction in how judges and caseworkers perceive children's participation and voice. It is seen as a right and something to be upheld, but it is also felt that it is not desirable in every circumstance. While the law does not distinguish between ages, age was a determining factor in how participation was viewed and exercised.

Routledge International Handbook of Children's Rights Studies, London, Routledge, 2015, p. 185; N. Thomas, 'Towards a Theory of Children's Participation' (2007) 15 *International Journal of Children's Rights*, p. 199.

3. EFFECTIVENESS OF PARTICIPATION

3.1. REGARDING REPRESENTATION BY LEGAL COUNSEL

Unlike the majority of other jurisdictions in Canada, Quebec is quite unique as the law provides that children, at all ages, should be represented by a lawyer. This seems like a perfect way to ensure indirect participation for children for whom it is not advisable to come to court. Traditionally a lawyer would meet with a client and act according to the client's instructions, ensuring the court knows the client's position. However, this is often not the case with children's lawyers. It goes without saying that not all children are capable of instructing a lawyer, usually because of their young age and lack of understanding of the proceedings, the options available, and the consequences of certain decisions. The Quebec Court of Appeal and the Quebec Bar have provided guidance on the role of the child's lawyer.[16] According to these bodies, a lawyer should represent a child according to their instructions if the child has sufficient maturity. It is for the lawyer to verify each child's capacity to instruct them. Yet, this guidance is not always followed. In this research, judges were particularly critical of the practice of many lawyers who do not meet with their child client, or meet with them only briefly in court, just before the hearing.

Representation by legal counsel also calls for distinctions to be made based on age. This indirect form of participation is effective when it comes to adolescents, who know their lawyer and instruct them. It is less effective for younger children. Some lawyers will not meet with seven- to 12-year-old children to assess their capacity to instruct a lawyer and will rather represent them based on the DYP's report and on what they believe to be in the best interests of the child and respectful of their rights. Lawyers of young children may correctly assume they should represent their client based on their best interests, but it is still important that they meet with them and hear them. Even a five-year-old can have an opinion, which the court should know. This does not mean that the lawyer should base their representation on this opinion.

One judge stated it is the five- to 10-year-old children who are the most abandoned, as many of them could express their opinion and could have

[16] Quebec Court of Appeal, *F.(M.) c L.(J.)*, [2002] RJQ 676 (CA), 211 DLR (4e) 350, 2002 CanLII 36783 (QC CA); Barreau du Québec, 'La représentation des enfants par avocat dix ans plus tard' (2006) Mémoire, <http://collections.banq.qc.ca/ark:/52327/bs61009>; Barreau du Québec, *Guide des meilleures pratiques en droit de la jeunesse*, Barreau du Québec, 2018, <https://www.barreau.qc.ca/media/1590/guide-droit-jeunesse.pdf>.

things to say, but they are often not heard or even met by their lawyer. On the contrary, children aged 13 or 14 years or older will know their lawyer and be able to meet with them in preparation of a hearing. Adolescents also tend to be more vocal, aware of their rights and will ensure their lawyer knows what they think and what they want. However, many participants deplored the fact that the lawyer will only meet with the adolescent in the courthouse, just before the hearing. Some children also noted that their lawyer did not convey everything they said to the judge.

Legal representation provides a great opportunity for children to be heard by the decision-maker, but, while the law makes no distinctions based on age, a certain practice has been developed excluding children under a certain age to really express their views and be heard. While they are represented by a lawyer, their voice may not be heard by the decision-maker. The age at which a child will be heard and met varies from one lawyer to another.

3.2. REGARDING CHILD TESTIMONY

Child testimony is the most direct way of hearing a child, as provided for in the law. When a child testifies, they are present at the hearing in court and speak directly to the judge.

While this is a form of direct participation, which is encouraged by the Committee on the Rights of the Child,[17] it may not be the best way for a child to express their opinions. This is so for many reasons, but especially because of the lack of freedom to express oneself. Testimony follows specific procedural rules, and while some adaptations are made for children, testimony has one major objective, which is to establish facts. Thus, the child will answer questions asked by their lawyer, and then will be cross-examined by other parties' lawyers. In child protection proceedings, the judge also has an investigative role and may ask the child questions. Therefore, testimony is not an opportunity for the child to express their opinion freely, but simply to answer questions to help the court establish facts.

Moreover, the child may not feel completely free to express themselves because testimony will happen in the presence of others. Depending on the nature of the case and on the child's level of anxiety, the parties may be present at the hearing, or they may be asked to leave the room. In the

17 Above n. 1, General Comment No. 12, para. 35.

latter case, their lawyers stay, and depending on courts, the parents may be able to listen to their child's testimony in another room. In any case, the child will know the other parties will be made aware of the contents of the testimony. Testimony can thus be stressful, and many caseworkers gave examples of how children's behaviour changes before the hearing if they are called to testify: there may be increased anxiety, crying, or insomnia, for example. The court will thus try to avoid child testimony when facts can be established through other means. Consequently, the majority of children do not testify. Therefore, this is not a reliable and systematic method to hear the child's opinion.

4. IMPROVEMENTS RELATING TO THE SIGNIFICANCE AND EFFECTIVENESS OF PARTICIPATION

There are recommendations for improvements stemming from suggestions made by research participants, as well as my observations and analysis based on child rights principles. While this contribution does not cover all recommendations discussed by participants, five categories of improvements are outlined to possibly make participation more meaningful and respectful of children's rights.

First, it is evident that we must *diversify opportunities* for the child to be heard and to participate in judicial child protection proceedings. There are examples from other jurisdictions that could be adapted to Quebec practice. One is the 'judicial interview' or child hearing, which is an opportunity for the child to meet with the judge without this being in the context of formal testimony.[18] Some professionals and children in this research already talked about informal discussions that sometimes happen between the child and the judge during the court hearing. However, this can only apply when the child is already present at the hearing, meaning that it is mainly adolescents that benefit from such an opportunity. In practice, the judge may ask the child if they have questions or something to say; the judge may also ask the child questions or explain to them the judge's expectations and decision when the decision is taken in the presence of the child. Again, this concerns adolescents, as younger children do not follow hearings. Thus, it

[18] See e.g. R. Birnbaum, N. Bala, and L. Bertrand, 'Judicial Interviews with Children: Attitudes and Practices of Children's Lawyers in Canada' (2013) *N.Z.L. Rev.*, p. 465.

would be interesting to develop this practice further in a way that it can become accessible to all children.

In addition to widening the practice of informal exchange with the judge to children of all ages, the setting could be more child friendly. The conversation between the child and the judge happens within the framework of the formal court hearing, in the presence of all parties, which is not optimal. According to the Committee on the Rights of the Child, hearing a child should be in the form of a talk, and not in an open court.[19] Of course, applying the idea of judicial interviews in Quebec is limited by the fact that children are parties to protection proceedings and, therefore, a private meeting between the judge and the child could be seen as affecting the judge's independence vis-à-vis the other parties. However, I would argue that protection proceedings are different from other court proceedings, as the decision must always be in the child's best interests. Thus, there is no real 'winner' or 'loser' in such cases, as the decision must always be to the child's advantage. I would suggest that procedural guarantees of parties, while having to be respected, should be examined through a different lens – the best interests of the child. Other solutions that have been implemented elsewhere include letters written by the child and addressed to the judge, or expert reports on the child's views.[20] The latter can be especially helpful to find out about younger children's opinions if lawyers' common practice of not meeting with younger children does not change.

Secondly, it is of utmost importance to discuss the *role of the child's lawyer*. Having legal provisions that mandate the appointment of an independent legal counsel to the child is one of the great advantages of the Quebec judicial child protection system. Quebec lawyers apply a distinction in the way they represent children: they have either a legal mandate or a conventional mandate. With a legal mandate, they represent the child who is incapable of instructing them, on the basis of the child's rights and what they believe to be in the child's interests. With a conventional mandate, they represent the child based on the child's wishes. Lawyers determine the child's capacity to instruct them; however, many lawyers will not meet or contact the child to make that determination. They often seem to make this decision based on the child's age. It would therefore be crucial to bring

---

19 Above n. 1, General Comment No. 12, para. 43.

20 See examples in family law proceedings in Canada: C. Houston and N. Bala, *Article 12 of the Convention on the Rights of the Child and Children's Participatory Rights in Canada*, Department of Justice 2015, pp. 12–13, <https://www.justice.gc.ca/eng/rp-pr/other-autre/article12/index.html>.

some uniformity to lawyers' practice through special rules of conduct when they are faced with a child client, and to provide mandatory professional training on ways to conduct meetings with all children. Many participants, especially judges, said lawyers should meet with the child in the child's own environment (e.g. foster care home or school), or in a neutral place, instead of the courthouse. It was also suggested that the lawyer spend enough time to hear the child, as often the meeting is restricted to barely 15 minutes before a hearing. Meeting the child earlier would also allow for better preparation of the child in case they attend a hearing or testify in court. One must strive towards such rights-respecting practice, while being fully aware of the current circumstances of tight deadlines and overloaded dockets. This would be very difficult without an overhaul of the judicial system.

Thirdly, the *judicial system* itself was criticized by research participants. It was noted that it is ill-suited to solve child protection issues, and social action is the best course of action. In fact, the YPA prioritizes voluntary measures, with decisions to be made together with the child's parents and the caseworker. However, in reality, cases end up in court mostly because of disagreements between the DYP and the parents. A judge noted that many of the cases brought before them should not be in court and should be dealt with in the community. They stated that the services are there, but they are underutilized. However, it was also noted that services are not always readily available, and that there may be waiting times to access them. Some participants were in favour of resorting to alternative modes of dispute resolution, such as mediation, arbitration, or settlement conferences. Such conferences are chaired by a judge, whose role is to facilitate the discussion between the parties. While training on settlement conferences is available to judges, and some practice this regularly, it is not mandatory for judges to offer or practice such facilitation. Alternative dispute resolution is faster and less adversarial, so it should be favoured over judicial proceedings, but not at the expense of child participation. We should ensure children have the right to participate and be heard in all modes of dispute resolution.

Fourthly, it was felt that the *physical space* in the courthouse makes participation more stressful for children. Courthouses were described by judges as cold and dehumanizing. One judge explained there is no other public space that looks like that. Another described what the child sees on arrival, such as the lawyers and judges dressed in black or black and red. One young person noted that there are just chairs in the waiting room. Another said the presence of security officers with guns was intimidating. Most courthouses in Quebec are not adapted to children;

there are generally no special waiting rooms for children with toys or books. Many participants wished that some spaces be adapted to children. Some children also suggested there could be books, a television, or even beanbags on the floor for children to relax. This is all the more important as children sometimes have to spend the whole day waiting for their hearing or their turn to testify. There are no fixed times for hearings, and children are told to come in the morning even if their case is heard in the afternoon. Additionally, there are frequent cancellations, and after hours of waiting, the parties may be told the case is postponed to months later. One young participant explained how having to wait, and not having anything to do to kill time, increases stress and anxiety. It makes children think about why they are there and worry about what will happen. Some participants, children, and caseworkers also said animal therapy should be available more, as the presence of a dog would reduce stress in court. Improving the spaces and services available in courthouses would have a positive impact on child participation in protection proceedings.

Finally, it is important to find ways to include children in a *dialogue*. This entails providing children with adequate information and asking them if they would like to be present in court, to meet the judge and/or to testify. As explained above, the law requires children be given the opportunity to be heard. However, it does not specify who should inform the child of this right. There is no guarantee the caseworker will inform the child about this since their role is generally limited to the social sphere of action. As to the lawyer, they only represent the child once the court is seized of a case. One author believes children should have access to legal counsel even outside the judicial procedure, as the lawyer can inform the child of their rights also in relation to the intervention initiated by the DYP.[21] Some caseworkers also noted that answering the child's questions about the legal procedure and legal rights should primarily be the lawyer's responsibility. Knowing that many lawyers do not make time to meet with children who might not be of an age to instruct their lawyer, but who can voice their opinions, it is quite likely that there are many children who are not informed about opportunities to have their voice heard. The child's lawyer should explain what options are available for the child to exercise their right to be heard, and make sure the child can make a choice within the possible scope. While the law includes provisions on giving children information in an appropriate language considering the child's age

---

[21] A. Fournier, 'Le droit de l'enfant à la représentation par un avocat en matière de protection de la jeunesse' (1996) 37(4) *Les Cahiers de* Droit, p. 971.

and understanding,[22] nothing in the law makes it possible to ascertain who is responsible for ensuring the child has access to information. This includes information about the court's decision. While adolescents may hear the decision directly from the judge at the hearing, children are not always present when the decision is made, and some decisions are only written. There is no practice of the judge writing a decision in a child-friendly language and the lawyer usually does not contact the child to inform them of the decision. It is unclear how the child learns about the decision (from their caseworker or parent) and in what terms. If the judge does not directly inform the child, the lawyer could play an important role in giving this information to the child in a child-friendly language.

It seems there is an assumption that it is best for children not to be present in court, and not to testify, because it can be stressful for them, because it makes them miss school, because it places them in the centre of a conflict, etc. Yet, adults' perceptions and children's feelings may not always coincide. It is important to make sure each child is asked whether and how they want to participate and that they are informed of the modalities and possible consequences of participation. For instance, in relation to testimony, which is the only method of direct participation provided for in the YPA, most children interviewed stated that they were initially stressed, but they felt relieved after. One young participant said she was less stressed after having met the judge. All were of the opinion that their views were important because the case was all about their lives. Children's views should thus be sought in relation to the application of the right to be heard.

5. CONCLUSION

In conclusion, it must be recognized that Quebec has long since introduced legislation that is favourable to children's participation in judicial child protection proceedings. Yet, there are many gaps in practice, and the vagueness of the law in certain respects allows for variations in practice that are not always to the child's advantage. While there is general recognition of the importance of hearing the child's voice, professionals find many arguments to limit children's participation. These arguments can certainly be justified in some cases. However, if it is not in a child's best interests to participate in a certain way, for example, through testimony in court, it does not mean the child should not voice their opinion in other ways.

22 Article 2.4(2) of the YPA.

It is therefore important to establish concrete ways in which children, at different ages and in different circumstances, can be heard by the decision-maker, and to involve children in decisions about modalities of participation. Additionally, improvements can be made to current practice in terms of the roles of different actors, particularly children's lawyers, and the context of the judicial proceedings. This context includes the rules around the adversarial process, deadlines, delays, and backlogs, as well as the lack of services in courthouses, and the inadequate nature of the physical spaces. Each of these aspects could be improved even minimally, and within the framework of current legislation, bringing practice closer to full implementation of children's participation rights in the context of child protection proceedings.

PART II

CHILDREN'S ACCESS TO JUSTICE IN JUDICIAL AND NON-JUDICIAL PROCEDURES

CHILDREN'S ACCESS TO AND PARTICIPATION IN THE FAMILY JUSTICE SYSTEM IN FRANCE

Limits, Paradoxes and Recommendations

Blandine MALLEVAEY

1. INTRODUCTION

Since minor children are subject to parental authority,[1] it is their parents who make decisions relating to them. If the child is capable of acting with discernment, their parents are required to involve them in their decision-making. This principle flows from Article 12 of the Convention on the Rights

[1] French law defines parental authority as a set of rights and obligations aimed at the child's best interests (Article 371(1)(1) and (2), C civ).

of the Child (CRC),[2] which establishes the right of the child to participate in decisions that concern them, if they are capable of forming their own views. The Committee on the Rights of the Child has raised the child's right to be heard to the status of a general principle of the CRC,[3] in the same way as their right to have their best interests constitute a paramount consideration for all decisions concerning them.[4] The Committee has emphasised the importance of the child's participation, highlighting it as a prerequisite to the decision-making that make the best interests of the child a paramount consideration.[5] Thus, the child is considered one of the best experts for their needs and interests.

A child's right to take part in decisions regarding them has been integrated into the French Civil Code, among the provisions regarding parental authority, which call upon the parents to involve their child in the decisions concerning them, according to their age and level of maturity.[6] The parents are the prime guarantors of the child's participation in family decisions that concern them and, as a result, of respect for their best interests. That being said, the statistics of the Ministry of Justice suggest a trend toward the judicialization of family relationships, with the result that the decisions bearing on the daily life of the child, on their place in their family, and on their family relationships, are ever more frequently taken in the context of legal proceedings in which their parents are adversaries.[7] This trend leads one to wonder about children's access to and participation

2 Convention on the Rights of the Child, 20.11.1989, 1577 UNTS 3 [CRC].

3 Committee on the Rights of the Child, General Comment No. 5 [2003]: General measures of implementation of the Convention on the Rights of the Child, [27.12.2003] Doc off CRCNU, 34th session, CRC/C/GC/2003/527, para. 6, Articles 4, 42 and 44, Section 12.

4 Above n. 2, Article 3(1).

5 Committee on the Rights of the Child, General Comment No. 12 [2009]: The right of the child to be heard, [20.07.2009], CRC/C/GC/12, pp. 70–74; Committee on the Rights of the Child, General Comment No. 14 [2013]: On the rights of the child that their best interests be paramount consideration, [29.05.2013] Doc off CRCNU, 62nd session, CRC/C/GC/14, pp. 43, 53; For a detailed study see: B. Mallevaey, 'Regards sur 30 ans d'application de l'article 12 de la Convention de New York sur la participation de l'enfant' (2020) 2 RTD civ p. 291.

6 Article 371-1 al 4 C civ.

7 In France in 2018, family court judges had before them 148,627 applications related to parental authority and to rights of access, compared to 133,169 applications in 2013 – an increase of 11.5% in five years. Ministry of Justice, *Les chiffres clés de la Justice*, 2014 and 2019, <http://www.justice.gouv.fr/statistiques-10054/chiffres-cles-de-la-justice-10303/>.

in the family justice system, in particular with regard to family court, to which French law confers the jurisdiction for hearing actions related to the exercise of parental authority.[8]

The French law brings a twofold response to this issue. The child's access to the family justice system is governed by different rules depending on whether proceedings concerning them have been brought before a family court judge. Before the family court, access to the court and the right to participate in proceedings are recognized, by means of a child hearing in court. However, this access may face numerous barriers. Since minor children may not take legal action, they are denied any access to the family court in the absence of prior proceedings taken forward before it.

2. CHILDREN'S LIMITED ACCESS TO FAMILY COURT IN THE CASE OF PRE-EXISTING PROCEEDINGS

When legal proceedings concerning a child have been brought before the family court, the child may be heard by the magistrate if they are capable of 'discernment' or forming their own views. This hearing allows the child to make their needs known to the judge, so that the latter may be in a position to make decisions that are most in line with their best interests. Hearing of the child thus constitutes a means for them to have access to the family justice system, as embodied in the family court judge. This access is nevertheless imperfect, given that hearing the child does not make them party to the proceedings,[9] with the result that they can neither have access to the docket nor avail themselves of remedies.[10] In addition, this access is limited by several legal or material obstacles.

---

8 Article L. 213-3 2° of the Code de l'organisation judiciaire [C org jud]. Thus, the family court has jurisdiction to decide disputes bearing on the one hand on the conditions for exercising parental authority, and on the other hand, on the forms of exercise of parental authority. See V. Larribeau-Terneyre and M. Azavant, 'Autorité parentale' (2020) 9 *Rép. pr. civ. Dalloz.*

9 Article 388-1 al 3 C civ.

10 The child may be accompanied by a lawyer when they are heard (Article 388(1) sub-para. 2, C civ). Since the lawyer cannot have greater procedural prerogatives than their young client, they have no additional access to the record of the proceedings.

2.1. THE LEGAL OBSTACLES PERTAINING TO THE HEARING OF THE CHILD BY THE FAMILY COURT JUDGE

Children's right to participate in decisions made by the family court was introduced by the French legislature within the Civil Code, which states that a minor capable of discernment be heard by the judge in all proceedings concerning them.[11] These provisions drew directly on Article 12.2 of the CRC which replicated the child's right of expression to actions in court, and thus stipulated that the possibility to be heard must be given to the child in any legal proceedings in which they have an interest.[12] This right is likewise recognized by the European Convention on the Exercise of Children's Rights (ECECR), pursuant to which a child sufficiently capable of forming their own views has the right to be consulted and to express their opinion, in any proceedings before a judicial authority in which they have an interest.[13]

While drawing on the international and European treaties[14] – the subordination of the child being heard to their capacity of forming their own views raises numerous difficulties that adversely affect the child's right to participate in family court decisions. Indeed, by virtue of its lack of precision, the concept of 'discernment' is complex and gives rise to subjective haphazard interpretations on the part of magistrates. Even though the Court of Cassation denies trial judges the latitude of deciding whether a child is capable of discernment solely by reference to their age,[15] age remains, in practice, the decisive factor. This is explained by the fact that, before meeting the child, the judge is obliged to assess the child's capacity to form their own views at the time of receiving the application for a hearing. The family court judge (JAF) has to make a decision on the

---

11 Article 388-1 al 1 C civ.

12 Since 2005, Article 12.2 of the CRC, along with Article 3.1, are recognized by the Court of Cassation as being directly applicable, and may thus be invoked before the family court: Cass civ 1re, 18.05.2005, Bull civ I 180, No. 02-20.613; Cass civ 1re, 14.06.2005, Bull civ I 207, No. 04-16.942; Cass civ 1re, 8.11.2005, Bull civ I 338, No. 02-18.360 and Cass civ 1re, 22.11.2005, Bull civ I 370, No. 03-17.912.

13 European Convention on the Exercise of Children's Rights, Strasbourg 25.01.1996. *Committee of Ministers of the Council of Europe*, European Treaty Series No. 160 [ECECR], Article 3.

14 In the French version the concept of 'discernement' is used in the CRC and the ECECR. In the English-language versions of these treaties, reference is made to a child, 'who is capable of forming his or her own views' (CRC), or 'considered as having a sufficient understanding' (ECECR).

15 Cass civ 1re, 18.03.2015, Bull civ I 57, No. 14-11.392.

request to be heard solely from the information that they have available in the case file. Inasmuch as French law no longer sets any age threshold starting at which the child may be considered capable of forming their own views,[16] substantial disparities in practices may be observed from one court to another, and even within the same court. Thus, certain JAFs refuse to hear children before the age of 12 or 13, which corresponds to the age of starting secondary school, while others hear them from the age of six or seven, coinciding with the age of starting primary school.[17] This is a source of inequality of treatment and of legal uncertainty. Consequently, a research team, working on the hearing of children and on their capacity to form their own views before the JAF, has recommended legislative measures such that this criterion be supplemented by an objective criterion characterized by the child's age.[18] It is recommended positing a presumptive capacity of discernment on the part of children older than 10 years of age. Provided that a child older than 10 was deemed capable of forming their own views, the judge could not refuse to hear them without having to explain this decision in their ruling. This presumption would foster the participation of minors over 10 years of age in family court proceedings, without inhibiting the hearing of children under that age, provided they meet the aforementioned requirement. The French legislature has remained deaf to this recommendation, which has nevertheless been taken up by the Children's Ombudsman in its 2020 report devoted to the rights of the child.[19]

In addition, since JAFs are not specialized magistrates,[20] they have not received training on gathering children's opinions. They may experience a certain unease when faced with this delicate exercise, and even treat hearing the child with suspicion. Indeed, the subjectivity and imprecision of the notion of 'discernment' is what permits them to take shelter behind the child's lack of capacity to form their own views in order to refuse to

16 From 1975 to 1987, the legislature had set the threshold of 13 years of age as that beyond which the hearing of the child could only be overridden by a specifically substantiated decision (former Article 290(3) of the Civil Code).

17 B. Mallevaey, 'Audition et discernement de l'enfant devant le juge aux affaires familiales' (2018), *Mission de recherche Droit et Justice*, pp. 46–54 <http://www.gip-recherche-justice.fr/publication/audition-et-discernement-de-lenfant-devant-le-juge-aux-affaires-familiales-2/>.

18 Ibid., pp. 56–62.

19 C. Hédon, *Prendre en compte la parole de l'enfant: un droit pour l'enfant, un devoir pour l'adulte*, 11.2020, p. 16.

20 In France, the JAF – unlike the juvenile court judge (JE) – is not a specialized magistrate (Article L. 213-3 C org jud.).

hear them.[21] As a consequence, a functional specialization for JAFs is recommended, which would have as its corollary specific training in child and adolescent psychology and in listening to what they have to say.[22] This would help children's access to and participation in family justice.

2.2. THE MATERIAL OBSTACLES TO THE HEARING OF THE CHILD BY THE FAMILY COURT JUDGE

In theory, French law subordinates children's right to be heard to the fulfilment of two conditions: the proceeding concerns the child, and they are capable of forming their own views.[23] The effective enjoyment of this right is de facto limited in terms of its implementation mechanisms. First, whereas the legislature has obliged parents to involve their child in decisions, depending on their age and level of maturity,[24] it has not required the judge to have the child participate. Indeed, the Civil Code states that a minor capable of discernment may be heard in any proceeding that concerns them. The wording demonstrates that the JAF is not obliged to hear the child and is hardly ever required to invite the child for this purpose. It is only when the child formulates such a request that the judge is obliged to hear them[25] and to take their views into consideration.[26] French law requires an active effort from the child to make their voice heard, undeniably limiting their access to and participation in family proceedings. On several occasions in its reports on the application of the Convention in France, the Committee on the Rights of the Child expressed concern relating to the fact that the child must make an application to exercise their right, which gives rise to discrimination and discrepancies in practice.[27] In theory, the request to be heard is presented to the judge in

---

21 Even more problematic is the fact that the decision of the judge ruling on the applications to be heard is not subject to appeal on the part of the child (Article 338-5 al 1 C pr civ).

22 Above n. 17, pp. 174–78.

23 Article 338(4), sub-para. 1, C pr civ.

24 At least in theory, since this rule is not accompanied by any penalty in the event of its breach.

25 Article 388(1), C civ. A request to hear the child may also be formulated by the parties to the proceeding, and the judge may therefore deny it if they do not consider it necessary to the resolution of the dispute, or if it appears to them to not be in the best interests of the child (Article 338(4), sub-para. 2, C pr civ).

26 Article 373-2-11 2° C civ.

27 Committee on the Rights of the Child [2009]: Concluding Observations of the Committee on the Rights of the Child: France, [11.06.2009], Doc off CRCNU,

no particular form and at any point in the proceedings;[28] in practice many courts require this request to be addressed to them in writing at the outset of the proceedings, prior to the court session that convenes the parents.[29]

The fact that, pursuant to French law, the child must request a hearing in order to speak in court, is problematic as the child may only launch this action after having been informed beforehand of their right to be heard. Indeed, French law entrusts to the parents the responsibility of informing their child of their right to be heard.[30] However, when the parents are personally involved in the dispute, they do not appear to be the best suited to dispense full and objective information to the child. Nor is it uncommon that the parent presents being heard not as a right but as an obligation to the child, if this is favourable for the parent. The parent who does not wish their child to be heard fails to inform them of their right, or even dissuades them from exercising it.[31] The law provides that the judge ensure the child has been informed of their right to be heard and to be assisted by counsel.[32] In practice, the magistrates have no way of verifying that this information has reached the child, and that the child's parents have allowed them to participate in the proceedings.

Bearing in mind the difficulties raised by the child's request to be heard and their being informed, the authors of research on children's hearing have recommended arranging a system to directly notify the child of their rights, through a form that would be sent to them by correspondence, as is done in Belgium[33] or Scotland.[34] This correspondence would advise the child of their right to be heard by the judge, in presence of counsel, and it would permit them to make their wish to be heard or not known in proceedings concerning them, by sending back the filled-in form to the court, whether by email or by means of a postage-paid envelope.[35] Coupled with the aforementioned presumption for children over 10 years of age, this mechanism would facilitate the child's access to the family court and would strengthen their participation in judicial decisions.

51st session, 1425th meeting, CRC/C/FRA/CO/4, p. 39. Along the same lines, Concluding Observations of the Fifth Periodic Report of France, [23.02.2017] Doc off CRCNU, 71st session, 2104th meeting, CRC/C/FRA/CO/5, p. 29.

28 Article 338-2 C pr civ.

29 Above n. 17, pp. 82–91.

30 Article 338-1 C pr civ.

31 Above n. 17, p. 65.

32 Article 388-1 al 4 C civ.

33 Article 1004/2 C jud. (Belgium).

34 *Act of Sederunt (Sheriff Court ordinary cause rules 1993)* (UK), Rule 33.7(1)(h).

35 Above n. 17, p. 199.

When an action concerning the child has been brought, the child benefits from access to the family justice system, manifested in their hearing by the family court judge. Such access is available in case of proceedings already under way prior to the child wishing to take part in the decisions made about them. Conversely, the child is deprived of access to the family court when the latter has not been called on beforehand to settle a dispute.

3. ACCESS BY THE CHILD TO THE FAMILY COURT: IMPOSSIBLE IN THE ABSENCE OF PRE-EXISTING PROCEEDINGS

When there are no prior proceedings brought before the family court, the latter becomes inaccessible for the child, who does not have the capacity to refer a case to it. This incapacity leads to a curious paradox, since a child who would like to call into question their parent's decisions would have no other alternative but to put themselves in danger, in order to bring a case before the juvenile court.

3.1. THE CHILD'S INCAPACITY TO REFER THE MATTER TO THE FAMILY COURT

While French law allows the child to express their views to the JAF, this prerogative may only be implemented if the magistrate has had proceedings concerning the child brought before them. Most often, such a case is submitted to the family court on both parents' initiative or of one of them, involving a conflict regarding the child. The family court may likewise hear a case brought by a third party, in particular by the grandparents of the child,[36] their brothers and sisters,[37] or any other person[38] who might apply for rights of access and accommodation, or further by a third party asking that the exercise of parental authority be delegated to them.[39] The JAF may also have a case referred by the public prosecution service, to rule on the mechanisms for the exercise of parental authority[40] or on the delegation

36 Article 371-4 C civ.
37 Article 371-5 C civ.
38 Article 371-4 C civ.
39 Article 377 C civ.
40 Article 373-2-8 C civ.

of this exercise.[41] Although the child is the principal interested party for decisions on the exercise of parental authority, they are unable to bring an action before the family court. Minor children are affected by an incapacity to exercise the rights that they enjoy,[42] depriving them of the capacity to be a party to legal proceedings. Thus, the child is able to request to be heard when the family court has had proceedings brought that concern them but cannot take the initiative for such proceedings. As a consequence, in the absence of pre-existing proceedings, the child has no access to the family court, nor any right to express their views in court.

This produces a dubious paradox, since a child whose parents are in conflict sees their rights better respected than a child whose parents jointly make the decisions pertaining to them. Indeed, a child whose parents are feuding to the point of remitting the dispute to judicial arbitration can express their feelings to the JAF, who will rule in favour of their interests and needs. By contrast, a child whose parents agree on decisions that would appear to the child to be inconsistent with their interests, has no possibility of bringing a case before this same JAF. For example, a child whose parents are in agreement for them to live alternately with each parent, regardless of the long distances between the homes, is unable to refer the matter to the family court to obtain a ruling for living arrangements in line with their interests.

This observation leads us to contemplate an overhaul of the procedural framework for minor children. The States Parties to the ECECR – including France – are invited by the treaty to do so. It encourages them to consider recognizing children's right to completely or partially exercise the prerogatives of a party in proceedings affecting their interests before a judicial authority.[43] The latter include 'family proceedings, in particular those involving the exercise of parental responsibilities such as residence and access to children'.[44] In looking to improve their access to family proceedings and their participation, it would be necessary for the child to have the possibility to take initiative for proceedings before a family court judge. Several mechanisms may be envisaged to give the child the power to trigger the bringing of a case to the family court.[45] The most

41 Article 377 3 C civ.

42 Article 414 C civ. *a contrario.*

43 ECECR, Article 5. Along the same lines, the Council of Europe's Guidelines on Child-Friendly Justice, adopted in 2010, invite the States Parties to facilitate access to the court by children with sufficient understanding of their rights.

44 Ibid., Article 1.

45 For a detailed presentation, B. Mallevaey, *L'audition du mineur dans le procès civil*, doctoral thesis, University of Artois, 07.12.205 [unpublished], <http://www.theses.fr/2015ARTO0301>.

appropriate would be to give the child the possibility of applying to the public prosecution service to refer the matter to the family court. *De lege lata*, the public prosecution service may have a matter referred to it by a third party for it to refer the matter to the family court for a ruling on the forms of exercise of parental authority.[46] *De lege ferenda*, the public prosecution service could additionally have a matter referred to it by a child who is in disagreement with the decisions that their parents make concerning them, to request an intervention by the family court. The public prosecution service would be accorded a screening function, which would allow it to dismiss the child's request if it did not exhibit a serious character, or to refer the matter to the family court if it deemed such to be justified. As things stand in French law, the only possibility that the child might have would be to put themselves in danger in order to be able to bring a case to the juvenile court for the purpose of child protection measures.

3.2. THE POSSIBILITY OF THE CHILD BRINGING A MATTER BEFORE THE JUVENILE COURT

In French law, endangered children have the possibility of bringing the matter before the juvenile court for the purpose of protection measures. The Civil Code provides that if the health, safety, or morals of a minor child are in danger, or if the conditions of their upbringing or their physical, emotional, intellectual, and social development are seriously compromised, child protection measures may be ordered by the juvenile court, at the request of the father and mother, the person or agency in whose care the child has been entrusted, their legal guardian, the public prosecution service, or of the child themselves.[47]

This exceptional power that the legislature has ascribed to the child is felicitous: to the extent that the danger threatening the child results more often than not from the activities or negligence of their parents, it is indeed desirable that they be able to activate their own protection by referring the matter to the juvenile court. However, there are two limitations. First, the child may only bring the matter before the juvenile court on the condition that they are capable of discernment, as the Court of Cassation so

46 Article 373-8-8 civ.
47 Article 375 al 1 C civ.

requires.[48] Secondly, the child's initiative presupposes that they are aware of this possibility, even though no mechanism is envisaged to so inform them, whether in law or in practice. Thus, if the child is capable of forming their own views and is advised of the procedural initiative that they benefit from, their ability to refer the matter to the juvenile court offers them an access to justice that is quite remarkable under French law. Not only may they bring the matter before the court but, in addition, they have status as a party to the proceedings, giving them in particular access to the docket[49] and the possibility of appealing against the juvenile court's ruling.[50] Within the framework of proceedings before the juvenile court, children enjoy a right to participate – a right that is likewise unique. Indeed, unlike the family court, the juvenile court is required in any event to hear the child, if they are capable of forming their own views.[51] Since hearing the minor in the inquiry phase of child protection proceedings is a rule of public policy,[52] the children's judge (JE) of the juvenile court must summon the child to be heard, failing which their ruling may be overturned on appeal.[53] The right of the child to participate is thus fully guaranteed by them being heard and the JE must always strive to obtain the assent of the family, including the minor child, to the protection measure that they envisage decreeing.[54]

4. CONCLUDING THOUGHTS

While evidently beneficial, the opportunity for a child to bring a matter before the juvenile court gives rise to a new and regrettable paradox. Given the extent of the criteria mentioned above, a child opposed to the decisions that their parents have made concerning them would need to endanger

---

48 Cass civ 1re, 21.11.1995, Bull civ I 292, No. 94-05.102. In the absence of discernment, the child themself may not bring the matter before the JE; they must be represented by an ad hoc guardian (Article 388(2), C civ).

49 Pursuant to Article 1187, sub-paras 3 and 4, C pr civ.

50 Article 1191, C pr civ.

51 Article 1182 al 2 C civ. However, in practice this right is not always respected: recently Cass civ 1re, 02.12.2020, Bull civ I, No. 19-20.184, AJ fam. 2021, p. 127, above n. 17.

52 Cass civ 1re, 30.06.1981, Bull civ I 236, No. 80-80.006.

53 With the clarification that hearing the minor is required of the JE but not of the child themself, such that if they have been summoned for their hearing but did not appear, the child protection proceedings are not deemed invalid: Cass civ 1re, 3.10.2000, Bull civ I 152, No. 99-05.072.

54 Article 375-1 al 2 C civ.

themselves in order to make judicial intervention possible. By way of illustration: an imposition, by the parents, of religion which collides with the child's beliefs and harms their interests, may not be referred to the family court. If this situation causes suffering to the child such that they flee, mutilate themselves, take on suicidal behaviour, or consume alcohol or narcotic substances ... then the criterion of danger is met, making it possible for them to bring the matter before the juvenile court. Thus, under French law cure is better than prevention!

CHILD PARTICIPATION IN FAMILY DISPUTE RESOLUTION IN CANADA

Rachel Birnbaum and Nicholas Bala

1. INTRODUCTION

Social science research and the Convention on the Rights of the Child (CRC) support children's participation in post-separation disputes about their care, whether the disputes are resolved by the parents themselves, through negotiation, mediation, or litigation. In Canada, there is significant variation between jurisdictions in philosophy and resources (e.g., private and public) for involving children in family dispute resolution. Methods used include: having a mental health professional prepare a report of a full assessment of the parents and child; or a briefer report prepared by a professional based solely on a couple of interviews with the child; child legal representation; having a child meet with the judge or the mediator or parenting coordinator; a letter or other communication from the child with the court; or through witnesses testifying about what the children told them. There are special concerns in determining how to involve children in cases where there is high conflict, or there are allegations of domestic violence, or a child is refusing to visit their other parent. While it is important for children to be heard, and for them to say what they want, it is also important they should not feel pressured by the court process to 'take sides'.

This contribution explores the different methods of involving children in post-separation disputes between parents, the advantages and disadvantages of each, and the empirical research about the use of different methods of involving children in the family justice system in Canada. While there is no one method that is suitable for all cases, and for some cases it may be appropriate to use more than one method as the case evolves, children continue to experience challenges in being heard in the family justice system. Our central thesis and focus is that children should be involved in the decision-making process about the plans for their care in a way that respects their needs, interests, and wishes. Including children promotes their long-term welfare by ensuring that decision-makers are properly informed and by giving children a sense of agency and respecting their rights as recognized in the CRC. Hearing from children may also facilitate settlement of the parental dispute, reducing the financial and emotional costs of decision-making.[1]

---

1 R. Birnbaum and N. Bala, 'Children's Participation in Family Disputes in Canada', in W. Schrama, et al. (Eds.) *International Handbook on Child Participation*, Intersentia, Cambridge, UK, 2021; R. Birnbaum and M. Saini, 'A Scoping Review of Qualitative Studies on the Voice of the Child in Child Custody Disputes' (2012) 20(2) *Childhood*, p. 260; J. Cashmore, 'Children's Participation in Family Law Decision-Making: Theoretical Approaches to Understanding Children's Views' (2011) 33 *Children & Youth Services Rev*, p. 515; J. Cashmore and P. Parkinson, 'Children's and Parents' Perceptions on Children's Participation in Decision Making After Parental Separation and Divorce' (2008) 46 *Fam Ct Rev*, p. 91; K. Tisdall, et al., 'Children's Participation in Family Law Proceedings: A Small Step or a Step Too Small?' (2004) 26 *J Soc Welfare & Fam L* 17.

2. STATUTORY PROVISIONS FOR CHILDREN'S INVOLVEMENT

At least in theory, in Canada, provincial and territorial legislation and caselaw have long required courts to consider the views and preferences of children as a factor in making 'best interests' decisions about parenting arrangements, generally based on the dated concepts of 'custody' and 'access'.[2] In practice, however, until relatively recently, despite the stated principle that children's views were to be considered, the adults involved often did not introduce this type of evidence, and decisions were made without children's preferences and perspectives being taken into account.[3]

The amendments to Canada's Divorce Act, which came into force on 1 March 2021, introduce new concepts, including parenting time, parental decision-making, and parenting plans.[4] These amendments also require that in making 'best interests' decisions the courts shall consider, 'the child's views and preferences, giving due weight to the child's age and maturity, unless they cannot be ascertained.' However, this legislation *does not* provide any mechanism for ascertaining the child's views. Rather, children's participation remains dependent on provincial and territorial laws and government services that are not uniform or consistently funded across the country (e.g., child lawyers, publicly funded parenting assessments, views of child reports), and the attitudes of family justice gatekeepers (e.g., judges, lawyers, mental health professionals) which are also not uniform.[5]

---

2 The federal Divorce Act applies across Canada to parenting disputes when the parents were legally married and are obtaining a divorce. If the parents are not obtaining a divorce, usually because they were cohabiting without marrying or never cohabited, then the legislation of the child's province or territory applies to their dispute. As discussed in this contribution, there is now consistency in the federal and provincial/territorial laws requiring consideration of the views and perspectives of children. However, the manner in which children's views are to be considered, even in cases under the federal Divorce Act, is the responsibility of the provincial and territorial governments, which have varying legislation, resources, and programmes for child participation.

3 N. Semple, 'The Silent Child: A Quantitative Analysis of Children's Evidence in Canadian Custody and Access Cases' (2010) 29(1) *Can Fam LQ*, p. 1.

4 N. Bala, 'The 2020 Reforms to the Parenting Provisions of Canada's Divorce Act' (2020) 39(1) *Can Fam LQ*, p. 45.

5 R. Birnbaum and N. Bala, *Making Parenting Plans in Canada's Family Justice System: Challenges, Controversies and the Role of Mental Health Professionals*, Toronto, Thomson Reuters 2019.

3. DIFFERENT WAYS OF HEARING CHILDREN

There are a number of different methods that can be used to hear from children who are the subject of post-separation parental disputes:[6]

- Hearsay evidence,[7] related by a witness, such as a parent or social worker;
- A videorecording or audiotape of an interview with the child;
- Written statements from a child such as a letter or affidavit;
- A report or the testimony of a mental health professional as part of a parenting assessment;
- A report from a lawyer or social worker who has conducted an interview and prepared a Voice of the Child Report;
- Counsel for a child presenting the child's views to the court;
- Testimony by the child in court; and
- A private meeting with the child and the judge.

There are advantages and disadvantages to each of these methods of bringing the child's 'voice' into family proceedings. There is no empirical research that demonstrates that one method is better than another. The method selected in a case will depend on a number of factors, including the resources available for the particular case and the attitudes of the professionals involved.[8]

---

6 N. Bala, R. Birnbaum, and F. Cyr, 'Judicial Interviews of Children in Canada's Family Courts: Growing Acceptance but still Controversial' in T. Gal and B. Duramy (Eds.), *Promoting the Participation of Children across the Globe: From Social Exclusion to Child-Inclusive Policies*, Oxford, Oxford University Press 2015; N. Bala, V. Talwar, and J. Harris, 'The Voice of Children in Canadian Family Law Cases' (2005) 24 *Can Fam LQ*, p. 221.

7 Above n. 6, N. Bala, V. Talwar, and J. Harris. The term 'hearsay' evidence refers to testimony by a person relating statements made by another person who is not a witness. While hearsay evidence is presumptively inadmissible in common law courts, there are some important exceptions to the rule that allow witnesses, in some circumstances, to testify about a child's statements to them. Further, the hearsay rule is usually somewhat relaxed in family proceedings. However, judges in family cases may discount hearsay evidence from parents and other interested parties about what they say a child told them; the concern is not just about the reliability or honesty of parents or other interested parties, but also about the influence that they may have had on the child.

8 N. Bala and R. Birnbaum, 'Rethinking the Role of Lawyers for Children: Child Representation in Canadian Family Relationship Cases' (2018) 59(4) *Les Cahiers de Droit*, p. 787; N. Bala, R. Birnbaum, and L. Bertrand, 'Controversy about the Role of Children's Lawyers: Advocate or Best Interest's Guardian? Comparing Practices in Two Canadian Jurisdictions with Different Policies for Lawyers' (2013) 51(4) *Fam LQ*, p. 681; R. Birnbaum and N. Bala, 'Judicial Interviewing with Children in Custody

4. INDIRECT MODES OF CHILDREN'S PARTICIPATION

4.1. PARENTS, GUARDIANS, AND PROFESSIONALS

Parents, guardians, and professionals in family cases may be permitted to testify about what children told them about their views and preferences. However, judges in litigated family disputes are concerned about parents manipulating their children and, if there is conflicting evidence from parents, may put little or no weight on evidence from parents about what their children told them. Canadian judges discourage parents from presenting recordings of statements from their children, and often refuse to admit this type of evidence in family proceedings.[9]

It is more acceptable to Canadian courts to admit hearsay testimony from an independent professional, like a schoolteacher or school social worker, who may have spoken to a child and can share the child's views with the court.[10]

4.2. PARENTING ASSESSMENTS

For parents who have the financial resources, the court has the authority to order them to pay for a parenting assessment by a mental health professional (e.g., psychologist, social worker, psychiatrist). These assessments typically report on interviews with each parent and other significant figures, as well as interviews with the child, and they include parenting recommendations about a plan that would promote the best interests of the child. However,

---

and Access Cases: Comparing Experiences in Ontario and Ohio' (2010) 24(3) *Intl JL Pol'y & Fam*, p. 398; R. Birnbaum and N. Bala, 'A Survey of Canadian Judges about their Meetings with Children: Becoming More Common but Still Contentious' (2014) 91 *Can Bar Rev*, p. 637; R. Birnbaum and N. Bala, 'Views of the Child Reports: The Ontario Pilot Project' (2017) 31(3) *Intl JL Pol'y & Fam*, p. 344; above n. 7; R. Birnbaum, N. Bala, and F. Cyr, 'Children's Experiences with Family Justice Professionals and Judges in Ontario and Ohio' (2011) 25(3) *Intl JL Pol'y & Fam*, p. 398; R. Birnbaum, 'Views of the Child Reports: Hearing Directly from Children Involved in Post Separation Disputes' (2017) 5(3) *Social Inclusion*, p. 148; M. Hayes and R. Birnbaum, 'Voice of the Child Reports in Ontario: A Content Analysis of Interviews with Children' (2019) 61(5) *J Divorce & Remarriage*, p. 301.

9 See, for example, *Whidden v. Ellwood*, 2016 ONSC 6938 and *Maharaj v. Wilfred-Jacob*, 2016 ONSC 7925; M. Shaffer, 'Surreptitiously Obtained Electronic Evidence in Seven Simple Steps' (2019) 38 *Can Fam LQ*, p. 259.

10 Above n. 7.

these private assessments often result in delay in the resolution of proceedings, are expensive, and many parents cannot afford them. In some jurisdictions in Canada there are limited government-funded programmes to prepare these assessment reports by a social worker or psychologist (e.g., British Columbia, Alberta, Saskatchewan, Manitoba, Ontario, Quebec, Nova Scotia), though these programmes continue to lack sufficient funding to allow an assessment in most litigated cases. In some parts of the country these programmes are unavailable (e.g., Yukon, Nunavut, Northwest Territories, New Brunswick, Newfoundland and Labrador), or publicly funded assessment reports are available for only a very small portion of cases.[11] As a result, children may not always be heard during the parental dispute, and this can cause negative emotional and behavioural outcomes.[12]

4.3. CHILD LEGAL REPRESENTATION

In some Canadian jurisdictions, including Ontario, Quebec, Alberta, Yukon, and the Northwest Territories, there is a possibility that a government-paid lawyer may be appointed to represent the child whose parents are litigating about parenting issues. While judges may request the involvement of a lawyer for a child, judges generally do not have the authority to require the government to provide counsel for a child in a family proceeding.[13] Even in jurisdictions with established offices of child legal representation, like Ontario, resource restraints result in many parenting cases being resolved without a lawyer for a child, even if requested by the court.[14]

It is accepted that one of the roles of counsel appointed for children is to ensure that the views and preferences of the child are presented to the court. In some cases, this may be done by having a mental health professional, retained by the child's lawyer interview the child and report about the child's statements. It is generally accepted in Canada that a lawyer for the child may tell the court about a child's wishes and preferences, including telling the court about, 'the clarity, consistency, and independence of the children's views [as the basis] to inform the [child's lawyer's] own assessment of what position to take on behalf of the children'.[15] However,

11 Ibid.

12 Ibid.; above n. 1, R. Birnbaum and M. Saini.

13 *B(AC) v. B(R)*, 2010 ONCA 714; *JESD v. YEP*, 2018 BCCA 286. In most provinces, judges can order representation for a child in a child welfare proceeding.

14 Above n. 8, N. Bala and R. Birnbaum (2018).

15 *Ludwig v. Ludwig*, 2019 ONCA 680.

there are also sometimes judicial concerns about lawyers appointed for children 'giving evidence from counsel table' about statements from the child, for example, about alleged abuse or not wanting to visit with the other parent, because the lawyer is not subject to cross-examination.

There is variation in policy and practice about the extent to which lawyers appointed for children will advocate a position based on the child's wishes, or whether counsel for the child will advocate a position based on their own assessment of the child's interests, though also ensuring that the parents and court are aware of the child's preferences. There are particular concerns about a lawyer 'acting on a child's instructions' if the child appears to be unduly influenced by one of the parents, such as when there are concerns about alienation, though even in alienation cases it is important for a child's views to be known to the court and parents. In practice, lawyers appointed for children often try to promote a settlement by the parents that is consistent with the child's wishes.[16]

5. DIRECT MODES OF CHILDREN'S PARTICIPATION

5.1. JUDICIAL INTERVIEWS WITH THE CHILD

Although children regularly testify in criminal proceedings in Canada, and are occasional witnesses in child protection cases, they almost never testify in the family court in parenting disputes. If a parent wants to call a child as witness, with the possibility of being subject to cross-examination, there will be concerns about the effect that this will have on the child. Judges have the authority to refuse to allow a parent to have a minor child testify as a witness in a family proceeding. However, judges also have the authority to conduct a judicial interview with a child in a parenting dispute.[17] In some provinces, such as Quebec, judicial interviews with children who are the subject of parenting disputes are common, and often occur in the courtroom, with the parents excluded but their lawyers present. However, in most parts of Canada, there is wide variation in practice, with some judges doing this regularly, and others not at all. Some judges feel that it

---

16 Above n. 8, N. Bala, R. Birnbaum, and L. Bertrand; above n. 8, N. Bala and R. Birnbaum (2018).

17 N. Bala, et al., 'Children's Voices in Family Court: Guidelines for Judges Meeting Children' (2013) 47(3) *Fam LQ*, p. 379; above n. 8, R. Birnbaum and N. Bala (2010); above n. 8, R. Birnbaum, N. Bala, and F. Cyr.

is not their role to be gathering evidence in the parenting dispute and are concerned that they are not properly trained in interviewing children, but other judges are willing to interview children, without having had formal training.[18]

It is generally accepted in Canada that judicial interviews with children should not be 'forensic'; in particular, they should not be intended to ascertain the truth of a child's allegations of abuse or witnessing spousal violence. While children's testimony in court about abuse is common in criminal cases, in parenting disputes, evidence of the child's reports about abuse or neglect is rarely if ever introduced by having the child testify, and never by having a child meet with the judge outside of court.[19]

5.2. VOICE OF CHILD REPORTS

There is a growing use of Voice of the Child Reports in some parts of Canada, including in British Columbia, Saskatchewan, Manitoba, Ontario, Nova Scotia, and New Brunswick.[20] These are short, focused reports about what the child says about their views and preferences in a parenting dispute. A social worker or lawyer with training interviews the child and prepares a report for the court about what the child said. The report is meant to be a reporting of the child's statements and not an interpretation of the child's stated views. These reports are usually prepared for children 10 years of age and older, but some children as young as seven years of age participate in these types of interviews. The interviews typically take about one hour, with siblings being interviewed separately. There are usually two interviews, with the child brought to each interview by a different parent. No other information (e.g., reviewing court pleadings, contacting professional or personal collaterals) is collected about the child or the parents and no parenting recommendations are made. These reports are much less expensive than a full assessment, as only a few hours of professional time are required, and they can be prepared quickly. Often these reports also serve as a triage function to ascertain if a more

---

18 Above n. 8, R. Birnbaum, N. Bala, and F. Cyr; above n. 8, R. Birnbaum and N. Bala (2010).

19 Above n. 8, R. Birnbaum and N. Bala (2010).

20 Above n. 8, R. Birnbaum; above n. 8 R. Birnbaum and N. Bala (2017); R. Birnbaum, N. Bala, and J.-P. Boyd, 'The Canadian Experience with Views of the Child Reports: A Valuable Addition to the Toolbox?' (2016) 16 *Intl JL Pol'y & Fam*, p. 158; above n. 8, M. Hayes and R. Birnbaum.

complete parenting assessment is required as in cases with domestic violence, alienation, mental health concerns, or emotional neglect. In some provinces, such as British Columbia, Ontario, Manitoba, and Nova Scotia, the government may pay for these reports.

5.3. CHILDREN IN MEDIATION AND PARENTING COORDINATION

Children have not typically been involved in mediation or parenting coordination in Canada, though the practice is becoming more common and empirical evidence as to the positive benefits for children is slowly emerging.[21] Yasenik and Graham[22] developed the Child Centered Continuum Model for parents to assess the degree of their child's participation readiness in the mediation process. This latter approach is similar to child-inclusive mediation carried out in Australia that demonstrates that fathers, in particular, benefit from hearing from their children.[23]

6. ADVANTAGES AND DISADVANTAGES OF THE DIFFERENT METHODS

As stated, there is no 'best way' to hear from children and there is no research to date in Canada that demonstrates that any one method or any one family justice professional (e.g., judge, lawyer, social worker, psychologist, psychiatrist) is 'better' than another for involving children.[24] The method used in an individual case will depend on the stage of the process, the issues in dispute, the resources available, the attitudes of the professionals and parents, the age and communication abilities of

21 L. Yasenik and J. Graham, 'The Continuum of Including Children in ADR Processes: A Child-Centered Continuum Model' (2016) 54(2) *Fam Ct Rev*, p. 186; L. Yasenik, J. Graham, and L. Fieldstone, 'Child Voice in Parenting Coordination: Toward a Model of Inclusion' (2020) 58(3) *Fam Ct Rev*, p. 760.

22 Ibid., L. Yasenik and J. Graham.

23 J. McIntosh, C. Long, and L. Moloney, 'Child-Focused and Child-Inclusive Mediation: A Comparative Study of Outcomes' (2004) 10(1) *J Family Studies*, p. 84; J. McIntosh, et al., 'Child-Focused and Child-Inclusive Divorce Mediation: Comparative Outcomes from a Prospective Study of Postseparation Adjustment' (2008) 46(1) *Fam Ct Rev*, p. 105.

24 Above n. 7.

the child, and the views of the child about how to be involved or not. In practice, often more than one method is used over the course of a parenting dispute. There are advantages and disadvantages to each of these methods, and which method or combination of methods is used may depend on a number of factors such as:

- the issues in dispute;
- the resources available (e.g., private or publicly funded);
- the child's age and capacity (e.g., whether the child has any special needs, such as learning problems, fetal alcohol syndrome disorder (FASD), autism spectrum disorder (ASD) or epilepsy);
- whether the child wishes to participate and, if so, how;
- the stage of process (e.g., interim, case conference, trial);
- the nature of the dispute resolution process (e.g., mediation, negotiation, arbitration, litigation);
- concerns about fairness to parents and the child;
- the attitude of the family justice professionals (e.g., whether they are focused on children as objects or subjects); and
- the legal framework and attitude of the decision-maker.[25]

In deciding about how children's views should be received, there also needs to be a balancing of a number of competing factors, including:

- providing the court with as much information as necessary;
- minimizing the trauma or distress to the child;
- ensuring a fair process for the parents;
- ensuring a fair process for the child; and
- resolving the dispute in a way that is as cost-effective as possible for the parents, the child and the family justice system.[26]

An important distinction must also be made between evidence about the preferences of children and their statements about factual issues that may be in dispute. For example, hearing from children about where they want to live and how often they want to visit a parent is different from hearing about their own maltreatment or witnessing domestic violence (e.g., children's views and preferences versus children's experiences). While children's preferences are related to their experiences, there are significant

---

25 Above n. 1, J. Cashmore and P. Parkinson.

26 Above n. 8, N. Bala, R. Birnbaum, and F. Cyr.

differences about how their views and preferences are expressed and how the court will deal with them, with greater expectations for parental due process if children are providing evidence of factual matters in dispute.[27]

7. EMPIRICAL RESEARCH INTO THE DIFFERENT WAYS CHILDREN ARE HEARD

While there has been research into the experiences of family justice professionals with children in mediation, being interviewed by a judge, having a lawyer or mental health professional interview them, this section solely focuses on research with and for children.[28]

In the last two decades, there has been a significant increase in empirical research with and for children about the different ways they can be heard during the parental dispute. Children have been interviewed both retrospectively and prospectively to better understand their views and experiences with family justice professionals and the different methods used to facilitate their voice in the process. Birnbaum[29] collaborated with the Department of Justice, Canada to prospectively interview 40 children and youth between the ages of 10–17 years of age to better understand whether and how they should be consulted about parental separation and the different forms of communication that would be helpful for them to learn more about separation and divorce. Focus groups were held in two different Ontario cities. The vast majority of children and youth wanted to be involved in some way in the process. They also described that the best method to hear more about separation and divorce was through public information campaigns such as billboards on the roads, on government-run websites, or children's telephone helplines.

Birnbaum and Bala[30] retrospectively interviewed 11 young adults (aged 19–21 years) who had been represented as a child by a lawyer in a family dispute in Ontario in 2002. Many of these young adults reported having felt divided loyalties as a result of their parents' separation, particularly feeling that they were caught in the middle of their parents' dispute. They

27 Above n. 8, N. Bala and R. Birnbaum (2018).

28 Above n. 3, R. Birnbaum and M. Saini.

29 Canada, Department of Justice, R. Birnbaum, *Listening to Youths About their Needs and Preferences for Information Relating to Separation and/or Divorce*, Ottawa 2009.

30 R. Birnbaum and N. Bala, 'The Child's Perspective on Legal Representation: Young People Report on their Experiences with Child Lawyers' (2009) 25 *Can J Fam L*, p. 11.

reported both positive benefits and concerns about their lawyers. While the majority (7/11) were satisfied with their lawyer as they had someone to talk to who reassured them that their views would be communicated to the court, they also expressed the need for more information from their lawyer, a follow-up with them after court appearances, and more explanation of the process to them in more child-friendly language.

Birnbaum, Bala, and Cyr[31] retrospectively interviewed 32 children between 7–17 years of age in Ontario and Ohio who had either met with a judge, had a lawyer represent them, or spoken to a mental health professional for a parenting assessment. Regardless of which family justice professional the children spoke to, they all reported that they wanted to be involved in the decision-making process in some way, but most did not want to decide parenting arrangements. None reported negative effects as a result of their interviews with judges or other family justice professionals. All of those interviewed by a judge reported that they appreciated having had an opportunity to be heard by the judge, even those who did not get the outcome they wanted.

As part of a pilot project in collaboration with the Office of the Children's Lawyer and the courts, research into Voice of the Child Reports took place between 2016–2018 in Ontario. Birnbaum and Bala[32] retrospectively interviewed 33 children, 37 parents, 27 social workers, 31 parents' lawyers, and 27 judges.[33] The majority of the parents, parents' lawyers, judges, and most notably the children involved, believed that having children's views reported was a valuable and important process for hearing from children. Judges in particular found these reports a very helpful form of hearing from children about their views and preferences to assist in their decision-making. Further, a majority of the cases settled soon after the Voice of the Child Report was provided, generally in a way consistent with the views expressed by the child. What became clear during the interview and reporting process to parents was that they were often not fully aware of their children's views and that, once the parents were provided with accurate independent information, many were able to settle their disputes. However, it is important to acknowledge the limitations of these types of reports. For example, cases involving children where there are concerns of domestic violence, children who do not wish to visit with the other parent, have special learning needs, or have not had contact with the other parent

31 Above n. 8, R. Birnbaum, N. Bala, and F. Cyr.
32 Above n. 8, R. Birnbaum and N. Bala (2017).
33 This study was funded by the Law Foundation of Ontario.

for a long period of time, may require a more comprehensive parenting assessment.[34]

It is clear that more research into obtaining children's views about their participation in the family justice process is needed. Hearing from children and young people provides a powerful message that they want to be included and they have important information to convey not only to their parents but to the family justice system.

8. CONCLUSION

In this contribution we discussed the importance of children's participation, the advantages and disadvantages of the different methods used in hearing from children, and outlined a summary of the growing body of empirical research that examines what children and youth have to say about their participation in family disputes. While the CRC, which Canada ratified in 1991, promotes children as rights-bearing individuals who should be consulted about plans for their care in the context of parental separation and divorce, there remains wide discretion about whether and how children are really being heard in Canada. Amending the Divorce Act to focus on obtaining children's participation is a positive step forward, but lack accompanying funding to the provinces and territories to make their voices heard consistently across the country is a major concern. What is clear from the research is that children want to be involved in some way and have important information to provide not only to their parents but to the decision-maker as well. From a practice and policy perspective there is a need for more resources, greater commitment to hearing from children, and more research about how to do this effectively.

[34] Since 07.2018, the Ontario Office of the Children's Lawyer added Voice of the Child Reports to their suite of services they already provide.

ACCESS TO CRIMINAL JUSTICE FOR MINORS IN FRANCE

Philippe Bonfils

1. INTRODUCTION

Criminal justice is aimed at trying offenders, which is to say the authors of the behaviour that is the most seriously injurious to the social order. It may, therefore, convict them and sentence them to more or less harsh terms, in accordance with the severity of the offence. Criminal justice is thus strong, powerful justice, and striking justice as well, due to the issues that it reflects. Indeed, in criminal matters the freedom of an individual, their estate, their honour, or their reputation are at stake.

As such, criminal justice is not reserved for persons who have reached the age of majority. Minors may access it, against their will or – conversely – willingly, depending on the situation. Access to criminal justice for minors appears in effect in a radically different way, depending on whether one contemplates minors as the perpetrators of offences or as victims.

In the case of young offenders, it is indeed despite themselves that they 'access' the criminal justice system because they find themselves in a criminal procedure, as perpetrators or accomplices in an offence. The issue is thus not to say whether young offenders may gain access to the criminal justice system, but rather that of finding out how the criminal justice system will take into account young offenders' specificity. In this regard, since the beginning of the 20th century the juvenile criminal justice system has been gradually adapted and specialized, under the combined effects of the legislature and of case law.[1] Very recently, criminal law for young offenders has been profoundly modified by the adoption of a code specifically for minors, the Code for Juvenile Criminal Justice (CJPM).[2] Studying access to criminal justice for young offenders thus provides an opportunity to examine the changes made by this new legislation, and to ensure that the specificities of criminal justice for minors are always respected.

In the case of minors who are victims, the issue of access to the criminal justice system emerges in a radically different way. This in effect involves allowing minors to have their voices heard, notwithstanding their age and legal incapacity, as well as despite the trauma and paralysis that often result from the infraction. In fact, numerous obstacles may inhibit access to the justice system for child victims – like the embarrassment or even the shame of having been a victim (particularly with regard to sexual offences), or further, links with the perpetrators, who are in fact most often people who are close to the child, if not their parents. The legislature has provided major adaptations to the ordinary rules of law in order to accommodate the specificity of the situation of child victims, and to allow them to gain access to the criminal justice system. Study of access by minors to the

---

1 P. Bonfils and A. Gouttenoire, *Droit des mineurs*, Précis Dalloz, 2nd edn, 2014, No. 1355, p. 837.

2 P. Bonfils, 'Première approche du Code de la justice pénale des mineurs' (2019) 2 *AJ Pénal* p. 476. The entry into force of the Code, first set for 30.10.2020 and then for 31.03.2021, was pushed back on 30.09.2021, at the time of the review by Parliament of the ratifying law. At the time of writing, the law has yet to be promulgated, but its content has been laid down by the Joint Commission.

criminal justice system is aimed at presenting the adaptations made, so as to take their specificity into account.

2. ACCESS TO CRIMINAL JUSTICE FOR YOUNG OFFENDERS

The criminal law applicable to young offenders diverges substantially from the general law. The Constitutional Council, in a ruling of 29 August 2002,[3] even enshrined this autonomy on the part of juvenile criminal law at the constitutional level, by asserting on the one hand that, 'the criminal responsibility of minors must be attenuated in accordance with their age', and on the other hand that, 'the response of the authorities to offences committed by young offenders must seek, as far as possible, their educational and moral uplift, through measures adapted to their age and personality, and handed down by specialized courts or following modified legal proceedings'. Looking to ensure a criminal justice response that is adapted to young offenders, access to the criminal justice system is undertaken in specialist courts; it is also undertaken in line with a modified procedure.

2.1. ACCESS TO SPECIALIZED COURTS

2.1.1. Principle of Specialization

While the existence of substantial specific rules for minors goes back to Roman law, the specialization of courts for young offenders dates back around 100 years. In France, this is the law of 22 July 1912,[4] which for the first time established specialized courts, charged with trying young offenders, to ensure that the particularity of juvenile criminal law was effectively taken into account. Today, this specialization constitutes a fundamental guarantee of the juvenile criminal justice system,[5] as has been highlighted by the Constitutional Council in

3 Constitutional Council, 29.08.2002, Rec 204; 2002 461 DC, (note J.E. Schettl).

4 P. Bonfils, 'Le centenaire mouvementé du tribunal pour enfants' (2012) 148 *Gaz Pal*, p. 23.

5 M. Allaix, 'La spécialisation des magistrats de la jeunesse: une garantie pour les mineurs de justice' in A. Garapon and D. Salas (Eds.), *La justice des mineurs: évolution d'un modèle*, LGDJ, 1995, p. 73.

a decision of 11 August 1993[6] and the European Court of Human Rights in the judgment in *SC v. United Kingdom* of 15 June 2004.[7] But in its decision of 29 August 2002, the Constitutional Council considered that the fundamental principle recognized by the laws of the Republic meant a specialization of courts or an adaptation of the proceedings – a formula that the Code for Juvenile Criminal Justice has taken up in its preliminary article. This alternative explains that the specialization of courts for minors admits of some exceptions. Thus, trying for offences committed by minors in the first four classes is entrusted to the police court, and as part of the same approach, the liberty and custody judge – a non-specialist magistrate – is competent to order or extend the custodial remand of a minor. Albeit with some exceptions, the principle is very clearly the existence of specialized courts for minors, and the CJPM has enshrined it as a governing principle for proceedings (Article L. 12-1). Clearly a minor may only be tried before a specialist court, with some exceptions.[8]

2.1.2. Forms of Specialization

The specialization of criminal courts for minors may take two different forms – that of an adaptation of the courts under the ordinary rules of law, or that of the existence of specific courts.[9] In the first instance, the specialization is relatively reduced, since it often turns on the particular training of the judges (specialized investigating judges, for example), or on the performance of one of these judges (like the juvenile assize court, consisting as far as possible of children's judges as non-presiding judges). In the second case, the specialization is reflected in the existence of specific courts, and these courts must be acquainted with the essential points of disputes under criminal law for young offenders. The children's judge embodies the specialization of courts;[10] this is the

---

6 Constitutional Council, 11.08.1993, Rec 217, No. 93 326 DC, Law amending the law of 04.01.1993 reforming the Criminal Procedure Code, JO, 15.08.1993, p. 11599.

7 A. Gouttenoire, 'Mineurs délinquants' (2004) 78 *Dr. fam.*, *Alertes* No. 30.

8 Consequently, the judgment must be annulled of a magistrate's court if it mistakenly tried a minor who had appropriated the identity of a person of majority: *Cass Crim*, 30.03.1999, [1999], *Bull. crim* 144, No. 97-83.464. Similarly, in relation the Juvenile Assize Court, see also *Cass Crim*, 11.09.2002 [2002], *Bull crim* 607 No. 02-80.906.

9 See P. Bonfils, 'Les juridictions répressives pour mineurs' (2006) *Dr. fam.* Study No. 35; see also P. Bonfils, 'Les juridictions répressives pour mineurs' in V. Donier and B.L. Scheneider (Eds.), *L'accès à la justice de la personne vulnérable en droit interne*, L'épitoge-Lextenso, 2015, p. 103.

10 J.F. Dreuille, 'Spécialité et autonomie de la justice des mineurs: la justice pénale' in Y. Favier and F. Ferrand (Eds.), *La justice des mineurs en Europe, une question de spécialité?*, EFL, Paris 2011, p. 31.

central court for juvenile law, all the more so as it combines functions that are civil (as the judge for child protection), as well as criminal. In regard to criminal functions, the children's judge simultaneously constitutes a trial court, competent with regard to class five minor offences,[11] as well as misdemeanours, and a court of enforcement of sentences.[12] They preside in the juvenile court and are likely to participate as non-presiding judges in the juvenile assize court (competent for crimes committed by minors between 16 and 18 years of age). The other specific court is the juvenile court. This is a collegiate court, composed of three persons: a children's judge who presides, and two non-presiding judges, who are non-professional magistrates and who have been chosen for their interest in child-related issues. The court is competent to try class five minor offences and misdemeanours, as well as the crimes committed by minors under 16 years of age.

2.2. ACCESS IN LINE WITH A MODIFIED PROCEDURE

2.2.1. Adaptation of the Guiding Principles of the Ordinary Rules of Law

The procedure applicable to young offenders is extensively modified, with the aim of taking into account the specificities related to their age. This results first in an adaptation of the guiding principles of ordinary law, which are sometimes strengthened and sometimes weakened. Among the principles that are strengthened, the right to counsel may be mentioned. This is not solely a right – as for persons who have reached the age of majority – but an obligation.[13] Thus, in picking up on Article 4-1 of Order 45, Article L. 12-4 of the CJMP provides that, 'a minor who is charged or convicted shall be assisted by a lawyer', and this assistance is likewise mandatory in the case of being held in custody (Article L. 413-8). With a view to ensuring that this right is respected, a lawyer may be designated

11 In France there are three levels of offences: crimes, misdemeanours, and infractions *[les crimes, les délits, et les contraventions]*. The latter are subdivided into five classes (according to the amount of the fine incurred).

12 It should be noted that in the CJMP, the children's judge gives up the duties of investigation that they had as of Order 45. The procedural model of the new Code is thus that of abandonment of investigation in favour of a judgment phase, split by a caesura in the criminal trial. See N. Beddiar, 'La césure du procès pénal du mineur' (2019) 10 *AJ Pénal* p. 483.

13 *Cass. Crim.*, 28.06.2000, [2000] *Bull. crim.* 750, No. 00-80.253, No. 254.

by the Bar Association president (if the minor or their legal guardians have not chosen a lawyer), and there is a system of legal aid making this possible when the minor – and particularly their legal guardians – lack sufficient resources. Article L. 12-4 specifies in this regard that, 'the minor shall participate in the selection of their lawyer, or shall carry it out under conditions laid down by the present Code', and that 'when a lawyer has been appointed by the court, as far as possible the minor shall be assisted by the same lawyer at each stage of the proceedings'. The open nature of the proceedings may be mentioned under diminished principles of ordinary law. Indeed, in the extension of the solutions established under the 1945 Order, Article L. 12(3) of the CJMP provides that, 'the open nature of the hearings of the courts adjudicating with regard to minors is restricted, in accordance with conditions established by the present code'. Limited openness is a classic principle of juvenile criminal law, enshrined by the European Court of Human Rights[14] and by the Court of Cassation,[15] based on the already long history of the idea that open proceedings could compromise the potential for rehabilitation of the minor.

2.2.2. Existence of Specific Guiding Principles

Taking into consideration the particularity of crimes committed by minors has given rise to the establishment of specific guiding principles. This is the case, for example, of the principle of involvement of the minor's legal guardians, on the ground that the child's upbringing has perhaps been a contributing factor in their crime, and that better monitoring of their child might permit their rehabilitation. Thus Article L. 12-5 of the Code provides that:

> Under the conditions established by the present Code, the legal guardians receive the same information as that which must be communicated to the minor in the course of the proceedings. The minor shall be so informed. A minor who is a suspect or faces criminal charges has the right to be accompanied by their legal guardians, in accordance with the provisions of this Code.

---

14 CEDH, 16.12.1999, *T. and V. v. United Kingdom. Dr. fam.*, Comm. No. 46, obs. A. Gouttenoire.

15 *Cass. Crim.*, 08.11.1967, *Bull. Crim.* 673, No. 67-91.599; No. 287; D. 1968. 195, note P. Robert. See also *Cass. Crim.*, 24.06.1998, *Bull. Crim.* 580, No. 98-80.995, No. 205; *Dr. penal.* 1999, Comm. No. 15, obs. A. Maron. *Cassation Crim.* 06.12.2000, No. 00-82.660.

The general principle of involvement of the legal guardians is here envisaged in both senses – which is to say, for the legal guardians themselves (they receive the same information as the minor), and for the minor (a minor who is a suspect or faces criminal charges has the right to be accompanied by their legal guardians). The primacy of education over repression could be mentioned, as a specific guiding principle. Although this originally involves a substantive rule, which explains in particular the ancillary character of criminal sentences as compared to protection measures, the primacy of education over repression contains an essential procedural dimension,[16] which explains in particular why knowledge of the child's personality must be mandatory (Article L. 322-1 ff.), or why the legislature has instituted a unique personality file,[17] earmarked to receive all aspects in relation to the personality of a minor as collected over the course of the inquiries in which they have been the subject. Lastly, and above all, it is in the end the interest of the minor that constitutes the cardinal principle of juvenile criminal law.[18] Guaranteed by Article 3-1 of the Convention on the Rights of the Child, this principle appears as a kind of framework – or perhaps a compass – for access by young offenders to the criminal justice system. It is striking that on the occasion of review by Parliament of the ratifying law, the best interests of the child were integrated into the preliminary article of the CJMP.

3. ACCESS TO CRIMINAL JUSTICE FOR MINORS WHO ARE VICTIMS

Access to the criminal justice system on the part of minors who are victims of offences poses questions that are different from those for young offenders. There is for example no specialized jurisdiction for child victims, nor a specific guiding principle, and more broadly, one cannot really talk about any autonomy in the criminal law for minors who are victims.[19] As such, the vital need arose to put in place a mechanism for

16 On this principle, and particularly on its procedural dimension, see P. Bonfils, 'La primauté de l'éducation sur la Répression' in J.-H. Robert, *Mélanges*, LexisNexis, Paris 2012, p. 55; See also P. Bonfils, 'La nouvelle primauté de l'éducation sur la répression' (2018) 7(8) *Dr. Pén.* 16, Study No. 20.

17 See P. Bonfils, 'La réforme du droit pénal des mineurs par la loi du 10 août 2011' (2011) 33 *Recueil Dalloz* p. 2286.

18 Among extensive literature, we can mention A.C. Réglier and C.S. Blanc (Eds.), *L'intérêt de l'enfant, mythe ou réalité?*, Institut Universitaire Varenne, Paris 2018.

19 Above n. 1, p. 1050.

the procedural protection of minors who are victims, since their access to justice was strongly compromised by their incapacity to act, their links with the perpetrator, or the embarrassment associated with the disclosure of certain classes of offences (sexual offences). It is for this reason that for some 30 years the legislature had adaptations in place directed both to enabling access to criminal justice for minors who are victims, and to rendering it effective.

3.1. THE ACCESS PERMITTED TO THE CRIMINAL JUSTICE SYSTEM

3.1.1. Ad hoc Administrator and Community Interest Groups

When the victim of the offence is a minor, the launching of criminal proceedings pursuant to rules of general law is more difficult, or even impossible. The adaptations put in place by the legislature are oriented towards overcoming these obstacles, and to allowing access by minors to the criminal justice system. Since minors lack legal capacity, it would normally fall to their legal guardians – and thus, more often than not, their parents – to act in their place. But it is not at all uncommon that they themselves are the perpetrators of the crime. Also, the Criminal Procedure Code (CPC) envisages that the public prosecutor and the examining magistrate may appoint an ad hoc administrator, 'when the protection of the interests of the minor is not fully assured by their legal guardians, or by one of them' (Article 706-50). It is this court-appointed administrator who will thus exercise the child's rights in the proceedings, will appoint a lawyer, and will bring civil proceedings. In the same vein, we might mention the role of the Associations for the Defence of Minors, which may – on behalf of a collective interest that they represent (combatting child abuse or as well sectarian movements; Articles 2-3 and 2-17 of the CPC) – join an existing criminal proceeding, and even, in certain cases, initiate one.

3.1.2. Broad Approach of French Criminal Law

Another difficulty, which may inhibit access to criminal justice for minors who are victims, involves mechanisms for spatial enforcement of the criminal law. In addition to the principle of territoriality, the Criminal Code (CC) confers jurisdiction on the law and on French courts of law when the perpetrator (active personality) or the victim (passive personality) is French, even though the offence has been committed abroad. But the conditions laid down by the Code might prevent enforcement of the criminal law, if the legislature had not provided derogations to it. Thus, with regard to a misdemeanour, it is not required that the offence be punishable in the country where it was committed (derogation to Article 113-6) and no complaint from the victim or official accusation from the authority of the country where the offence was committed is required (derogation from Article 113-8). What is more, French law may be applied not only to French nationals, but also to foreigners customarily living in France. These mechanisms, which have to do with active personality (Articles 227-27-1, 222-22-3 and 225-12-3) and passive personality (Article 222-16-2) make it possible to effectively combat sex tourism, or further, the practice of certain forms of mutilation, such as female circumcision.

3.1.3. Adaptations of the Statute of Limitations

While the statute of limitations is a natural mechanism for termination of criminal proceedings, it may prove to be profoundly unjust when it concerns a child victim because the latter may not take legal action (as a result of their incapacity), nor act on a moral basis (due to the links that they very often have with the perpetrator of the offence). That is why, with regard to sexual offences committed against minors, the Criminal Procedure Code (CPC) envisaged two kinds of adaptations, thus making it possible for minors to overcome this obstacle and gain access to the criminal justice system. The first is the extension of the statute of limitations. The time limits under statutory law of six years in cases involving misdemeanours and of 20 years in criminal matters, become 10 or 20 years, as a function of the misdemeanour, and 30 years for crimes (Articles 7 and 8 of the CPC). The second adaptation, which augments the first, is that the starting point for the limitation period is moved to the age of majority of the victim. In other words, and even if it is possible to launch legal proceedings prior to the age of majority, it is only from the age of 18 years that the term of the statute of limitation commences to run, such that in criminal matters, the victim may be as old as 48 and still be able to commence an action. This is to say that access to criminal justice for minors who are victims is permitted, where it would – under ordinary law – be impossible. These rules thus come to make access to the criminal justice system possible. Others improve that access in a more qualitative manner by making it effective.

3.2. EFFECTIVE ACCESS TO THE CRIMINAL JUSTICE SYSTEM

3.2.1. *Hearing the Child*

It is one thing to gain access to criminal justice; it is another to do so effectively and fully, which is to say under the right conditions. Along these lines, French law envisages several provisions directed to facilitating or improving access to the criminal justice system on the part of minors. This is also true with regard to the child being heard, where the French mechanism – drawing on foreign legislation (Canadian in particular) – is now very effective. The hearing of a minor who is a victim must necessarily be recorded audio-visually (Article 706-52 of the CPC), whether it occurs at the inquiry phase or during an investigation, which makes it possible to avoid the minor having to be subjected to being heard several times in the course of the criminal proceedings, which proves to be very harrowing and trying for the victim.[20] In addition, recording provides much better knowledge of the child's attitudes or behaviour while they are being heard, than what is possible with a simple transcript of their testimony in a record of proceedings. Along the same lines, because narrating the offences suffered may involve additional trauma, a child victim may be assisted by a third party when they have their hearing (Article 706-53 of the CPC). This third party, who may be a psychologist, a doctor, the ad hoc administrator, or a family member of the minor, may thus reassure or comfort the victim. When the child victim is heard by an examining magistrate, they must, in addition, be assisted by counsel.

3.2.2. *Limitation of the Public Nature of the Proceedings*

A criminal hearing is a challenge, especially for minors who are victims of sexual abuse, and the prospect of open court might impair access to the justice system for child victims. That is why several moderating actions have been put in place to the principle of the public nature of the proceedings. First, the victim may request in camera proceedings, and the presiding judge may grant this request if they consider that an

---

20 See R. Rolland, 'La protection du mineur victime d'infraction sexuelle (Law No. 98-468 of June 17, 1998)' (1998) 4 *RDSS* p. 892; See also C. Etrillard, 'L'enregistrement audiovisuel des auditions de mineurs en France' (2004) 1 *RICPT* p. 43.

open hearing would be dangerous to order and serenity of the debate, to the dignity of the person, or the interests of a third party (Articles 306 and 400 of the CPC). Then, closed proceedings may be demanded by the victim 'when the proceedings are for charges of rape or torture and acts of savagery accompanied by sexual assault' (Article 306(3) of the CPC); when the victim is a minor, the request may be made by their legal guardian[21] or the ad hoc administrator. Finally, the press law of 29 July 1881 (Article 39) specifically prohibits publication of the identity of child victims.

3.2.3. Lawyer of the Child Victim

Looking to ensure effective access by the minor to the criminal justice system, French law has been concerned specifically with their being assisted by counsel. It is first envisaged that – for the most serious offences and in certain situations, such as sexual offences – assistance to the child victim by a lawyer shall be mandatory (Article 706-50 of the CPC). Then, appointment of the lawyer may be undertaken by means of a request from the minor's legal guardians, from the ad hoc administrator, or from the Bar Association president, with the case being referred by the examining magistrate. It is however questionable whether a child victim could themselves appoint their lawyer directly,[22] even though the power to instruct counsel is acknowledged for the juvenile offender (Article 4-1 of the 1945 Order) and for the minor at risk within the framework of child protection (Article 1186 of the CPC). In the same way, unlike a minor in child protection and a juvenile offender, a child victim does not automatically benefit from legal aid,[23] a situation that is very much open to criticism. Nevertheless, agreements exist in a number of bars making it possible to alleviate the lack of legal aid. Above all, legal aid is automatic for the victims of crimes of deliberate attempts to take a life, or of crimes against the inviolability of the person (Article 9-2) Law of 10 July 1991).

---

21 *Cass. Crim.*, 22.03.1989, [1989] *Bull. Crim.* 369, No. 88 84.580, No. 145; *RSC* 1989, p. 143, obs. G. Levasseur.

22 M. Picot, 'La participation de l'enfant victime au procès pénal' (2003) 11 *AJ fam* p. 373.

23 In the case of a juvenile offender, the benefit of legal aid is not automatic as such, but is granted if the parents fail to take an interest in the child, irrespective of the state of their resources.

4. CONCLUSION

Ultimately, access to the criminal justice system for minors in France appears today to be largely satisfactory. As for juvenile offenders, systematic assistance by a lawyer and the possibility for the parents to be present along with their child, constitute considerable improvements. In the case of child victims, the progress made by the legislation over a period of more than 20 years has made effective access possible, in spite of a number of obstacles relating in particular to their age and their vulnerability, or further to the links that they generally maintain with the perpetrators of the offences that they are the victims of.

CHILDREN'S ACCESS TO JUSTICE IN JERSEY

Obstacles and Impediments

Deborah McMillan

1. INTRODUCTION AND METHODOLOGY

Jersey is in the Channel Islands and is the most southerly island of the British Isles and yet, it is not part of the United Kingdom. Out of a population of 104,000, there are 20,469 0–17-year-olds. In 2019 the Commissioner for Children and Young People (Jersey) Law was passed and established the role of Children's Commissioner.

As the Commissioner I was asked by the Government to undertake research to consider the extent to which Jersey legislation complied with the Convention on the Rights of the Child (CRC). This was part of an ongoing collaboration between the Commissioner and the Government to make children's rights a reality by ensuring that all domestic legislation is fully compatible with the CRC and that the Convention's principles and provisions can be directly applied and appropriately enforced. I also launched the Child Friendly Justice project due to concerns raised about youth justice reported in the Independent Jersey Care Inquiry (IJCI)[1] in 2017. The focus of the project has been to consider if children's access to justice is sufficiently guaranteed and to identify the barriers to achieving access to justice.

This contribution will look at findings related to youth justice in Jersey, which have resulted from work undertaken by my office over the past three years. I will be drawing on three main themes to support my conclusions.

The first of these is the current level of compliance of Jersey legislation with the CRC. I will be referencing a substantial piece of research that was carried out in 2019 and 2020 on behalf of the Children's Commissioner in Jersey by Swansea University's Observatory on the Human Rights of Children. This year-long project was the first piece of work to be undertaken by the Commissioner using statutory powers and culminated in the publication of a Legislative Gap Analysis (LGA) in September 2020.[2] The LGA is based on an independent analysis of Jersey legislation and provides a comprehensive picture of the extent to which Jersey legislation complies with the CRC.

This means that, for the first time since ratifying the CRC in 2014, Jersey now has a clear understanding of where its laws meet the expectations of the CRC, and where they continue to fall short of them. The LGA is part of

---

1 Independent Jersey Care Inquiry 2017, <http://www.jerseycareinquiry.org/>.

2 S. Hoffman and S. Sellwood, 'Legislative Gap Analysis Welsh Observatory of Children's Human Rights 2020' (2020) *Children's Commissioner for Jersey*, <https://www.childcomjersey.org.je/media/1389/legislative-gap-analysis-oct-2020.pdf>.

an ongoing collaboration between the National Human Rights Institution (NHRI) for children and the Government of Jersey, the intended outcome of which is to achieve genuine progress – as opposed to nominal, tick-box compliance – with both the letter and the spirit of the CRC.

The second theme I will be drawing on in this contribution is the operational experience of the Office of the Children's Commissioner in Jersey during its first three years of operation. The office's casework team has taken on an average of one new case every other day since the beginning of its informal operations in 2018. Many of these cases have related specifically to the rights of children and young people in conflict with the law.

The third and final theme that underpins the findings of this contribution relates to cultural and structural influences on the criminal justice system in Jersey. Specifically, these might include: pervasive attitudes towards certain sections of young society in Jersey; the confusion that can arise from having both a national police force and a volunteer-led 'honorary' police force simultaneously carrying out different functions in relation to juvenile justice; the low minimum age of criminal responsibility in Jersey; and shortfalls in advocacy provision.

2. BACKGROUND

The Bailiwick of Jersey has been a signatory to the CRC since 2014; however, the post of Commissioner for Children and Young People has only existed in the island since January 2018, on an informal basis, and in statute since July 2019.

The Office of the Children's Commissioner Jersey was formally established as a National Human Rights Institution (NHRI) for children through the Commissioner for Children and Young People (Jersey) Law 2019.[3] I am the first Commissioner to take up this post, and as such, I have diverted a great deal of effort and resource into establishing awareness of the CRC, both in general terms, among the public of Jersey, and as a means for fellow professionals to view their ongoing work and policy-formation through a child-rights lens.

---

3 Jersey legal information board, 'Commissioner for Children and Young People (Jersey) Law (2019)' (last modified: 19.12.2019) *Jersey legal information board*, <https://www.jerseylaw.je/laws/enacted/Pages/L-08-2019.aspx>.

Children's rights have increasingly been used for analyzing and critiquing the youth justice system in England and Wales. In Jersey, over the last 10 years, 5,385 crimes have been recorded by the States of Jersey Police as being committed by children and young people. Of these, 30 were aged under 10 years and 1,424 were aged 10–13 years old.[4] The European Convention on the Exercise of Children's Rights and the CRC have provided a rights framework for those seeking to ensure that a culture of children's rights is evident in the justice system. We can see that international rights standards have also increasingly formed the basis of legal challenges brought by children and their advocates. General Comments 35 and 32[5] of the Human Rights Committee, the monitoring body of the International Covenant on Civil and Political rights (ICCPR), as well as documents of the UN Working Group on Arbitrary Detention should also be noted as being of further importance in examination of the current international standards on child justice. While these documents are not child-specific, they nevertheless have general application to everyone and identify children as a specific vulnerable group.

3. FINDINGS OF THE LEGISLATIVE GAP ANALYSIS

Following the publication of the LGA, it became apparent that current legislation in Jersey presents an obstacle to children's access to justice in the island, particularly in terms of the deprivation of their liberty and their guarantee of a fair trial. The research reported findings on CRC Articles 37 and 40, in particular, which guarantee the rights of children deprived of liberty and those of children caught up in the criminal justice system, respectively.

3.1. PRIORITIES AND FINDINGS RELATING TO DEPRIVATION OF LIBERTY (CRC ARTICLE 37(B)–(D))

For the purposes of this contribution, the key aspects of CRC Article 37 are that deprivation of liberty should not be unlawful or arbitrary, and

4 States of Jersey Police official data.

5 Human Rights Committee, General Comment No. 35, [2014]: Liberty and security of person, [23.10.2014], UN Doc. CCPR/C/GC/35; Human Rights Committee, General Comment No. 32, [2014]: Right to Equality before Courts and Tribunals and to Fair Trial, [23.08.2007], UN Doc. CCPR/C/GC/32.

that children who are deprived of their liberty should be treated with humanity and respect, and in a manner which takes account of the child's age and needs. Article 37 also emphasizes that children who are deprived of their liberty should be separated from adults unless it is in the child's best interests.

And finally, CRC Article 37 stipulates that children deprived of their liberty should be able to maintain contact with family, as well as access legal and other assistance, and they should also be given the ability to challenge the legality of the deprivation of their liberty before a court or other independent, impartial authority and to receive a prompt decision.

However, while States of Jersey legislation provides for deprivation of liberty to be in accordance with the law, several gaps in relation to the aforementioned CRC priorities were identified during the LGA research:[6]

- The Children Law does not require best interests to be taken into account as a primary consideration where a child is deprived of their liberty under the legislation.
- The Mental Health Law does not require best interests to be taken into account as a primary consideration where a child should be deprived of their liberty under the legislation.
- The Mental Health Law does not include provision to ensure a child detained under the Law can maintain contact with their family.
- The Mental Health Law does not permit a child to nominate a preferred 'nearest person'.
- There do not appear to be any express and specific standards in place concerning the treatment of children deprived of their liberty for mental health reasons.
- Children may be detained alongside adults in the secure estate or when detained under the Mental health Law.

3.2. PRIORITIES RELATING TO CHILDREN IN CONFLICT WITH THE LAW, CHILD VICTIMS AND WITNESSES OF CRIMES AND JUVENILE JUSTICE (CRC ARTICLE 40)

The Committee on the Rights of the Child recognizes different groups of children that require special protection because of their interaction with

6 Above n. 2, p. 106.

the law and juvenile justice, whether as a child in conflict with the law, a child victim of crime, or children who witness a crime.[7]

Legislation in Jersey introduces a comprehensive regime of youth justice. However, the LGA research identified the following gaps in legislation where legislation falls short of expectations of the CRC:[8]

- There is no overriding statement of principle ensuring that the best interests of the child are a priority in the youth justice system.
- The Young Offenders Law does not expressly require detention to be used as a measure of last resort.
- Legislation includes the possibility of detention 'during Her Majesty's pleasure' for the most serious offences.
- The Young Offenders Law has no provision requiring the child to be heard from directly in criminal proceedings.
- The minimum age of criminal responsibility of 10 years of age is too low.
- Legislation permits children to be tried alongside adults in some cases.
- There is no requirement that criminal charges are read and explained to children.
- Legislation does not specify time limits for criminal matters to be disposed of against children.
- Legislation does not require that children should benefit from the lightest sentence available, whether this be the sentence prescribed at the date if commission of an offence, or at time of sentencing.
- In some instances, children may be detained with adults, and legislation does not prevent this.
- Legislation does not ensure that children are provided with legal aid when charged with a criminal matter.

4. CULTURAL AND STRUCTURAL OBSTACLES

As the NHRI for children on the island, the Office of the Children's Commissioner has acted for a number of children caught up in the justice system. This work has provided us with evidence that, as well as legislation and procedures not meeting expectations of compliance with the CRC, there are other pervasive obstacles to children accessing justice. These can

---

7 See Committee on the Rights of the Child, General Comment No. 24 [2019]: on children's rights in the child justice system, [18.09.2019], UN Doc. CRC/C/GC/24.

8 Above n. 2, p. 116.

be broadly considered under two headings: 'cultural obstacles', which relate to attitudes and beliefs that have formed over time and which may still be affecting outcomes in Jersey's juvenile justice system; and 'structural obstacles', which relate to the way in which Jersey's criminal justice and policing systems are structured, and how those structures can affect children's ability to understand, access and participate in the justice system.

4.1. CULTURAL OBSTACLES

Cultural and attitudinal beliefs towards children and young people are a barrier to children accessing justice. In 2008 the Howard League for Penal Reform conducted a review of the Jersey youth justice system. This review followed an earlier review that concluded that the system for controlling children in custody would not be 'acceptable or lawful in England and Wales' and that 'it is doubtful that it would be in compliance with international obligations under human rights legislation'. The 2008 review stated, 'We have to say that we do not believe that custody for children in Jersey is currently used only as a "last resort"'.[9] It concluded: 'We hope and expect that within a relatively short time, children's custody in Jersey will be virtually eliminated.'[10]

Twelve years later, Jersey children are still being deprived of their liberty and the Young Offenders Law does not expressly require detention to be used as a measure of last resort. The Government of Jersey carried out a further youth justice review in 2018.[11] That review intended to address a recommendation of the Independent Jersey Care Inquiry (IJCI) that 'the youth justice system move to a model that always treats young offenders as children first and offenders second'.[12]

There is still no youth justice strategy for Jersey and there is no overriding statement of principle ensuring that the best interests of the

---

9 L. Ravenscroft and J. Fayle, 'Jersey Review: a review for the Jersey youth justice system' (2008) *Howard league for Penal Reform*, pp. 3 and 22, <https://www.gov.je/SiteCollectionDocuments/Caring%20and%20support/R_HowardLeagueReportNov2008_CS_190112.pdf>.

10 Ibid., p. 22.

11 Jersey Youth Justice Review Steering Group, 'Jersey Youth Justice Review' (2018) *Government of Jersey*, <https://www.gov.je/SiteCollectionDocuments/Crime%20and%20justice/R%20Youth%20Justice%20Review%2020190529.pdf>.

12 Independent Jersey Care Inquiry, 'Chapter 13: Recommendations for the States of Jersey' (2017) *Independent Jersey Inquiry*, p. 61, <http://www.jerseycareinquiry.org/Final%20Report/Ch%2013.pdf>.

child are a priority in the youth justice system. So why is it taking so long to make the necessary changes in Jersey towards a child-friendly justice system?

In order to answer that question, we need to turn to the findings of the IJCI report.[13] While the IJCI was primarily focussed on the experiences of people who had been cared for by the States of Jersey, the attitudinal and cultural fault lines that were found to underly some examples of abuse or neglect are likely also to have affected wider societal attitudes towards 'problem children' who are in conflict with the law. The IJCI reported on the provision of juvenile justice facilities as well as residential childcare settings and mental health residential settings.

The phrase 'the Jersey Way' featured several times in the IJCI report. It was described as 'the protection of powerful interests and resistance to change.' Witnesses to the inquiry complained of being treated as 'second-class' citizens, not just as children in care, but since leaving care too. Being labelled as having been in 'care' proved a serious handicap both in education and in seeking employment because being in 'care' was often erroneously associated with being 'in trouble with the law'. An ethos of its own subsequently developed, which carried a stigma and influenced government policy, as well as public and professional attitudes at all levels of care of vulnerable children in Jersey. Society, it was deemed, had been allowed to develop in a way that considered it acceptable to allow the rights of vulnerable children to become secondary to what were thought to be more important issues.

The IJCI made a series of recommendations. The first was to appoint a Children's Commissioner, and to enact legislation that would ensure that the Commissioner's role be underpinned with robust statutory powers. The following was stated:

> A 'commissioner with teeth' is required to ensure that Jersey has the best child protection and welfare system possible. The dangers of child abuse and neglect have not gone away, they are real and present. Whoever is appointed needs to have the ability to ensure that Jersey's leaders are delivering good management and best practices through the provision of resources.[14]

---

13 Government of Jersey, 'About the Independent Jersey Care Inquiry', <https://www.gov.je/Government/Departments/StrategicPolicy/RespondingtoIndependentJerseyCareInquiry/Pages/WhatistheIndependentJerseyCareInquiry.aspx>.

14 A. Collins, 'The Jersey Way and next steps for child protection following the IJCI' (12.07.2017) *Hugh James*, <https://www.hughjames.com/blog/the-%E2%80%9Cjersey-way%E2%80%9D-and-the-next-steps-for-child-protection-following-the-independent-jersey-care-inquiry>.

The IJCI recommended that the Commissioner hold broad powers to support all children on the island and not just those in alternative care and in juvenile justice or mental health settings.

4.2. STRUCTURAL OBSTACLES

Children and young people encounter the justice system in many ways. This can be for family matters, in both public and private law – for example, divorce or care orders; in administrative justice for nationality or immigration issues; or in criminal justice, as victims, witnesses, or perpetrators of crimes. However, the criminal justice system in the island, particularly, is complicated and, as such, is apt to create a structural barrier to children's access to justice in the island, as illustrated below.

4.2.1. Policing

Jersey has 13 independent police forces within a geographical area of 45 square miles. A dozen of these forces, known as the Honorary Police, are attached to the Island's 12 administrative parishes, and as such are parochial in scope and voluntary in nature. In addition to the Honorary force is a paid police force, whose remit covers the whole island: this is the States of Jersey Police. Each of the Honorary forces has a separate chain of command, emanating from that particular parish's Chef de Police, while the States of Jersey Police is structured in a much more readily recognisable way to other UK national police forces, with a Chief Officer, Superintendent, Detective Superintendent, and so on.

Added to this complex policing structure is the fact that Jersey's Probation and After Care Service is an agency of the Royal Court of Jersey, thereby making it yet another discrete operation with its own procedures, autonomies, and systems of working.

The combination of these factors can mean that, for many children (especially those coming into conflict with the law for the first time), the justice system in Jersey is too complex to readily understand. When faced with this system, children can find themselves thrown into an adult world with little guidance, which can be frightening and overwhelming.

It is imperative, then, that Jersey creates a justice system that guarantees the respect and effective implementation of all children's rights. In practice, this would mean a justice that is: accessible; age appropriate; speedy; diligent; adapted to and focused on the needs of the child; respecting the right to due process; respecting the right to participate in and to understand the proceedings; respecting the right to private and family life; respecting the right to integrity and dignity.

4.2.2. The Minimum Age of Criminal Responsibility

The minimum age of criminal responsibility in Jersey is 10 years of age. The Committee on the Rights of the Child has formally noted that this threshold is too low.[15] This also constitutes a structural barrier to children accessing justice in Jersey.

The Committee's General Comment No. 24[16] is highly regarded as an international standard on child justice. It encourages States Parties to increase the minimum age to at least 14 years of age. There should be an exploration of how a move to raise the age of criminal responsibility could be supported by an appropriate, welfare-based model that protects children's rights via appropriate judicial oversight. A whole-system approach that focuses on prevention and diversion and the provision of rights respecting interventions can create positive outcomes for children.

4.2.3. Children's Lack of Knowledge of their Rights

Lack of knowledge of rights is another obstacle to children accessing justice. Prior to the creation of a Children's Commissioner role in the island, Jersey's children had been largely unaware of their rights and were therefore in a poor position to mount effective challenges when those rights were violated. We know that this is the case because the Commissioner's island-wide survey in 2018 reported that just 22% of children and young people knew about children's rights.[17] The UNICEF Rights Respecting Schools Award[18] is now being delivered in all island schools, however, and the latest survey reports that 77% of children now know about their rights.

---

15 Above, n. 2, p. 111.

16 Above, n. 7.

17 Children's Commissioner for Jersey, *Island-Wide Consultations: The Findings*, 07.2018, p. 18, <https://www.childcomjersey.org.je/media/1167/island-wide-consultation-findings-full-report.pdf>.

18 UNICEF- United Kingdom, 'Rights respecting schools: creating safe and inspiring places to learn' (2020) *UNICEF-United Kingdom*, <https://www.unicef.org.uk/rights-respecting-schools/>.

4.2.4. A Lack of Child-Friendly Information about the Justice System

Information about the justice system has not routinely been provided in a child-friendly, accessible format, which also constitutes an obstacle to children's access to justice. In my conversations with children and professionals, I have identified that few children make complaints about the system, and some children whose rights are violated, do not come forward and seek redress, let alone obtain effective remedy. The charity National Society for the Prevention of Cruelty to Children is also concerned that there may be under-reporting of child sexual abuse on the island.

As NHRI for children, the Commissioner's office can act for children and support them to make a complaint, but Government complaints mechanisms are not child-friendly. The Office of the Children's Commissioner has established a child-friendly complaints mechanism as a good practice model.[19]

4.2.5. Advocacy for Children Caught Up in the Justice System

Children repeatedly report that they do not know where to go for help and support, and this is another obstacle for children accessing justice.[20] State-funded legal aid is not available in Jersey. Eligibility of legal aid for a child is based on the financial circumstances of their parent(s). Legislation does not ensure that children are provided with legal aid when charged with a criminal matter.

The quality of advocacy in youth proceedings should never be variable. Representation of children and young people, in any court setting, is an area of practice which requires considerable skill and expertise. The consequences for children who cannot properly engage with the process and communicate or be understood can have negative impacts for them. Practitioners must be empowered to effectively advise children in such a way as to enable them to engage fully with the process and to understand what is happening to them. In order to assist this, they need access to resources to use with children as they prepare for a youth justice case.

---

19 Children Commissioner for Jersey, 'Telling us there's a problem- how to make a complaint' (2020) *Children Commissioner for Jersey*, <https://www.childcomjersey.org.je/media/1364/jersey-complaints.pdf>.

20 Covid 19 survey 2020 Children's Commissioner Jersey, <https://www.childcomjersey.org.je/publications/research-and-papers/joint-survey-with-government-of-jersey/>.

4.2.6. Training for Youth Justice Actors does not Focus on Rights and Trauma

Those in the justice system lack training on child rights and childhood trauma. Often, we see that the response to juvenile offending focuses on presenting behaviour of children and young people rather than understanding that the behaviour is often the symptom of a trauma or adversity, not the cause of it. A recent survey undertaken on behalf of the Commissioner as a precursor to trauma-informed training demonstrated that there is little awareness or understanding amongst youth justice professionals of the existence and impact of Adverse Childhood Experiences (ACEs) and trauma on brain development and the resulting behaviour. The outcome of this is that professionals working in the youth justice arena are missing a significant opportunity to build meaningful relationships and seek sustainable solutions.

An effective youth justice service cannot be designed, implemented, and delivered without a foundation of training to provide a universal understanding of the impact of trauma and adversity on the development of the brain and how this behaviour sometimes manifests in aggressive conduct problems.

Specialist training is required for a wide range of professionals, volunteers, and people who have contact with children in Jersey's juvenile justice system. This should be high-quality, evidence-based, specialist training on how best to communicate and engage with young people. The content of the training should include an understanding of what children's rights are and how children's rights should be applied in practice, as well as an understanding of ACEs, child development, trauma-informed practice, and developing resilience. The Committee on the Rights of the Child General Comment No. 24 on children's rights in the child justice system states that, '… the developmental and neuroscience evidence indicates that adolescent brains continue to mature even beyond the teenage years, affecting certain kinds of decision-making.'[21]

The Committee comments further:

> It is essential for the quality of the administration of child justice that all the professionals involved receive appropriate multidisciplinary training on the content and meaning of the Convention …. It should include established and emerging information from a variety of fields on, inter alia, the social and other causes of crime, the social and psychological development of children, including

---

21 Above n. 7, para. 22.

current neuroscience findings, disparities that may amount to discrimination against certain marginalized groups such as children belonging to minorities or indigenous peoples, the culture and the trends in the world of young people, the dynamics of group activities and the available diversion measures and non-custodial sentences, in particular measures that avoid resorting to judicial proceedings.[22]

5. WHAT THE CHILDREN'S COMMISSIONER CAN DO

As the first Children's Commissioner for Jersey, my priority is to develop and embed a culture of children and young people's rights in Jersey by helping children and young people to know and understand their rights, and by working with the Government to provide expert advice on the rights of children and young people. These are important steps towards breaking down ingrained cultural barriers, and thereby supporting children's access to justice.

Stimulating discussion and debate is also a valuable part of my role in raising awareness of the current obstacles to children's access justice in Jersey. And on a wider level, it helps to establish an Island community that respects children and young people and places a real value on offering them the opportunities they need to fulfil their potential. Jersey's approach to children's rights is paternalistic, viewing that children are requiring protection first and foremost and seeing children as incompetent becomings. My work is to encourage the emancipation approach to see children as beings not becomings, citizens in their own right, and being competent and to encourage participation.

Similarly, by supporting public bodies and civil society organizations to ensure that they incorporate children and young people's views in everything they do, my office helps other agencies be more vigilant and effective in their efforts to improve children's chances in the justice system.

6. CONCLUSION

A child rights-based approach must continue to be the cornerstone of any, and all, progress towards removing statutory, cultural, and structural

---

22 Ibid., para. 112.

obstacles to a child-friendly justice system in Jersey. The justice system must guarantee the respect and effective implementation of all children's rights.

Meaningful participation of children and young people to inform, shape, co-design, and co-produce services that have a true child rights-based approach should be at the heart of developing a child-friendly justice system.

Service redesign must be underpinned by a proven evidence-based methodology which includes looking outside Jersey for developments in services. Applying this approach will guarantee that service redesign is carried out transparently, strategically, based on best practice and, most importantly, in a way that is built around a child rights-based approach.

The justice system must be adapted for children, must be independent, and must be efficient.

This is an opportunity to create a child-friendly justice system that guarantees the respect and effective implementation of all children's rights. My role as Children's Commissioner for Jersey is to continue to work tirelessly to advocate for the removal of these obstacles to children accessing justice, using my statutory powers where necessary and continuing to raise awareness of children's equitable access to justice.

CHILDREN'S ACCESS TO PROCEDURAL JUSTICE IN SCHOOL DISCIPLINE PROCESSES IN ONTARIO, CANADA

Jean-Frédéric Hübsch

1. INTRODUCTION

The Convention on the Rights of the Child recognizes children's right to education as well as children's right to be heard in administrative proceedings affecting them.[1] Disciplinary measures in school are to be 'administered in a manner consistent with the child's human dignity'[2] which includes giving children a voice in school.[3] In Canadian law, a fair administrative proceeding is one in which, 'those whose interests were affected had a meaningful opportunity to present their case fully and fairly'.[4] Children facing discipline in school should have the opportunity

[1] Convention on the Rights of the Child, General Assembly resolution 44/25 of 20.11.1989, Articles 12, 28, and 29.

[2] Ibid., Article 28(2).

[3] Committee on the Rights of the Child, General Comment No. 12 [2009]: The right of the child to be heard, [07.20.2009], UN Doc. CRC/C/GC/12.

[4] *Baker v. Canada (Minister of Citizenship and Immigration)*, [1999] 2 S.C.R. 817, 1999 CanLII 699 (SCC), para. 30.

to be heard before school officials decide how to respond to an incident of alleged misconduct. Unfortunately, the discipline procedures set out in Ontario's Education Act that may result in the exclusion of a child from school[5] do not systematically reflect these principles.[6] Children in school cannot on their own challenge suspensions and expulsions, meaning those who manage their own education for whatever reason have no guarantee of being meaningfully heard when faced with exclusionary disciplinary measures.[7]

In addition to being contrary to principles of fairness, the failure to systematically include children's voices in school discipline procedures offends children's subjective sense of justice. Tom Tyler, an American psychologist, argues, 'voice, neutrality, respect, and trust' are core principles of procedural justice.[8] These principles apply equally in the school context.[9] Fairness in school is about educators showing they care by respecting children and communicating with them. It is also about consistently and transparently applying rules and explaining decisions.[10] Echoing Tyler's procedural justice principles, children in Ontario and elsewhere 'are concerned with fairness' when it comes to school discipline and in school life generally.[11] Children who face discipline in school want information about their rights, the ability to meaningfully participate in the decisions affecting them, and want decision-makers to take into account their individual circumstances when determining the extent of disciplinary measures.[12] Janet Mosher, a Canadian legal scholar, describes

5 RSO 1990, c E.2, Part XIII.

6 J.-F. Hübsch, 'The Self-Represented Child in School Discipline under Ontario's Education Act' (2020) 7(1) *Canadian Journal of Children's Rights* 73.

7 Justice for Children and Youth, 'Children's Right to be Heard in Canadian Judicial and Administrative Proceedings' (2013), Submission for the Committee on the Rights of the Child, General Day of Discussion Group 1: The Child's Right to be Heard in Judicial and Administrative Proceedings, <http://jfcy.org/wp-content/uploads/2013/10/UNDiscussionPaper.pdf>.

8 T.R. Tyler, 'Procedural Justice and the Courts' (2007) 44 *Court Review* 26, p. 30, <http://digitalcommons.unl.edu/ajacourtreview/217>.

9 T.R. Tyler and R. Trinkner, *Why Children Follow Rules: Legal Socialization and the Development of Legitimacy*, Oxford UP, Oxford 2018, p. 170.

10 Ibid.

11 R. Raby, *School Rules: Obedience, Discipline, and Elusive Democracy*, UT Press, Toronto 2012, p. 123. See also: J. Rudduck and J. Flutter, *How to Improve Your School: Giving Pupils A Voice*, Continuum, London 2004; J.E. Mosher, 'Lessons in Access to Justice: Racialized Youths in Ontario's Safe Schools' (2008) 46 *Osgoode Hall LJ* 807; S.A. Hussain, *The Effects of Ontario's Safe Schools Policy on Racialized Students (2000–2013)*, Ph.D. Thesis, Queen's University, 2015.

12 Above n. 6.

the 'language of justice' spoken by youth as one of '[u]nderstanding, mutual respect, and second chances'.[13]

Suspensions and expulsions are not the only options open to educators when responding to misconduct in schools.[14] Ontario's 'progressive discipline' approach – implemented after the province's previous 'zero tolerance' approach was shown to have a disproportionate impact on racialized children and children with disabilities[15] – 'emphasizes the promotion of positive student behaviour and allows principals to determine the most appropriate consequences for student misconduct'.[16] This includes 'a much wider range of preventative and progressive alternatives, including peer mediation and anti-bullying initiatives'.[17]

After briefly describing the processes set out in the Education Act, I look to the Ministry of Education's policy guidance with respect to progressive discipline as an opening for alternatives to exclusionary discipline practices that otherwise 'undermine (...) students' bonds with the school'.[18]

2. PROGRESSIVE DISCIPLINE LAW AND POLICY

Ontario has adopted a progressive discipline paradigm in its publicly funded schools. The Education Act, school board policies and procedures, and school-level codes of conduct form the 'three political and administrative layers [that] guide school personnel' when responding to student misconduct.[19]

---

13 Above n. 11, J.E. Mosher, p. 814.

14 L. Sandals, et al., 'Shaping a Culture of Respect in our Schools: Promoting Safe and Health Relationships', Queen's Printer for Ontario, 2008, p. 23, <http://www.edu.gov.on.ca/eng/teachers/RespectCulture.pdf>; J. Jean-Pierre and S. Parris-Dumont, 'Alternative School Discipline Principles and Interventions: An Overview of the Literature' (2018) 53(3) *McGill Journal of Education* 414, p. 418.

15 M.G. Hill, *Step by Step to a Safer School*, 2nd edn, LexisNexis, Markham, ON, 2013, p. 1.

16 Above n. 11, R. Raby, p. 7.

17 Ibid.

18 Above n. 11, R. Raby, p. 71. See also above n. 14, J. Jean-Pierre and S. Parris-Dumont, p. 417; M.H.A. Bailey, 'Restorative Justice: Moving from Punitive Sanctions to Proactive Interactions' in F.J. Villegas and J. Brady (Eds.), *Critical Schooling*, Springer International Publishing, 2019, 47–74, p. 48; B.E. Morrison and D. Vaandering, 'Restorative Justice: Pedagogy, Praxis, and Discipline' (2012) 11(2) *J Sch Violence* 138, p. 140; K. Evans and D. Vaandering, *The Little Book of Restorative Justice in Education*, Good Books, New York 2016, pp. 11, 84.

19 Above n. 11, R. Raby, p. 6.

The Education Act states the purpose of progressive discipline includes encouraging a positive school climate, promoting early intervention, and 'establish[ing] disciplinary approaches that promote positive behaviour and use measures that include appropriate consequences and supports for pupils to address inappropriate behaviour'.[20] According to Policy/Program Memorandum No. 145 (PPM 145), progressive discipline 'combines prevention and intervention strategies and discipline with opportunities for students to continue their education'.[21] This involves promoting 'respectful and caring relationships' in the school community through, for example, 'curriculum, school climate, teaching practices, policies, and procedures'.[22] The intent is to create a 'positive school climate' through 'an effective continuum of strategies'.[23] These strategies are to be 'developmentally and socio-emotionally appropriate'.[24] PPM 145 also sets out policy statements that school boards are required to include in their own policies and procedures with respect to progressive discipline.[25] School boards then develop their own policies in line with the Ministry's guidance, which then lead to local school-level codes of conduct.[26]

The only school discipline processes explicitly prescribed in the Education Act relate to disciplinary measures resulting in the short- or long-term exclusion of a student from school. Such discipline is divided into two categories: activities leading to possible suspension[27] and activities leading to mandatory suspension with possibility of expulsion.[28] Suspensions may be appealed to the school board while expulsions may be appealed to the

---

20 Section 300.0.1.

21 Ontario Ministry of Education, 'Policy/Program Memorandum No. 145 – Progressive Discipline and Promoting Positive Student Behaviour' (05.12.2012) [PPM 145], p. 1, <https://www.ontario.ca/document/education-ontario-policy-and-program-direction/policyprogram-memorandum-145>. Other related policies include Ontario Ministry of Education, 'Policy/Program Memorandum No. 144 – Bullying Prevention and Intervention' (05.12.2012) [PPM 144], <https://www.ontario.ca/document/education-ontario-policy-and-program-direction/policyprogram-memorandum-144> and Ontario Ministry of Education, 'Policy/Program Memorandum No. 128 – The Provincial Code of Conduct and School Board Codes of Conduct' (05.12.2012) [PPM 128], <https://www.ontario.ca/document/education-ontario-policy-and-program-direction/policyprogram-memorandum-128>.

22 Ibid., p. 2.

23 Ibid., p. 2.

24 Ibid., p. 3.

25 Ibid., p. 6.

26 Sections 302, 303.

27 Sections 306–309.

28 Sections 310–311.7.

provincial Child and Family Services Review Board.[29] When imposing discretionary suspensions, conducting investigations following mandatory suspension, or considering an expulsion recommendation, the decision-makers must take into consideration mitigating and other factors. These include the student's ability to understand the foreseeable consequences of their behaviour; their age and history; whether the behaviour in question is related to a disability or to harassment contrary to the Ontario Human Rights Code; and the effect of the disciplinary measures on the student's ongoing education.[30] This list of factors has been understood as a way of 'accommodating student differences in determining appropriate disciplinary outcomes'.[31]

In both suspension appeals and expulsion proceedings, the affected child may attend the hearing and make a statement.[32] However, the child is not a formal party to the proceeding unless they have turned 18 years old or are 16 or 17 years old and have withdrawn from parental control. Otherwise, only the parent or guardian may initiate an appeal and be a party to suspension appeals and expulsion proceedings.[33] The same applies to appeals to the Review Board.[34] In the circumstances, only those children whose parents have the means to challenge school authorities benefit from the procedural protections of the Education Act.[35]

In contrast to its detailed suspension and expulsion procedures, the Education Act provides no specific guidance with respect to alternatives to these exclusionary practices. However, among the statements that school boards are required to include in their own school policies are two that explicitly open the door to alternatives to formal disciplinary processes. First, school boards are required to include 'a continuum of

29 Section 311.7 of the Education Act; Ontario Regulation 472/07 – *Behaviour, Discipline and Safety of Pupils*, sections 1, 4.

30 Ibid., sections 2, 3.

31 E. Milne, *Loosely Cultivating Discipline: From Zero Tolerance to Progressive Discipline in an Ontario School Board*, M.A Thesis in Sociology, McMaster University, 2011, p. 115. See also M. Paré and T. Collins, 'Government Efforts to Address Bullying in Canada: Any Place for Children's Rights?' (2015) 25 *J L & Social Policy* 54, p. 66.

32 Sections 309(9) and 311.3(4) of the Education Act.

33 Sections 309(8) and 311.3(3).

34 J. Scott, 'Expulsion Appeals: Framework for the Legal Analysis', Paper presented at OBA Institute 2019 Education Law Section Program, Ontario Bar Association, Toronto, 2019, p. 1, citing to *Appellants v. Respondent School Board*, 2016 CFSRB 42.

35 Above n. 18, M.H.A. Bailey, pp. 69–70; above n. 14, J. Jean-Pierre and S. Parris-Dumont, p. 417; E. Milne and J. Aurini, 'A Tale of Two Policies: The Case of School Discipline in an Ontario School Board' (2017) 183 *Cdn J Ed Admin & Policy* 30, p. 39.

prevention programs, interventions, supports, and consequences [that] build upon strategies that build skills for healthy relationships and promote positive behaviours'.[36] Second, progressive discipline strategies 'must include learning opportunities for students in order to reinforce positive behaviours and help students make good choices'.[37] More than just developing responses to misconduct in schools, school boards are encouraged to ensure their progressive discipline strategies contribute to student learning and personal development.[38]

A very small sample of policies from four of Ontario's 72 school boards indicates the Ministry's guidance has had an impact.[39] For example, two school boards' policies speak specifically to learning and development opportunities in the progressive discipline context. In Eastern Ontario Catholic schools, '[o]pportunities for student leadership such as student government, peer mediation, and/or peer mentorship will be provided'.[40] In Toronto's public school board, '[s]chools shall (...) provide opportunities for students to improve the school climate by assuming leadership roles (e.g., peer mediation, mentorship)' and 'apply interventions which may include (...) peer mediation'.[41]

In Toronto's Catholic school board, the continuum of interventions is described in the context of addressing 'underlying causes of inappropriate behaviour. Some examples of ongoing interventions are meeting with the parent(s), requiring the student to perform volunteer service in the school community, conflict mediation, peer mentoring, and/or a referral to counselling'.[42] In addition, its Victims Rights Policy contemplates a 'Restorative Conflict Mediation Circle'[43] as a form of

---

36 Above n. 21, PPM 145, p. 6.

37 Ibid.

38 Above, n. 35, E. Milne and J. Aurini, p. 31.

39 Toronto District School Board, Toronto Catholic District School Board, Ottawa-Carleton District School Board, and Catholic District School Board of Eastern Ontario.

40 Catholic District School Board of Eastern Ontario, 'Administrative Procedure B2:3 – Progressive Discipline', p. 4, <https://www.cdsbeo.on.ca/policies/B2-3_Progressive_Discipline.pdf>.

41 Toronto District School Board, 'Operational Procedure PR702 – Progressive Discipline and Promoting Positive Student Behaviour', pp. 2–3, <http://ppf.tdsb.on.ca/uploads/files/live/98/1801.pdf>.

42 Toronto Catholic District School Board, 'Policy No. S.S.10 – Progressive Discipline', p. 4, <https://www.tcdsb.org/Board/Policies/Documents/SS10.pdf>.

43 Toronto Catholic District School Board, 'Policy No. S.S.13 – Victims Rights', p. 4, <https://www.tcdsb.org/Board/Policies/Documents/S.S.13.pdf>.

progressive discipline.[44] Similarly, Ottawa's public school board includes restorative justice practices directly in its progressive discipline policy:

> Restorative justice uses peer mediation, healing circles and, at its most formal, group conferences. These methods can address a wide range of issues: bullying and harassment, vandalism, swearing at teachers, fighting, assault, theft and weapon offences. Sometimes the process replaces suspensions and sometimes it runs alongside them. It is useful for incidents between students, between students and teachers or between students and other staff.[45]

A study conducted in an Ontario school board found the implementation of progressive discipline policies led educators to view incidents of student misconduct as creating 'opportunities for students to learn socially appropriate behavioural patterns' and helping educators 'to learn about individual students, what their specific needs are, and what support mechanisms may help them achieve success'.[46] An educator in another study stated involving children in conflict resolution and discipline processes gives them voice and builds self-confidence.[47] A study in three Ontario secondary schools found the policies 'gave school administrators more leeway to implement restorative responses in conflict situations to promote proactive peacebuilding approaches in their schools'.[48] One of the schools in particular had implemented 'a range of proactive preventive measures as well as post-incident restorative and dialogue approaches'.[49]

Progressive discipline is not a panacea and policy statements are only as effective as their implementation. Variable exercise of discretion by educators,[50] inconsistent guidelines and communication,[51] disagreements

---

44 Toronto Catholic District School Board, 'Safe Schools Protocols, Policies, Legislation', <https://www.tcdsb.org/FORPARENTS/ParentInvolvement/cpic/Documents/Safe%20Schools%20Presentation%20November%206.pdf>.

45 Ottawa-Carleton District School Board, 'Procedure PR.660.SCO – Progressive Discipline and Promoting Positive Student Behaviour', pp. 1–2, <https://weblink.ocdsb.ca/WebLink/0/edoc/2008838/PR%20660%20SCO%20-%20Progressive%20Discipline%20And%20Promoting%20Positive%20Student%20Behaviour.pdf>.

46 Above n. 31, E. Milne, pp. 69–70.

47 Above n. 35, E. Milne and J. Aurini, p. 38.

48 D. Barnes, *Restorative Peacemaking Circles and other Conflict Management Efforts in Three Ontario High Schools*, Ph.D. Thesis, Ontario Institute for Studies in Education, 2015, p. 150.

49 Ibid., p. 76.

50 Above n. 31, E. Milne, pp. 75–76; above n. 35, E. Milne and J. Aurini, p. 35.

51 Ibid., p. 36; D.D. Vaandering, *Towards Effective Implementation and Sustainability of Restorative Justice in Ontario Public Schools: A Critical Case Study*, Ph.D. Thesis, University of Western Ontario, 2009, p. 136; above n. 31, E. Milne, pp. 64–67.

over the effectiveness of various approaches,[52] resistance from educators to implementing new procedures,[53] and a continued focus on adult power over children[54] are factors that can undermine the implementation of progressive discipline approaches.

3. PRACTICING PROGRESSIVE DISCIPLINE

The following discussions of restorative justice and peer mediation define the term in question, address children's perspectives as reported in relevant empirical studies, and discuss the limitations of each approach's implementation in schools. The studies I refer to were selected based on two primary criteria: they relate to restorative justice or peer mediation in schools; and they include the views of children in their findings. In addition, preference was given to studies concerning schools in Ontario.

3.1. RESTORATIVE JUSTICE

While there is no one definition of restorative justice,[55] relevant practices generally find their inspiration from Indigenous conflict resolution practices.[56] Unlike exclusionary discipline practices:

> Restorative justice procedures provide a forum to address inappropriate behaviors so that students are aware of the effects of their action in disrupting the class. The student has the opportunity to explain what caused the inappropriate action and listen to advice and suggestions from their peers about alternative ways to express their frustration and anger.[57]

---

52 Above n. 35, E. Milne and J. Aurini, p. 30.

53 Above n. 31, E. Milne, pp. 64–67.

54 Above n. 51, D.D. Vaandering, p. 126.

55 K. Reimer, 'An Exploration of the Implementation of Restorative Justice in an Ontario Public School' (2011) 119 *Cdn J Ed Admin & Policy* 1, p. 4; above n. 14, J. Jean-Pierre and S. Parris-Dumont, pp. 423–24.

56 Above n. 18, M.H.A. Bailey, pp. 65–66.

57 Ibid., p. 63, citing to B. Costello, J. Wachtel, and T. Wachtel, *The Restorative Practices Handbook: For Teachers, Disciplinarians and Administrators*, International Institute for Restorative Practices, Bethlehem, PA, USA, 2009. See also above n. 14, J. Jean-Pierre and S. Parris-Dumont, p. 424.

Restorative justice is about relationships[58] and empowers the community 'to collectively create safe and just schools'.[59]

Restorative practices in schools can range from informal in-class use of restorative language by educators, to classroom-based restorative discussions, to structured restorative circles involving not only children but any other community members affected by an incident.[60] Restorative practices can be used to prevent conflict by including restorative principles in the curriculum or to repair relationships following conflict through circles in which the offender, victim(s), and others come together based on agreed guidelines. Such circles are often led by a trained facilitator as participants identify the harm caused by the behaviour in question, seek to have the offender take responsibility for their actions, and together come to a consensus on what steps need to be taken to repair the harm caused.[61] As one participant in a study put it, in school-based restorative justice 'students reach answers and are not given answers'.[62]

Children in an Ontario study who were the subject of past suspensions contrasted restorative approaches with their own experiences. When suspended, they were unable to speak with those with whom they had been in conflict and therefore were not given an opportunity to repair the relationship in any structured way.[63] However, children who were given the opportunity to participate in restorative practices left with strengthened relationships among children and staff alike, and they felt future violence was prevented.[64] In another school from the same study, a child 'liked that one person could speak at a time, and as a result she could hear everyone's perspectives and the story could get clarified'.[65] Another student found the process fair 'because everyone had the same amount of time to say what they had to say'.[66]

---

58 Above n. 55, K. Reimer, p. 6; above n. 48, p. 24.

59 Above n. 55, K. Reimer, p. 6. See, in the youth criminal justice context, S.A. Moore and R.C. Mitchell, 'Theorising Rights-Based Restorative Justice: The Canadian Context' (2011) 19(1) *Intl J Child Rts* 81; S.A. Moore and R.C. Mitchell, 'Rights-Based Restorative Justice in Canada: From Silence to Citizenship' in M. Freeman (Ed.), *Law and Childhood Studies*, Oxford UP, Oxford, 2012, pp. 202–18. See also T.R. Tyler, 'Restorative Justice and Procedural Justice: Dealing with Rule Breaking' (2006) 62(2) *J Soc Issues* 307.

60 Above n. 55, K. Reimer, p. 7; above n. 48, p. 64.

61 Above n. 14, J. Jean-Pierre and S. Parris-Dumont, p. 423.

62 G. Rideout, et al., 'Measuring the Effect of Restorative Justice Practices: Outcomes and Contexts' (2010) 21(2) *EAF Journal* 35, p. 55.

63 Above n. 48, p. 143.

64 Ibid., pp. 125, 150.

65 Ibid., p. 136.

66 Ibid.

The implementation of restorative responses to conflict can be challenging. In some schools, children were not proactively educated on restorative justice despite related statements in school codes of conduct.[67] In other cases, educators instrumentalized restorative language without fully implementing restorative practices,[68] or undermined the community-based nature of restorative justice by failing to include all affected individuals.[69] Despite mobilizing restorative language, discipline conferences in one school left 'little space for student voice, since counselling was based on explaining why students were suspended'.[70]

In a study conducted prior to the advent of progressive discipline in Ontario, once funding specifically for restorative justice training stopped after three years, so did the expansion of restorative justice practices within the school board's schools.[71] Later studies into restorative justice schools show little evidence that matters have improved since progressive discipline became provincial policy. Moreover, restorative justice as a philosophy is not simply a tool for educators; its success depends on how well it is 'integrated into [educators'] overall practice and pedagogical relationship with students in school communities'.[72]

3.2. PEER MEDIATION

Peer mediation is about restoring relationships in schools.[73] Instead of the community coming together in a discussion facilitated by a trusted adult, it involves specially trained children acting as neutral third parties to facilitate a resolution among peers.[74] Peer mediation models discussed in studies from Australia[75] and the United States[76] describe it as a consensual

67 Ibid., p. 139.

68 Above n. 62, p. 58.

69 Above n. 48, p 131.

70 Ibid., p. 70.

71 Above n. 55, K. Reimer, pp. 14–15.

72 Above n. 51, D.D. Vaandering, pp. 124, 289. See also above n. 18, B.E. Morrison and D. Vaandering, pp. 144–45; above n. 18, K. Evans and D. Vaandering, pp. 70–71, 104–06.

73 N. McWilliam, 'A school peer mediation program as a context for exploring therapeutic jurisprudence (TJ): Can a peer mediation program inform the law?' (2010) 33 *Intl J L & Psychiatry* 293, p. 294.

74 Above n. 48, p. 27.

75 Above n. 73, p. 296.

76 K. Bickmore, 'Good Training is Not Enough: Research on Peer Mediation Program Implementation' (2002) 31 *Journal of Social Alternatives*.

and confidential process whereby each party is given the opportunity to present their version of events without interruption, and where the mediator assists the parties to identify relevant issues and cooperatively resolve the dispute. School-based peer mediation programs generally 'use a "cadre" approach to peer mediation: a small group of students in each school are trained, outside of regular classes, to provide the mediation service'.[77]

Mediation can be more or less formal depending on various factors, in particular the age of the children involved.[78] Peer mediators can frame disputes in age-appropriate language; children can talk out problems without fear of judgment from an adult authority figure; and children are empowered to come up with their own solutions.[79] Moreover, peer mediation can have a long-term positive impact in schools as children as mediators retain the skills they learned and are able to apply them to different situations.[80]

Implementing peer mediation programs requires attention to ethical challenges. For example, bullying incidents by definition involve power imbalances.[81] Since '[t]he mediation process presumes that the parties are able to negotiate with each other on relatively equal terms',[82] mediators must be trained on techniques for managing the power imbalances. Ground rules such as ensuring only one person speaks at a time and avoiding interrupting speakers, preventing attacks, restating positions to help balance voice, and giving positive reinforcement when parties participate and cooperate can help account for power imbalances.[83] Mediation also presumes the mediator will remain impartial. This, coupled with having to account for power differentials, means peer mediators must strike the right balance to avoid an apprehension of bias.[84]

---

77 Ibid.

78 Ibid.

79 F. Schrumpf, D.K. Crawford, and R.J. Bodine, *Peer Mediation: Conflict Resolution in Schools – Program Guide*, Revised Edition, Research Press, Champaign, IL, 1997, p. 47.

80 Ibid., p. 40; above n. 73, p. 300, fn omitted; D.W. Johnston and R.T. Johnson, 'Conflict Resolution and Peer Mediation Programs in Elementary and Secondary Schools: A Review of the Research' (1996) 66 *Review of Education Research* 459, quoted in R. Jacobson and A. Rycroft, *Managing Conflict in Schools: A Practical Guide*, LexisNexis, Markham, ON, 2007, p. 102.

81 Above n. 21, PPM 144, pp. 4–5.

82 B. Landau, L. Wolfson, and N. Landau, *Family Mediation, Arbitration and Collaborative Practice Handbook*, 5th edn, LexisNexis, Markham, ON, 2009, p. 58.

83 Ibid., pp. 58–59.

84 Above n. 80, R. Jacobson and A. Rycroft, pp. 94–95.

A study conducted in Hamilton, Ontario found that structured peer mediation during elementary school recess resulted in significant decreases in aggressive playground behaviour.[85] It noted the decrease in such behaviour was only sustained as long as the peer mediation program was kept at full strength.[86] According to the Australian study, 'without the appropriate training and information, a participant cannot optimise their experience of the process'.[87] Moreover, in one study peer mediators did not always follow their training, 'unconsciously imitat[ing] traditional patterns of discipline that contradicted the principles of peer mediation'.[88]

In terms of access to peer mediation programs, schools must be aware that 'students' cultural, class, or family backgrounds may make them more or less inclined to favour a participatory approach'.[89] As mediation is a consensual process, any peer mediation program must engage with more marginalized students and avoid punishing them for resisting participation.[90] Peer mediation 'fails if it simply becomes another mechanism to perpetuate and reward middle class values'.[91] To have a positive impact on school climate, peer mediation 'must be viewed not as isolated interactions between individuals, but as [part of] a pervasive, systemic cultural change'.[92]

4. ACCESS TO JUSTICE AND FAIRNESS IN SCHOOL DISCIPLINE

Fairness and justice for children in school discipline is about being treated respectfully. Respect is shown by teaching children their rights, accounting for their individual circumstances, and giving them opportunities to be heard and to improve.

Restorative practices, when implemented properly, are student-centered.[93] Based on a school-wide understanding of the principles underlying

---

85 C.E. Cunningham, et al., 'The Effects of Primary Division, Student-mediated Conflict Resolution Programs on Playground Aggression' (1998) 39(5) *J Child Psychol Psychiat* 653.

86 Ibid. See also above n. 76.

87 Above n. 73, p. 303.

88 Above n. 76.

89 Above n. 11, R. Raby, p. 227.

90 Ibid., p. 245.

91 Ibid.

92 Above n. 79, p. 6.

93 Above n. 18, M.H.A. Bailey, p. 70.

restorative justice, children can come together in safe spaces to share their feelings, account for their actions, and come to solutions acceptable to the whole community. While adults will usually still be involved in restorative justice circles, children are given the space and time to find their own solutions, and those who harmed the community are given the opportunity to make reparations for their actions and move forward.

In peer mediation, children drive the process. With appropriate training, mediators work with their peers to resolve conflict and come to mutually agreeable solutions. Prior to any mediation, a mediator will ensure the parties understand the ground rules, are participating voluntarily, and will be treated respectfully. Once everyone has told their story, the mediator will work with their peers to identify common issues and seek common ground for resolution. Given its consensual and peer-based nature, children 'could judge the peer mediation process as fair even when the outcome of the process was unfavourable from their standpoint. Students reported that being given the opportunity to voice their opinions and ideas in relation to issues, at peer mediation, was a very satisfying feeling'.[94]

Both restorative justice and peer mediation appear to reflect well what children understand to be fair and just in school discipline. Given the benefits to children and to the school community of progressive discipline approaches over the formal exclusionary processes set out in the Education Act, there is little reason to default to top-down approaches to school discipline. As '[e]ducation is living, not the preparation for living[, s]tudents must be involved in dealing with real problems in order to learn what they need to know now and later'.[95] Indeed, children have expressed a desire and appreciation for being able to resolve their own conflicts.

5. CONCLUSION

School climate is defined by its relationships,[96] and a positive school climate comes about through a culture of mutual respect.[97] Both restorative justice and peer mediation contribute to a culture of mutual respect, because they offer children space to work together to understand the underlying context

94 Above n. 73, p. 301.
95 Above n. 79, p. 11.
96 Above n. 21, PPM 144, p. 3, footnote omitted.
97 Ibid.

of a conflict situation.[98] Only by meeting underlying needs can discipline be effective over the longer term.[99] An important element of respect according to children is having their individual circumstances considered. Children feel 'that they should be held accountable for their actions, but that compassion should be exercised and the circumstances of particular situations taken into account when consequences are being administered'.[100] Fortunately, the 'shift toward progressive discipline suggests an increasing attention to context'.[101] Context-sensitive inclusionary approaches to discipline can be more effective than traditional exclusionary approaches because responses to specific incidents 'emerge from an understanding of the challenges students face and the causes underlying their behaviour'.[102]

Implementation of progressive discipline procedures requires collective effort, consistency, and caring relationships.[103] Inclusionary discipline processes seek 'to bring the students' voices into the decision-making process of school and to encourage them to promote the changes they want by assuming responsibility for their ideas'.[104] Children themselves have said, 'anti-violence efforts need to be peer-led because people only listen to people to whom they can relate' and 'child participation [supports] the identification of violence and generate[s] new responses'.[105] However, 'if teachers are not fully inclined or willing to relinquish power to students, the successful implementation of the (…) student-driven model can be challenging'.[106] Moreover, when implementing progressive discipline practices, boards have the flexibility to take into account local needs and circumstances,[107] which can lead to very different access to programs in different school boards. Developing alternatives to suspensions and expulsions as part of progressive discipline also takes time;[108] requires

---

98 Above n. 80, R. Jacobson and A. Rycroft, p. 4; above n. 18, K. Evans and D. Vaandering, p. 82.

99 Ontario Ministry of Education in collaboration with the Ontario Human Rights Commission, 'Supporting Bias-Free Progressive Discipline in Schools: A Resource Guide for School and System Leaders', Queen's Printer for Ontario, 2013, p. 10, <http://www.ontla.on.ca/library/repository/mon/27009/324101.pdf>.

100 Above n. 11, R. Raby, p. 67.

101 Ibid., p. 131.

102 Above n. 99, pp. 9–10.

103 Above n. 14, J. Jean-Pierre and S. Parris-Dumont, p. 418.

104 Ibid., p. 422.

105 T.M. Collins and M. Paré, 'A Child Rights-Based Approach to Anti-Violence Efforts in Schools' (2016) 24 *Int J Child Rights* 764, p. 770.

106 Above n. 14, J. Jean-Pierre and S. Parris-Dumont, p. 423.

107 Above n. 21, PPM 145, p. 5.

108 Above n. 79, p. 6.

staff resources, including training and dedication to the program;[109] and community buy-in through information and communication.[110]

The design of any school conflict resolution strategy should be to promote a healthy system with a variety of dispute resolution options to choose from that meet the nature of the dispute and the parties' willingness to engage.[111] Attention must also be paid to the congruence between various disciplinary approaches within a school community in order to avoid contradictory results, such as imposing exclusionary measures despite stated adherence to an inclusionary model.[112] In addition, inclusionary measures must be truly inclusive and 'support diverse students to participate in activities so all can have opportunities to build peer conflict management capacity and increase their sense of belonging to a school'.[113] Indeed, 'for transformative reform to be sustained, the reform must become normative within the culture, not an alternative'.[114] If Ontario's public school system takes seriously the idea that progressive discipline 'promote[s] responsible citizenship by encouraging appropriate participation in the civic life of the school community'[115] and 'active and engaged citizens are aware of their rights, but more importantly, they accept responsibility for protecting their rights and the rights of others',[116] inclusionary discipline measures become an integral part of both school conflict resolution and of citizenship education more broadly.

---

109 Ibid., pp. 14–15; above n. 14, J. Jean-Pierre and S. Parris-Dumont, p. 427; above n. 18, K. Evans and D. Vaandering, p. 24.

110 Above n. 80, R. Jacobson and A. Rycroft, p. 114.

111 J. Lande, 'Principles for Policymaking About Collaborative Law and Other ADR Processes' (2007) 22 *Ohio St J Disp Resol*, p. 619, quoted in J.C. Kleefeld, et al., *Dispute Resolution: Readings and Case Studies*, 4th ed., Emond Montgomery, Toronto, 2016, pp. 817–18.

112 Above n. 48, pp. 93, 109.

113 Ibid., p. 107.

114 Above n. 55, K. Reimer, pp. 38–39. See also above n. 105, p. 789; H. van Gurp, *Peer Mediation: The Complete Guide to Resolving Conflict in our Schools*, Portage & Main Press, Winnipeg, MB 2002, p. 6, quoted in above n. 80, R. Jacobson and A. Rycroft, p. 108; above n. 18, K. Evans and D. Vaandering, p. 109.

115 Above n. 21, PPM 128, p. 4.

116 Ibid., p. 2.

CHILDREN'S RIGHTS TO ACCESS JUSTICE AT THE INTERNATIONAL LEVEL

Challenge and Opportunity

Ursula Kilkelly

1. INTRODUCTION

International law is clear that children are rights holders, entitled to a range of rights under the Convention on the Rights of the Child (CRC) and numerous other international and regional instruments. Interestingly, the Convention is silent on whether the child has a right to access justice, although the Committee on the Rights of the Child has made it clear that children are entitled to remedies for breaches of their rights.[1] In setting out this position, the Committee has focused on the availability and effectiveness of national rather than international mechanisms. However, the adoption of the Optional Protocol to the Convention on

---

1 Committee on the Rights of the Child, General Comment No. 5 [2003]: General measures of implementation of the Convention on the Rights of the Child (Articles 4, 42 and 44, para. 6), UN Doc. CRC/GC/2003/527, para. 24.

a Communications Procedure has now brought international remedies firmly into view.

Liefaard remarks that the concept of access to justice has 'neither been carefully conceptualized, nor contextualized in relation to children'[2] and this is particularly true at the international level where there is a significant gulf between the acceptance of the child's right to access justice and children's experience. It is the aim of this chapter to advance our understanding of these issues through an exposition of the child as a legal actor under the CRC.

2. THE CHILD AS A LEGAL ACTOR UNDER THE CONVENTION ON THE RIGHTS OF THE CHILD

As a legally binding international instrument, with almost universal ratification,[3] the CRC is the benchmark against which a State's treatment of its children is measured. The breadth of the Convention – which covers the full spectrum of rights including social, economic, and cultural rights, and civil and political rights – means children's rights must be protected, promoted and fulfilled in all aspects of their lives.[4] The Convention confirms the status of children as rights holders and is clear that, notwithstanding the supporting role played by the child's family, the responsibility to vindicate children's rights rests with the State. Article 4 recognizes that the State, as duty bearer, must take all appropriate measures to implement the Convention.[5] Under Article 5, States recognize it is the responsibility of parents to provide the child with appropriate direction and guidance in the exercise of their rights in a manner consistent with their evolving capacities. While the Convention accepts the child may need parental support to exercise their rights,[6] it is clear as children develop that they

---

2 T. Liefaard, 'Access to Justice for Children: Towards a Specific Research and Implementation Agenda' (2019) 27 *International Journal of Children's Rights* 195–227, p. 197.

3 The Convention was adopted and opened for signature, ratification, and accession by General Assembly resolution 44/25 of 20.11.1989 and entered into force on 02.09.1990, in accordance with Article 49. Only the United States of America has not ratified the instrument. See, <https://indicators.ohchr.org/>.

4 For a comprehensive analysis of the Convention see J. Tobin, *The UN Convention on the Rights of the Child: A Commentary*, OUP, New York, 2019.

5 See above n. 1, Article 4.

6 E. Sutherland, 'The Enigma of Article 5 of the United Nations Convention on the Rights of The Child Central or Peripheral?' (2020) 28(3) *International Journal of Children's Rights*, pp. 447–70.

will gradually assume full responsibility to exercise and seek vindication of their rights.

Various provisions of the CRC recognize the procedural rights of children in legal proceedings. The Convention recognizes that the child has a role in criminal proceedings (Article 40), in family law proceedings (Article 9) and in the review of alternative care (Article 25). More generally, Article 12 requires States parties to assure to the child who is capable of forming their own views the right to express those views freely in all matters affecting them.[7] To this end, Article 12(2) requires that the child be 'provided the opportunity to be heard in any judicial and administrative proceedings affecting the child, either directly, or through a representative or an appropriate body, in a manner consistent with the procedural rules of national law'. Article 12(1) has had a significant influence on the attitude to children's rights, signifying the increased visibility and influence of children in decision-making.[8] Article 12(2) is equally important, however, reflecting the status of the child as a legal actor and a participant in legal proceedings affecting them. According to the Committee on the Rights of the Child, the child's right to be heard applies 'without limitation' to all relevant administrative and judicial proceedings affecting the child[9] and it applies equally to those initiated by the child – such as complaints against ill-treatment – as well as those initiated by others which affect the child, such as parental separation or adoption.[10] The Committee recognizes a child cannot be heard effectively where the environment is 'intimidating, hostile, insensitive or inappropriate' and recommends that proceedings must be 'accessible and child-appropriate.'[11] It recommends that particular measures are taken to ensure that the environment in which proceedings take place is consistent with the child's participation.

The Convention requires States to put in place the conditions to realize the child's Article 12 rights. However, the requirements to safeguard the child's procedural rights appear most commonly invoked in proceedings about the child, but to which the child may not be a party. In fewer situations, if any, is it envisaged children will have initiated these

---

7 Committee on the Rights of the Child, General Comment No. 12 [2009]: The right of the child to be heard, [07.20.2009], CRC/C/GC/12.

8 G. Lansdown, *Every Child's right to be heard. A resource Guide on the UN Committee on the Rights of the Child's General Comment No 12*, UNICEF and Save the Children, London 2011.

9 Above n. 7, para. 32.

10 Ibid., para. 33.

11 Ibid., para. 34.

proceedings themselves. For instance, the Convention says little about the child's entitlement to bring proceedings in their own name and although the CRC provides some guidance on the legal capacity of children, it does not recognize the unequivocal right of the child to legal representation or assistance, at least not outside the context of the criminal justice system.[12] It is hard to separate this conclusion from the fact that, although the Convention recognizes the child's procedural rights, unlike other international human rights treaties,[13] it is silent on the fundamental right to an effective remedy.[14]

Yet, according to Freeman, '[r]ights without remedies are of symbolic importance, no more'.[15] For this reason, the Committee on the Rights of the Child recognized early on that it is implicit in the Convention that, 'for rights to have meaning, effective remedies must be available to redress violations'.[16] It goes on to note that children's 'special and dependent status creates real difficulties for them in pursuing remedies for breaches of their rights', requiring States parties to ensure there are 'effective, child-sensitive procedures available to children' including 'child-friendly information, advice, advocacy'. It specifically references the importance of the child having access to 'independent complaints procedures and to the courts with necessary legal and other assistance.'[17] Where rights are found to have been breached, the Committee says, there should be appropriate reparation. It also regards it as 'essential' that domestic law set out entitlements in sufficient detail to enable remedies for non-compliance to be effective.[18] Having set out the child's right to a remedy under the CRC, this contribution now turns to the concept of child-friendly justice in order to examine the contribution this makes to our understanding of children's access to justice.

---

12 Above n. 2, p. 204.

13 For example, see Article 2(3) of the International Covenant on Civil and Political Rights. UN Human Rights Council, *Access to justice for children. Report of the United Nations High Commissioner for Human Rights* [2013], UN Doc. A/HRC/25/35, para. 10.

14 Above n. 2, p. 196.

15 M. Freeman, 'Why It Remains Important to Take Children's Rights Seriously' (2007) 15 *International Journal of Children's Rights* 5–23, p. 8.

16 Above n. 1.

17 Ibid.

18 Ibid., para. 25.

3. THE EMERGENCE OF CHILD-FRIENDLY JUSTICE

The concept of child-friendly procedures was developed in the Guidelines on Child-friendly Justice adopted by the Council of Europe in 2010.[19] According to Liefaard, the Guidelines are 'a practical tool' to help States adapt their 'judicial and non-judicial systems to the specific rights, needs and interests of children'.[20] According to the Guidelines, child-friendly justice guarantees:

> the respect and the effective implementation of all children's rights at the highest attainable level, bearing in mind the principles listed below and giving due consideration to the child's level of maturity and understanding and the circumstances of the case. It is, in particular, justice that is accessible, age appropriate, speedy, diligent, adapted to and focused on the needs and rights of the child, respecting the rights of the child including the rights to due process, to participate in and to understand the proceedings, to respect for private and family life and to integrity and dignity.[21]

The Guidelines set out the role and place of the child in legal proceedings, and aim to ensure in any such proceedings 'all rights of children … are fully respected with due consideration to the child's level of maturity and understanding and to the circumstances of the case'.[22] The instrument sets out the rights to which children are entitled before, during, and after legal proceedings and include rights relating to information, representation, participation, and protection. The Guidelines were inspired by legal developments around the effective participation of children in legal proceedings such as that found in the case law of the European Court of Human Rights (ECtHR) as well as the views of children themselves.[23] The Guidelines provide that, as bearers of rights, children should 'have recourse to remedies to effectively exercise their rights or act upon violations of

---

19 Guidelines of the Committee of Ministers of the Council of Europe on Child-friendly Justice adopted by the Committee of Ministers of the Council of Europe on 17.11.2010, <http://www.coe.int>.

20 T. Liefaard, 'Protection and Participation of Children in the Justice System' (2016) 88 *Temple Law Review* 905–27, p. 905.

21 Above n. 19, p. 16.

22 Ibid., p. 16.

23 T. Liefaard and U. Kilkelly, 'Child-friendly justice: past, present and future' in B. Goldson (Ed.), *Juvenile Justice in Europe. Past, Present and Future*, Routledge, London and New York 2018, pp. 57–73.

their rights'.[24] They provide that, 'the domestic law should facilitate where appropriate the possibility of access to court for children who have sufficient understanding of their rights and of the use of remedies to protect these rights, based on adequately given legal advice'.[25] The Guidelines require that, '[a]ny obstacles to access to court, such as the cost of the proceedings or the lack of legal counsel, should be removed' and go on to make extensive provision for the child's right to legal representation. The Guidelines contain a novel and important focus on the relationship between the child and their lawyer[26] highlighting the importance of lawyers who represent children being specially trained and capable of communicating with children 'at their level of understanding'. Lawyers who represent children are required to provide them with all necessary information and explanations regarding their role in the process and its possible consequences for them[27] and their role is to bring forward the opinion of the child. The Guidelines consider children should be 'fully fledged clients with their own rights' and they recognize the importance of children being adequately and separately represented especially in proceedings involving other parties, like parents, whose interests may conflict with the child's.[28]

The Guidelines thus mark a significant advance in the articulation of the child as a legal actor. They support the concept of the child as a litigant and as a party to legal proceedings, even if representation, advocacy, or guardianship is required to support children through the legal process. Although they recognize that legal and other proceedings can present challenges to children's rights, the Guidelines equally acknowledge that if modified to take account of children's circumstances, they can play an important role in enabling children to claim their rights. In this way, child-friendly justice is not just about adapting the legal process to which a child happens to be subjected but is a vital step in helping children to actively use the justice process to claim their rights. Having established the international standards on child-friendly justice, the paper now moves on to consider what we know about how children experience justice in practice.

24 Above n. 19, p. 26.
25 Above n. 19, p. 26.
26 Above n. 19, p. 27.
27 Ibid.
28 Ibid.

4. BARRIERS TO CHILDREN'S ACCESS TO JUSTICE

While it is vital that international standards establish children's access to justice, it is evident that children seeking access to justice at an international level face a number of acute barriers exercising this right.[29] The first barrier reflects children's poor awareness of their rights; if children are not aware of their rights, they will not be able to take steps to exercise them.[30] Importantly, Article 42 of the CRC addresses this issue, compelling States parties to make the principles and provisions of the Convention 'widely known, by appropriate and active means, to adults and children alike'. The Committee on the Rights of the Child has connected this obligation to the broader concept of human rights education, recommending to States parties that it is integrated into the school curriculum to promote greater awareness among children of their rights.[31] Even where children are aware of their rights, additional barriers may impede their access to remedies for breaches of their rights. Particularly, children who are not familiar with available remedies will not be able to access them. Adults have a key role to play in directing children's attention to the available remedies for breaches of their rights. In this respect, the Committee has repeatedly highlighted the need to embed the Convention in professional training and development among all those who work with and for children, recommending lawyers in particular receive systematic and ongoing training in children's rights.[32] There is no comprehensive international data on the children's rights training received by lawyers and other professionals. However, one study of practice in the European Union found training on the rights of children was either not available for professionals working in the legal system or where it was available, it varied in terms of its 'obligatory or voluntary nature and its availability to specific groups of professionals'.[33]

---

29 Above n. 13, UN Doc. A/HRC/25/35, paras. 13–17.

30 R. Smith, 'The Third Optional Protocol to the Convention on the Rights of the Child – Challenges Arising Transforming the Rhetoric into Reality' (2013) 21 *International Journal of Children's Rights* 305–22, p. 309.

31 Committee on the Rights of the Child, General Comment No 1. [2001]: Article 29(1) The aims of education, [17.04.2001], UN Doc. CRC/GC/2001/1, para. 15.

32 See for example, above n. 1, para. 53; above n. 7, para. 49; Committee on the Rights of the Child, *Children's Rights in the Child Justice System* [2019], UN Doc. CRC/C/GC/24, para. 49.

33 N. Kennan and U. Kilkelly, *Children's involvement in criminal, civil and administrative judicial proceedings in the 28 Member States of the EU. Policy Brief*, Publications Office of the European Union, Luxembourg 2015, p. 26.

Smith notes that making an international complaints system available is not the same as making it effective or accessible to children.[34] Even if children are aware of their rights and are familiar with how to avail of those remedies, access to them may be impeded by systemic or institutional barriers. Barriers at a national level may impede a child's access to the international remedy because they must be overcome as part of the process of exhausting domestic remedies. The application of age limits is one such barrier.[35] For instance, many States limit the right to litigate or make a complaint to those above a certain age, meaning children can, by definition, be excluded from taking such proceedings in their own name.[36] Thus, even if international mechanisms have no such age limits, their imposition at a national level may limit the admissibility of a child's complaint, if the international body requires the exhaustion of national remedies. This situation may be ameliorated where the child's parent or guardian acts on the child's behalf, but this is not always possible or appropriate. Especially vulnerable children – such as those deprived of liberty, in alternative care or who are the subject of discrimination or stigmatisation or fear reprisal – will find it particularly difficult to navigate remedies or indeed to have the confidence or trust to invoke them where they are available.[37]

The appointment of an intermediary like a guardian *ad litem* is one practical way to ensure children can access remedies for breaches of their rights, but international support for this seems limited to certain situations.[38] Moreover, opposition among professionals to the appointment of independent representation for children and to their right to participate in legal and administrative proceedings about them continues to persist. For instance, one recent study in Sweden found ambivalence about the right of the child to litigate.[39] The desire to protect children from the harm that such participation might entail appeared to explain this reluctance.[40]

---

34 Above n. 30.

35 S. Rap, E. Schmidt, and T. Liefaard, 'Safeguarding the dynamic legal position of children: a matter of age limits? Reflections on the Fundamental Principles and Practical Application of age limits in light of international children's rights law' (2020) *Erasmus Law Review*, pp. 4–12.

36 Above n. 33, pp. 31–32.

37 Above n. 13, UN Doc. A/HRC/25/35, para. 17.

38 Committee on the Rights of the Child, General Comment No. 6. [2005]: Treatment of Unaccompanied and Separated Children Outside their Country of Origin, [01.09.2005], UN Doc. CRC/GC/2005/6, paras. 33–38.

39 E. Hultman, S. Höjer, and M. Larsson, 'Age limits for participation in child protection court proceedings in Sweden' (2020) 25 *Child and Family Social Work*, pp. 304–12.

40 Ibid., pp. 309–10.

5. INTERNATIONAL REMEDIES FOR BREACHES OF CHILDREN'S RIGHTS

It is interesting to note the Committee on the Rights of the Child's focus on remedies has traditionally been directed to the national context, reflecting the duty on State parties to implement the Convention. The availability of remedies at a domestic level is vital to ensure children can access mechanisms best placed to respond efficiently and effectively to their complaints. For children, any delay in dealing with a breach of their rights can result in reparation losing its value and timeliness and it has been argued that strengthening national complaints procedures would have 'more effect' than adding an international complaints mechanism to the CRC.[41] At the same time, it has been somewhat ironic that until recently, the Committee criticized States parties for the absence of effective remedies at a national level, when no such system existed at an international level. Even though the same barriers impeding children's access to justice at a domestic level can play out at international level too,[42] it is important to the credibility of the CRC system that the Committee can now receive complaints from children about breaches of their rights under the Convention.

5.1. REGIONAL MECHANISMS

The Human Rights Council has noted that complaint mechanisms at the regional and international level, 'reinforce and complement the national system'.[43] Although Nolan and Kilkelly highlight the progressive impact of the CRC on the regional mechanisms for human rights protection, these systems of individual petition are not generally specific to children and have in the main struggled to adapt to the particular circumstances of child applicants.[44] The Rules of Court of the European Court of Human Rights, for example, make provision for the court to act with urgency

41 L. Smith, 'Monitoring the CRC' in G. Alfredson, et al., (Eds.) *International Human Rights Monitoring Mechanisms: Essays in Honour of Jakob Th Muller*, Martinus Nijhoff, 2009, p. 115, in above n. 30.

42 Above n. 30, p. 315.

43 Above n. 13, UN Doc. A/HRC/25/35, para. 32.

44 A. Nolan and U. Kilkelly, 'Children's rights under regional human rights law – A tale of harmonisation' in C.M. Buckley, A. Donald, and P. Leach (Eds.), *Harmonisation of International Human Rights Law*, Brill, London 2017, pp. 296–322.

where circumstances demand it, but there is no specific duty to act with expedience where children's rights are the subject of ECtHR proceedings, or indeed where the child is the applicant.[45] The result is that children's cases under the European Convention on Human Rights (ECHR) which have been growing in significance in recent years,[46] can take several years to conclude, reducing the effectiveness of the remedy achieved. This is particularly acute for children whose sense of time requires more urgency in how their complaints are handled. A similar conclusion can be made with respect to the decisions of the European Social Rights Committee, which hears collective complaints under the European Social Charter. Notwithstanding that there is nothing in the Charter to preclude children from invoking its collective complaint procedure, evidenced from the increasing relevance of the Committee's work to children's rights, its procedures appear to ignore the particular circumstances of children who are party to such complaints. It is particularly disappointing that neither the Court nor the European Social Rights Committee appear to have taken account of the Guidelines on Child-friendly Justice in the adaptation of their procedures to children, notwithstanding that all three instruments emanate from the Council of Europe.[47]

The one regional mechanism specific to children's rights is the African Charter on the Rights and Welfare of the Child, adopted by the Organisation of African Unity (OAU) in 1990. This provides for the Committee of Experts on the Rights and Welfare of the Child to receive communications from any person, group, or non-governmental organization recognized by the OAU.[48] Under Article 45 of the Charter, the Committee may 'resort to any appropriate method of investigating any matter falling within the ambit of the Charter', and this has been interpreted as the authority to adjudicate on petitions or complaints regarding the breach of Charter

45 European Court of Human Rights, *Rules of Court*, 01.01.2020, <http://www.coe.int>. However, see J. Watts, 'European states ordered to respond to youth activists' climate lawsuit' (2020) *The Guardian*, <https://www.theguardian.com/environment/2020/nov/30/european-states-ordered-respond-youth-activists-climate-lawsuit>.

46 U. Kilkelly, 'The CRC in litigation under the ECHR' in T. Liefaard and J. Doek (Eds.), *Litigating the rights of the child: the UN Convention on the Rights of the Child in Domestic and International Jurisprudence*, Springer, 2015.

47 See *Handbook on European Law Relating to the Rights of the Child*, Publications Office of the European Union, Luxembourg 2015.

48 J. Sloth-Nielsen, 'Children's rights litigation in the African Region: lessons from the communications procedure under the ACRWC' in above n. 46, T. Liefaard and J. Doek (Eds.).

rights.[49] The Committee's Revised Complaints Guidelines, adopted in 2014, has interpreted Article 45 to include collective complaints obviating the need for an identifiable victim for the complaint to be admissible.[50] Although the Committee's work in this area is described as 'significant' from a children's rights perspective, concern has been expressed at the low number of communications emanating so far from individuals, grassroots organizations, and children themselves.[51]

5.2. THE CRC COMMUNICATIONS PROCEDURE

In 2011, the United Nations adopted the Optional Protocol to the Convention on a Communications Procedure, recognizing the competence of the Committee on the Rights of the Child to receive communications from children and their representatives with regard to violations of Convention rights.[52] The Protocol provides for children to make complaints to the Committee with respect to alleged breaches of their rights under the Convention and its protocols and under Article 5, this communication can be submitted 'by or on behalf of an individual or group of individuals' claiming to be victims. Under Article 3, the Committee's procedures must align with 'the principle of the best interests of the child' and, 'have regard for the rights and views of the child', those views being given due weight in accordance with the child's age and maturity. Article 3(2) provides that safeguards must exist to 'prevent the manipulation of the child by those acting on his or her behalf' and the Committee may 'decline to examine any communication it considers not to be in the child's best interests'. Concern has been expressed that the process may be abused through vexatious complaints that are not instigated by children[53] and the failure to make provision for a guardian or litigation friend who might act legitimately to bring communications on behalf of the child is regrettable.[54] Smith notes

49 A. Skelton, 'International Children's Rights Law: Complaints and Remedies' in U. Kilkelly and T. Liefaard, *International Human Rights of Children*, Springer, 2018, p. 79.

50 Ibid.

51 Ibid., p. 83.

52 The Protocol was adopted and opened for signature, ratification, and accession by General Assembly resolution A/RES/66/138 of 19.12.2011 and entered into force on 14.04.2014. For ratifications, see <https://indicators.ohchr.org/>.

53 Above n. 30, p. 314.

54 Ibid., p. 315.

how difficult it can be to distinguish the rights of parents from those of their children[55] and questions, similarly, how a child could be expected to prove a complaint against the wishes of their parents 'especially when the child lacks legal capacity'.[56] For younger children, she says, the problem is even more acute.

Although the Protocol has some protective measures, it does remarkably little to accommodate the specific characteristics of children. As Egan explains, the drafters' efforts to ensure the complaints procedure was 'child-friendly' fell short in a number of respects.[57] There are 'no meaningful allowances made for children in respect of the time limits provided' for responding to complaints or in the follow-up procedure.[58] Requirements about response times are loose, with repeated references to 'as soon as possible' and 'as quickly as possible' (Article 10(1)), highlighting a failure to invoke the kind of urgency that is to be expected of hearings involving children. Only where the Committee has requested interim measures under Article 6 is it required to 'expedite the consideration of the communication' (Article 10(3)). The admissibility criteria set out in Article 7 of the Protocol are in some respects 'more rigorous than other complaint mechanisms', something Egan describes as 'the ultimate failure' to 'make concessions to the special position of children'.[59] Additionally, the requirement that the Committee must consider the 'reasonableness of State actions and the variety of possible alternatives' as part of its assessment of communications concerning economic, social, and cultural rights must be seen as a further blow to children's right to seek remedies for breaches of the full gambit of children's rights protected by the Convention. This mechanism, which was opposed by the Committee on the Rights of the Child on the grounds that it would be 'unworkable' to distinguish between the different categories of rights, clearly diminishes the Protocol's effectiveness as an international remedy for the breach of children's rights.[60]

While it is welcome that the Protocol allows inter-state communications under Article 12 and includes an inquiry mechanism for grave or systematic violations under Article 13, the absence of a collective

55 Ibid., p. 316.

56 Ibid., p. 320.

57 S. Egan, 'The New Complaints Mechanism for the Convention on the Rights of the Child: A Mini Step Forward for Children?' (2014) 22 *International Journal of Children's Rights*, pp. 205–25.

58 Ibid., p. 223.

59 Ibid., p. 214.

60 Ibid., p. 220.

complaints mechanism is seen as the greatest failure to accommodate the challenges faced by children seeking to access international remedies. As Skelton notes, a collective procedure would have eliminated the difficulties identifying 'individual victims and avoided their re-victimisation in the application process'.[61]

Notwithstanding these criticisms, it is interesting to see the use of the communications procedure appears to be gathering momentum with cases being taken against a number of different states parties. Apart from the substantive topics – which include rights issues associated with immigration, education, voting and environmental rights and access to justice – the Committee has also begun to interpret the rules around admissibility in a way that gives greater clarity to those seeking to access the remedy. While the Committee appears to have set the bar high with regard to the requirement to exhaust domestic remedies – in a point that echoes the concerns elsewhere in this contribution – it is important that it has taken some progress steps in other areas including extra territorial jurisdiction and with the apparent grouping of individual applications to promote a more efficient, collective approach. Only time will tell whether the Committee's approach in these and other areas bears fruit in improving children's access to justice at an international level.

6. CONCLUSION

Notwithstanding the recognition of children as rights holders, and the accepted importance of children being supported to claim their rights, children continue to encounter significant barriers accessing justice, especially at an international level. While the adoption of the Communications Procedure enables the Committee on the Rights of the Child to consider children's complaints about the breach of their rights, the fact that the first international child-specific mechanism falls short of children's rights standards reveals the international community's reluctance to take children's access to justice seriously. By contrast, the adoption of the Guidelines on Child-friendly Justice by the Council of Europe articulates a much stronger vision for children's rights in the justice system. But this has not been applied even to the Council of Europe's own treaty bodies in the development of child-specific complaints procedures. Can it be that international bodies are more comfortable setting out the standards to

---

61 Above n. 49, p. 74.

be applied by states at a national level, than enshrining effective means for them to be held to account in the international sphere? Or is there something more difficult involved – conceptually or practically – in articulating and implementing children's right to an effective remedy at an international level?

Although it is disappointing that the Committee's Rules of Procedure under the Optional Protocol have so far failed to adopt a child-friendly approach,[62] there is still scope for the Committee to revaluate its handling of complaints. Leadership has so far been shown by the 46 States parties to the Protocol, mainly from Europe and South America who have ratified the Optional Protocol[63] and it is important the Committee brings pressure to bear on others to follow suit. How the Committee handles the complaints from children will speak volumes to states about the efficacy of the procedure and to children themselves. The communications considered by the Committee have, so far, been dominated by children's rights in the migration and refugee law area.[64] Although early, there is evidence the Protocol can indeed have real impact. In 2020, the Committee commended Denmark for acting promptly to review the matter that was the subject of a complaint received under the Protocol, granting asylum to the children concerned.[65] According to the Committee, the swift response from the State party 'set a benchmark to show how the CRC's complaints mechanism could efficiently remedy violations of children's rights'.[66] This is to be commended, but the Committee must now quickly show true leadership in how it manages these complaints, by renewing the commitment to child-friendly justice in its own procedures. Only by applying its own standards will the Committee have the credibility to demand child-friendly justice from States parties. And only then will children's access to justice start to become a reality.

---

62 Committee on the Rights of the Child, *Rules of procedure under the Optional Protocol to the Convention on the Rights of the Child on a communications procedure*, [2013], UN Doc. CRC/C/62/3.

63 See <https://indicators.ohchr.org/>.

64 Case notes on the handling of communications by the Committee are available from the Leiden Children's Rights Observatory, <https://childrensrightsobservatory.nl>.

65 Decision adopted by the Committee under the Optional Protocol to the Convention on the Rights of the Child on a communications procedure, concerning communication No. 52/2018, CRC/C/83/D/52/2018.

66 'UN Committee welcomes Danish asylum for Syrian mother of six', Press Release, 08.04.2020, available at <https://www.ohchr.org/EN/NewsEvents/Pages/DisplayNews.aspx?NewsID=25780&LangID=E>.

PART III

OBSTACLES TO CHILDREN'S ACCESS TO JUSTICE AND AVENUES FOR SOLUTIONS

CHILDREN'S ACCESS TO AND PARTICIPATION IN THE JUSTICE SYSTEM IN LIGHT OF NATIONAL CHARACTERISTICS

Kamel KHIARI

'Your children are not your children, they are the sons and daughters of life's longing for itself.'

Khalil Gibran, The Prophet

1. INTRODUCTION

The adoption of the Convention on the Rights of the Child (CRC)[1] represents a historic moment for children, particularly in respect to their

---

1 Convention on the Rights of the Child, General Assembly resolution 44/25 of 20.11.1989, entry into force 02.09.1990, Article 12.

access to and participation in the justice system. Adopted on 20 November 1989,[2] the CRC came into effect less than one year later, and at present constitutes the most ratified human rights treaty in history. Throughout its 54 articles, it sets itself the objective that, 'the child should be fully prepared to live an individual life in society', by incorporating to that purpose measures of both enfranchisement and protection concerning them.

The essential points of the philosophy of this binding instrument[3] are summarized in its Article 12.1, which specifies, 'States Parties shall assure to the child who is capable of forming his or her own views the right to express those views freely in all matters affecting the child, …'. Its other provisions articulate various rights of the child – in particular those dealing with the administration of justice:

- Article 12.2 states that the child '… shall in particular be provided the opportunity to be heard in any judicial and administrative proceedings affecting the child, …'.[4]
- Article 37[5] insists that deprivation of liberty must be 'in conformity with the law and shall be used only as a measure of last resort and for the shortest appropriate period of time'. Minors are to be treated humanely during this period and be able to readily access assistance, in particular, legal assistance.
- Article 40[6] emphasizes the right for the child to a particular justice.

If indeed there is a very broad consensus for considering access to and participation in the justice system on the part of the child as a major concern internationally, nevertheless it is not inappropriate to consider whether beyond declarations and official positions, this fundamental

---

2 Year of the 30th anniversary of the Declaration of the Rights of the Child and the 10th of the International Year of the Child.

3 Conversely, for example, the 'Beijing Rules', which despite having laid down the broad parameters for the CRC with regard to juvenile justice, are limited in their implementation by their character as 'soft law', Adopted by General Assembly resolution 40/33 of 29.12.1985, <https://www.ohchr.org/documents/professionalinterest/beijingrules.pdf>.

4 For a discussion on its implementation, see M. Paré, 'L'accès des enfants à la justice et leur droit de participation devant les tribunaux: quelques réflexions' (2014) 44(1) *Revue générale de droit*, pp. 81–124.

5 For a discussion on this article, see T.S. Barry, 'L'examen de l'article 37 de la Convention relative aux droits de l'enfant et des règles et principes des Nations Unies relatifs à la privation des libertés des enfants en conflit avec la loi' (2017) *Revue de l'Université de Moncton*, Special Issue, pp. 83–104.

6 Ibid.

right is perceived and implemented in the same way irrespective of a country's political regime, economic level, security situation, and cultural specificities.

This research proposes to respond to these issues. Referring to the CRC, it deals with the effectiveness[7] of formally consensual rules within different national contexts. It is intended as a contribution to identification of the difficulties that may inhibit or hold back children's access to and participation in the justice system in certain States parties.

2. CHILDREN'S ACCESS TO AND PARTICIPATION IN JUSTICE IN LIGHT OF THE POLITICAL REALITIES

Speaking of justice is speaking of democracy,[8] and hence, of the independence of the legislative, executive, and judicial branches, which regrettably is far from being the case in numerous developing countries (DCs), where, 'there is often no clear separation of power, [and] the judiciary is usually controlled by the executive'.[9] In contradiction to the provisions of their own constitutions, often these are nothing but sham democracies, where justice is abused on an ongoing basis by the interference of the executive and by endemic corruption. In effect, 'while elections have become the norm rather than the exception, many undemocratic regimes use them to legitimize themselves in the eyes of their national and international partners'.[10]

In Africa, for example, various studies have shown the deplorable state of justice, where it is accused 'of being an institution plagued by a corruption (…) that continues to mushroom, in full view of the public authorities'.[11] The complaints against it have to do at the same time with 'its limited independence – in particular as regards politics – its

---

7 The term 'effectiveness' being understood as, 'the character of a legal rule that is actually applied'. See H. Reid, *Dictionnaire de droit québécois et canadien*, 2nd ed., Wilson et Lafleur, Montréal 1996.

8 Use of this term evokes elements, '… such as Basic Welfare, Access to Justice, Gender Equality, Social Group Equality and Absence of Corruption – which link to sustainable social, human and economic development'. International IDEA, *State of democracy in the world (summary)*, Strömsburg (Sweden) 2019, p. 10, <https://www.idea.int/sites/default/files/publications/the-global-state-of-democracy-2019.pdf>.

9 Ibid., p. 21.

10 Ibid., p. 26.

11 M.T. Alou, 'La justice au plus offrant, Les infortunes du système judiciaire en Afrique de l'Ouest (autour du cas du Niger)' (2001) 83(3) *Politique africaine*, p. 6.1.

absence of impartiality, its remoteness from the population, its excessive formalism and legal machinations, the poverty of its courts in finances and documentation, and the inadequate professional and moral training of the magistrates'.[12] This is a justice system the population frequently abstains from using, since it is 'hard to access [and] they are distrustful of it or unaware that it exists'.[13] We may even speak of an 'exhausted justice system', the source of the 'legal and judicial chaos' of a continent.[14] In the Arab countries, corruption, the lack of well-trained judges, and the clogging up of the courts also bring suspicion on the part of the population towards the judicial institutions.[15]

The examples cited above are unfortunately illustrative of the norm prevailing in the DCs with regard to justice. So we can question whether a justice system classified as chaotic for adults could be welcoming and efficient for children. It would be unrealistic to think so, since these ills have to do with the whole judicial apparatus and its practices. Some of the comments of the Committee on the Rights of the Child regarding the administration of justice for minors are illustrative. For example, in the Concluding Observations concerning Rwanda's Report,[16] 'the Committee urges the State party to bring its child justice system fully into line with the Convention'.[17] This Observation eloquently summarizes the status of application of the CRC by the DCs, and it is found in the most recent Concluding Observations addressed to a number of countries, including Mozambique,[18] Botswana,[19] Guinea,[20] and Mauritania.[21]

---

12 J. du Bois de Gaudusson, 'La justice en Afrique: nouveaux défis, nouveaux acteurs. Introduction thématique' (2014) 250(2) *Afrique contemporaine*, pp. 13–14.

13 Ibid., p. 14.

14 Ibid.

15 Institute of the Arab World (webdoc), 'Vous avez dit Arabe?', <https://vous-avez-dit-arabe.webdoc.imarabe.org/religion/le-droit-musulman/existe-t-il-un-droit-et-une-justice-modernes-dans-les-pays-arabes>.

16 Committee on the Rights of the Child, Concluding observations on the combined fifth and sixth periodic reports of Rwanda [28.02.2020], UN Doc. CRC/C/RWA/CO/5-6, para. 4.

17 Ibid., para. 48.

18 Committee on the Rights of the Child, Concluding observations on the combined third and fourth periodic reports of Mozambique [27.11.2019], UN Doc. CRC/C/MOZ/CO/3-4, para. 47.

19 Committee on the Rights of the Child, Concluding observations on the combined second and third reports of Botswana [26.06.2019], UN Doc. CRC/C/BWA/CO/2-3, para. 67.

20 Committee on the Rights of the Child, Concluding observations on the combined third to sixth periodic reports of Guinea [28.02.2019], UN Doc. CRC/C/GIN/CO/3-6, para. 46.

21 Committee on the Rights of the Child, Concluding observations on the combined third to fifth periodic reports of Mauritania [26.11.2018], UN Doc. CRC/C/MRT/CO/3-5, para. 45.

In addition to this general finding, in its observations, the Committee draws the attention of the States parties, in particular to the following points.

- *Legal aid.* The Committee said in 2019 it 'is concerned that children are provided less protection than international law guarantees for adults. The Committee recommends that States provide effective legal representation, free of charge, for all children who are facing criminal charges'.[22] It is also concerned that 'many children (…) are deprived of liberty, without having the benefit of legal representation'.[23] These practices contravene the provisions of Article 37(d) of the CRC, which clearly states imprisoned children have, 'the right to prompt access to legal and other appropriate assistance'.
- *Detention.* In its General Comment No. 24, the Committee indicates its 'concern that, in many countries, children languish in pretrial detention for months or even years'. It thus urges Rwanda, 'to ensure that detention is used as a measure of last resort only, and for the shortest possible period of time'.[24] It asks Mozambique to, 'ensure that detention is used as a last resort and for the shortest period of time possible'.[25] It is concerned about reports in Mauritania, 'of children facing long periods of pretrial detention'[26] and notes that in Guinea, 'deprivation of liberty is the most common sentence for children in conflict with the law, including for minor offences'.[27]

These examples demonstrate how little consideration is accorded by these States to the provisions of Article 37(b) of the CRC, which specifies the imprisonment of children may only be 'used only as a measure of last resort and for the shortest appropriate period of time'.

- *Abuse.* In its Concluding Observations with regard to this point, the Committee notes: in Mozambique, 'the extensive use of corporal punishment';[28] in Botswana, 'the use of corporal punishment as

---

22 Convention on the Rights of the Child, General Comment No. 24 [2019]: on children's rights in the child justice system, [18.09.2019], UN Doc. CRC/C/GC/24, para. 51.
23 Ibid., para. 50.
24 Above n. 16, para. 48(c).
25 Above n. 18, para. 47(e).
26 Above n. 21, para. 44.
27 Above n. 20, para. 45(c).
28 Above n. 18, para. 25.

a sentence';[29] and in Rwanda, 'reports of the ill-treatment and beatings of children during pretrial detention'.[30]

These practices are contrary in particular to paragraphs (a) and (c) of Article 37 of the CRC, which indicate a child deprived of their liberty may not be submitted 'to … cruel … treatment or punishment …' and they must be 'treated with humanity …'.

3. CHILDREN'S ACCESS TO AND PARTICIPATION IN THE JUSTICE SYSTEM IN LIGHT OF ECONOMIC REALITIES

It is due to their economic resources that the developed countries are able to offer quality services to their inhabitants. While this is seldom the case in the DCs, this is precisely due to the modesty of these resources. The run-down state of premises, the scarcity of resource materials and technological tools, and the low level of training of judges, are a reflection of the paucity of resources experienced by a population confronted with hunger and lack of medical care. In these conditions, children's access to justice is not at the top of the list of concerns.

The few statistical examples that follow provide us with an idea of the gap in economic terms between rich and poor countries and help to understand the state and functioning of the justice systems in these countries. Taking by way of example a comparison between two developed countries (Canada and France) and two DCs (Niger and Chad), the finding that emerges is as follows: Canada's per capita GDP is 83 times that of Niger and 63 times that of Chad. Life expectancy in Canada and in France is 28 years higher than that of Chad and 20 years higher than that of Niger. There is 67.6% more infant mortality in Chad than in Canada, and 44.5% more in Niger than in France. While in France and in Canada illiteracy has been eradicated for many years, it is 71.6% in Niger and 60.2% in Chad.[31]

In these circumstances, for many DCs it is difficult to expect that children's access to and participation in the justice system would be included among their priorities, especially due to malnutrition, diseases, and lack of schooling. According to the figures from the UNICEF Institute

---

29 Above n. 19, para. 61(d).

30 Above n. 16, para. 47(d).

31 PopulationData.net, <https://www.populationdata.net/>.

for Statistics, 258 million children were not in school during the 2018 school year.[32]

With regard to health, the coronavirus pandemic has aggravated an already dramatic situation. UNICEF, basing itself on a study from the American Johns Hopkins University published in *The Global Health Lancet* in 2020, reports that in 'the countries marked by failing health systems, COVID-19 disrupts supply chains for medicines and access to food.'[33]

A report published in January 2021 by the UNICEF Office of Research and by the World Food Programme[34] reports that 39 billion school meals have been missed worldwide due to school closures since the beginning of the COVID-19 pandemic, with these meals being 'for many their only nutritious food of the day.' The pandemic has aggravated an already very worrying situation: 'Pre-pandemic survey data from 68 countries show that, before COVID-19 hit, around 50 percent of children aged 13 to 17 years-old reported feelings of hunger.'

Another report released in October 2020 by UNICEF, WHO, the World Bank Group, and the United Nations Department of Social and Economic Affairs, reports each year close to two million children are stillborn. 'In 2019, three in four stillbirths occur in sub-Saharan Africa or South Asia.'[35]

The CRC has not disregarded the problem of economic realities, making reference to it in its Article 4, which sets out that:

> States Parties shall undertake all appropriate legislative, administrative, and other measures for the implementation of the rights recognized in the present Convention. *With regard to economic, social and cultural rights, States Parties shall undertake such measures to the maximum extent of their available resources and, where needed, within the framework of international co-operation.* (emphasis added)

These resources are often very far from what may be imagined in a developed country, which brought about reservations lodged to the CRC

---

32 UNESCO ISU, 'Out-Of-School Children and Youth', <http://uis.unesco.org/en/topic/out-school-children-and-youth#:~:text=About%20258%20million%20children%20and,million%20of%20upper%20secondary%20age>.

33 Le Temps, 'La Covid-19 pourrait tuer indirectement jusqu'à 6000 enfants par jour en six mois' (13.05.2020), <https://www.letemps.ch/monde/covid19-pourrait-tuer-indirectement-jusqua-6000-enfants-jour-six-mois>.

34 UN Info, 'More than 39 billion school meals missed during COVID-19 pandemic' (28.01.2021), <https://news.un.org/fr/story/2021/01/1087912>.

35 WHO, 'One stillbirth occurs every 16 seconds, according to first ever joint UN estimates', Press release of 08.10.2020, <https://www.who.int/fr/news/item/0810202016>.

on this point, including for example that of Oman: 'The provisions of the Convention should be applied within the limits imposed by the material resources available.'[36]

It is particularly these economic conditions that account for the state of the human and material resources of the justice systems, as noted by the Committee on the Rights of the Child. In its General Comment on the rights of the child within the justice system, the Committee notes that:[37] 'State party reports indicate that many States parties still require significant investment to achieve full compliance with the Convention, particularly regarding (…) implementation of diversion measures, the minimum age of criminal responsibility and the reduction of deprivation of liberty'.[38] In certain Concluding Observations, the Committee notes in particular, 'the lack of specialized juvenile justice personnel in the justice system and the police'[39] in Botswana, and that in Guinea, 'juvenile courts are not available outside of Conakry'.[40] It 'is also concerned about the limited availability of juvenile courts and separate detention facilities for children'[41] in Mauritania, and urges Rwanda 'to designate specialized judges for children in all courts and to ensure that such specialized judges, as well as prosecutors, police officers and other professionals, receive training on the provisions of the Convention'.[42] To make good these shortcomings, resources need to exist that these States often lack.

4. CHILDREN'S ACCESS TO AND PARTICIPATION IN THE JUSTICE SYSTEM IN LIGHT OF SECURITY REALITIES

The armed conflicts prevalent in certain regions of the DCs further exacerbate the already catastrophic situation for children, while at the

36 UN Treaty Collection, Convention on the Rights of the Child (Declarations and Reservations), <https://treaties.un.org/Pages/ViewDetails.aspx?src=IND&mtdsg_no=IV-11&chapter=4>.

37 Above n. 23.

38 Ibid., para. 4.

39 Above n. 19, para. 66(c).

40 Above n. 20, para. 45(a).

41 Above n. 21, para. 44.

42 Above n. 16, para. 48(a).

same time relegating to the background the issue of their access to and participation in the justice system. A 2019 report of the agency Save the Children,[43] based on a study by the Peace Research Institute of Oslo, reports appalling figures in this regard. In 2017, close to 420 million children were living in regions affected by conflicts. More than 100,000 die there each year, due in particular to attacks on schools, the recruitment of child soldiers, sexual crimes, and murders. Between 2013 and 2017, 550,000 infants died in these conflict zones by virtue of famine, poor hygiene, or lack of access to health care, which amounts to more than three times the estimated number of combatants in the 10 countries studied. This NGO estimates the total number of deaths for children under five years of age at 870,000. A recent report from UNICEF warns in this regard that several African countries are threatened in 2021 with 'imminent famine', in particular due to conflicts.[44]

In its 2019 Report, The United Nations High Commissioner for Refugees reports that at the end of 2018 it identified 70.8 million displaced persons worldwide. This agency says in its 70 years of existence, it has never seen such a high number of, 'people being forced to flee their homes against their will'.[45] In 2020 in the Sahel alone, there was 'a sad record'[46] of more than two million displaced persons, as well as the deaths of more than 2,400 persons.

And yet, the CRC's Article 38 clearly commits the States parties, in the event of armed conflict, to respect the rules of international humanitarian law, including that, 'protection is extended to children', and in this regard to, 'take all feasible measures to ensure protection and care of children who are affected by an armed conflict' and that those under 15 years of age, 'do not take a direct part in hostilities'. These provisions evidently have not resonated with the war-torn countries, which are countries that have

---

43 Save the Children, *Stop the war on children, Protecting children in 21st century conflict*, 2019, <https://www.stopwaronchildren.org/report.pdf>.

44 UN Info, 'Millions of children in crisis hotspots "on the brink of famine", warns UNICEF', <https://news.un.org/en/story/2020/12/1081102>.

45 PopulationData.net, '70.8 million people uprooted worldwide in 2019', <https://en.populationdata.net/2019/06/28/70-8-million-people-uprooted-worldwide-in-2019/>.

46 D. Traoré, 'En 2020 plus de civils ou de suspects non armés ont été tués par des forces de sécurité que par des groupes Extrémistes', Le Monde, Paris 2021, <https://www.lemonde.fr/afrique/article/2021/02/14/sahel-en-2020-plus-de-civils-ou-suspects-non-armes-ont-ete-tues-par-des-forces-de-securite-que-par-des-groupes-extremistes_6069932_3212.html>.

signed the CRC. This can be seen through the following observations from the Committee on the Rights of the Child:

> States parties should refrain (...) from charging and prosecuting [children] for expressions of opinion or for mere association with a non-State armed group, including those designated as terrorist groups.[47]
>
> The Committee is deeply concerned about the continuing violations of the rights of a significant number of children in the context of armed conflict. These include (...) arrest, detention and, in some instances, torture and ill-treatment of children and adolescents who are accused of associations with groups designated as terrorist organizations [and] the targeting of very young girls and boys for sexual violence.[48]

Thus, more than three decades following the entry into force of the Convention, matters have only gotten worse in this area. It is difficult to consider children's access to and participation in the justice system to be an everyday concern in these countries.

5. CHILDREN'S ACCESS TO AND PARTICIPATION IN THE JUSTICE SYSTEM IN LIGHT OF CULTURAL REALITIES

The question which must be considered here is that of whether the concern for children's access to and participation in the justice system is the same in all countries – whatever the nature, weight, and place of the cultural and religious traditions in their socio-political organization.

One of the pillars of the CRC is its Article 12.1, which very clearly commits the member States to ensuring children the right to express their views freely on matters affecting them, which logically includes questions of justice. May one affirm on this basis that all children, irrespective of the culture, can – without being constrained by the latter – freely express their opinion before the justice system, on matters affecting them? We do not think so, since there are cultures that do not encourage such freedom of opinion.[49] Two situations must be differentiated.

---

47 Above n. 23, para. 101.

48 Committee on the Rights of the Child. Supplement No. 41 [2020], UN Doc. A/75/41, para. 35.

49 Of course, this does not involve a value judgement that we express, but rather a sociological finding.

5.1. CULTURAL PRACTICES

The first concerns cultural practices liable to adversely affect the psychological and physical integrity of children, and that the children are required to accept because they are within cultural traditions.

The following comments from the Committee on the Rights of the Child are particularly apt. With reference to Article 12:

> The Committee notes that, in most societies around the world, implementation of the child's right to express her or his view on the wide range of issues that affect her or him (...) continues to be impeded by many long-standing practices and attitudes (...). The Committee also remains concerned about the quality of many of the practices that do exist.[50]

On the subject of Mozambique, the Committee invites this country to 'strengthen its efforts to train parents, teachers, professionals working with children and the public on positive, non-violent forms of discipline'.[51] In addition, it expresses, 'deep concern about the extremely high rate of child marriage, including forced marriage, and the practice of initiation rites for girls'.[52] It recommends in this regard to this State to 'implement legislation explicitly prohibiting all traditional practices harmful to the physical and psychological well-being of children and take all necessary measures to eliminate child marriage and the harmful aspects of initiation rites for girls'.[53]

5.2. RELIGION

The second situation hindering the child's freedom of opinion is that of religion.

It has been well established that the way in which Islam, for example, traditionally conceives the place of the child in society is not always in step with the Western way of thinking. Therefore, it becomes quite easy

---

50 Committee on the Rights of the Child, General Comment No. 12 [2009]: The right of the child to be heard, [07.20.2009], CRC/C/GC/12.

51 Above n. 18, para. 25(c).

52 Ibid., para. 28.

53 Ibid., para. 28(a).

to understand the reason why a number of Islamic countries adopted reservations examined below. Indeed:

> The protection of the child and of their rights is not absent in Islamic law, but it responds to other concerns and draws on other values than those that prevail in the West. Above all Islam stresses much more collective rights and the duties of the individual toward society, than individual rights. Consequently, the autonomy of the child is minimized and is perceived within a group, a family unit, rather than being a fully-fledged subject of law.[54]

Would it be truly realistic to expect, for example, that the freedom of religion prescribed by the CRC could be effectively applied in certain countries where – once branded as apostasy, it disowns its perpetrator and renders them potentially punishable under the law with the death penalty, since it is their obligation to 'follow the religion of their father'?[55] The child may not be a party to legal proceedings addressing a threat to their freedom of opinion on the matters concerning them – but is liable to prosecution and sanctions.

This reality is at the origin of the reservations formulated against the CRC provisions concerning freedom of conscience, especially on the part of the Islamic countries.[56] These are of two kinds. The first category of reservations is of a general nature, without reference to any specific article. These arise in particular from countries such as Saudi Arabia which voices 'reservations with respect to all such articles as are in conflict with the provisions of Islamic law', Afghanistan which 'reserves the right to express, upon ratifying the Convention, reservations on all provisions of the Convention that are incompatible with the laws of Islamic Shari'a', and Iran which makes 'reservation to the articles and provisions which may be contrary to the Islamic Shari'a'.

The nature of these reservations has induced reactions from countries like Austria, which points out, regarding those expressed along these lines by Somalia, that:

> By referring to the General Principles of Islamic Sharia [this country] has made a reservation of a general and indeterminate scope. This reservation does not

[54] J. Tugault-Lafleur, *Analyse comparative des conceptions de l'enfant et des institutions de l'adoption dans le monde arabo-musulman et en Occident: une réconciliation est-elle possible?*, Université de Montréal, Faculty of Law, Master's dissertation in law, 02.2011, p. 21.

[55] Ibid., p. 28.

[56] Concerning the issue of reservations and the Vienna Convention on the Law of Treaties of 23.05.1969, the following authors may be consulted: N.Q. Dinh, P. Daillier, and

> clearly define for the other States Parties to the Convention the extent to which the reserving State has accepted the obligations of the Convention. Austria therefore considers the reservation to be incompatible with the object and purpose of the Convention and objects to it.[57]

The second category of reservations issued by these countries is aimed at precise provisions of the CRC, like Article 14 dealing specifically with freedom of thought, conscience, and religion. These[58] are authored by: Algeria, Brunei Darussalam, United Arab Emirates, Iraq, Jordan, Morocco, Oman, Qatar, Syria, Malaysia, Somalia, or the Republic of Maldives, which: '... expresses its reservation to paragraph 1 of article 14 of the said Convention on the Rights of the Child, since the Constitution and the Laws of the Republic of Maldives stipulate that all Maldivians should be Muslims.'

6. CONCLUSION

From the Aristotelian conception that considers children as beings 'lacking in reason' and comparable to an animal – to that, with the CRC, of a person holding specific rights, particularly those concerning access to and participation in the justice system – the road has been long, slow, and very often rocky for the child and their rights.

The CRC is a revolutionary text in the history of the rights of the child, but does its existence equate its implementation for all in States parties, whatever their particularities in political, economic, security, and cultural terms? The nuanced response given to this question throughout this contribution does not in any way challenge the utility of this Convention for children. Quite to the contrary, it sees itself rather as a constructive criticism of its actual efficacy, a situation in the absence of which its rules are but statements of intent, at least on the part of several States.

We believe beyond the number of its signatories and the official discourses lauding it, that the concrete implementation of this Convention – in particular its provisions regarding access to the justice system for

A. Pellet, *Droit international public*, 5th ed., L.G.D.J., Paris 1994, pp. 177–83; and C. Rousseau, *Droit international public*, 10th ed., Dalloz, Paris 1984, pp. 49–51. For the particular reservations, see UN Treaty Collection, <https://treaties.un.org/Pages/ViewDetails.aspx?src=IND&mtdsg_no=IV-11&chapter=4>.

57 Ibid. UN Treaty Collection.

58 Depending on the countries, these reservations are aimed at Article 14 in its totality or at one or both of its two paragraphs.

children – depends on a welcoming environment. This latter is certainly not that of countries submitted on a daily basis to arbitrariness, poverty, disease, and armed conflicts. Conversely, it is of those countries – rich and at peace, where democracy and the rule of law prevail. Clearly the logics, concerns, and priorities are not the same between the former and the latter.

A consensual and clear instrument, as is this one, is only able to alter a reality if the prevailing conditions favour its implementation. Neither the Universal Declaration of Human Rights nor the other international human rights instruments have put an end to abuse and arbitrariness in countries having signed them. The developed countries may be able to do much to change the conditions experienced in the DCs, which will undoubtedly facilitate application of the CRC and its provisions regarding access to and participation in the justice system. They may do so by providing economic support, by not supporting dictatorial regimes, and by ceasing to supply them with arms.

IMPEDIMENTS TO ACCESS BY THE CHILDREN OF INDIGENOUS PEOPLES TO THE JUSTICE SYSTEM IN CAMEROON

Eléazar Michel Nkoué

1. INTRODUCTION

Access to the justice system is defined as a 'right of all citizens to have unimpeded access to justice for defence of their interests, even if their submission should be declared improper, inadmissible or ill-founded'.[1] It provides the possibility for the author of a claim to be heard in order for the judge to deliver their ruling. Access to justice is a *sine qua non* for the achievement of 'justice rights', such as the right to a trial or the rights of the accused (offences and penalties must be defined by law; presumption of innocence; etc.).

Access to justice has been enshrined globally, regionally, and nationally. It is a fundamental human right guaranteed by a number of international

[1] G. Cornu, *Vocabulaire juridique*, 12th ed., Paris, PUF 2018, p. 9.

human rights instruments, in particular the Universal Declaration of Human Rights, Article 8 of which provides that, 'Everyone has the right to an effective remedy by the competent national tribunals for acts violating the fundamental rights granted him by the constitution or by law.'[2] The International Covenant on Civil and Political Rights sets out this same principle in its Article 2(3).[3] At the regional level, Cameroon has ratified the African Charter on Human and Peoples' Rights, which in its Article 7(1)(a) enshrines a guarantee of unimpeded access to the justice system for all citizens of a State.[4] At the national level, the Constitution of Cameroon includes the right of access to the justice system, by specifying in its preamble that, 'the law shall ensure the right of every person to a fair hearing before the courts'.[5] Its implementation is defined by laws such as the Criminal Code and the Code of Criminal Procedure.

In reference to the judgment in *Golder v. United Kingdom of Great Britain and Northern Ireland*,[6] access to the justice system must not be simply theoretical, but concrete, and not be compromised by legal or financial impediments linked to the litigant's lack of resources. An impediment is the 'fact (…) of preventing the exercise of an activity authorized or required by

---

2 Universal Declaration of Human Rights, General Assembly Resolution 217 A(III), 10 December 1948, Article 8.

3 International Covenant on Civil and Political Rights, 16 December 1966, 999 UNTS 171. According to article 2 (3), 'Each State Party to the present Covenant undertakes:

'(a) To ensure that any person whose rights or freedoms as herein recognized are violated shall have an effective remedy, notwithstanding that the violation has been committed by persons acting in an official capacity;
(b) To ensure that any person claiming such a remedy shall have his right thereto determined by competent judicial, administrative or legislative authorities, or by any other competent authority provided for by the legal system of the State, and to develop the possibilities of judicial remedy;
(c) To ensure that the competent authorities shall enforce such remedies when granted'.

4 African Commission on Human and Peoples' Rights, 27.06.1981, OAU Doc. CAB/LEG/67/3 rev. 5, 21 I.L.M. 58 (1982), Article 7(1)(a), <https://www.achpr.org/legalinstruments/detail?id=49>. According to Article 7(1), 'Every individual shall have the right to have his cause heard. This comprises:

(a) The right to an appeal to competent national organs against acts of violating his fundamental rights as recognized and guaranteed by conventions, laws, regulations and customs in force'.

5 In particular Law No. 2008/001 of 14.04.2008, amending and supplementing certain provisions of Law No. 96/06 of 18.01.1996, amending the Constitution of 2.06.1972. Const. of Cameroon, 1972, rev. 2008, <https://www.constituteproject.org/constitution/Cameroon_2008?lang=en>.

6 *Golder v. United Kingdom*, 21.02.1975, Series A No. 18.

law'.[7] It is also any action or situation that may inhibit the free exercise of access to the justice system.

Children in court proceedings may be victims, witnesses, or defendants. They may also be involved in proceedings involving protection or inheritance. An individual below the age of majority, as set in Cameroon at 21 years of age, is a minor. Nevertheless, an individual of 18 years of age is fully accountable criminally. A minor over 14 and under 18 years of age is criminally liable, but benefits from mitigating circumstances. A child from 10 to 14 years of age is criminally liable, and may only be subject to special measures, while those under 10 years of age are not criminally liable.[8] In the context of this contribution, we will concentrate on the case of children of the indigenous peoples of Cameroon. Pursuant to the criteria for identification of indigenous peoples as contained in Convention No. 169 of the International Labour Organization (1989), the ethnic groups regarded as indigenous peoples in Cameroon are: the 'M'bororo'[9] and the 'Pygmies'.[10] Convention No. 169 establishes the specificity of tribal cultures, and from that derive particular political rights. But in Cameroon, 'it appears that one is still far from what needs to be done'.[11]

Given their vulnerability, children should benefit from a procedure adapted to them. Thus, the treatment of children during legal proceedings

---

7 Above n. 1, p. 363.

8 See Article 80 of Law No. 2016/007 of 12.07.2016, setting forth the criminal code.

9 The M'bororo, 'traditionally they were nomads, constantly on the move from one place to another to find pastures for their herds. Today, a number of them are transhumant herdsmen, who migrate on a seasonal basis but return to their temporary dwelling. The M'bororo live throughout Cameroon, but they are mostly to be found in the West, East, and Northwest regions, and in the northern part of the country.' International Labour Organization, *Indigenous peoples in Cameroon: A guide for media professionals*, (2015), p. 14 <https://www.ilo.org/wcmsp5/groups/public/---dgreports/---gender/documents/publication/wcms_438854.pdf>.

10 Ibid., p. 14. The pygmies are peoples who live in the forests, with several tribes being called the Baka, the Bakola or Bagyeli, and the Bedzang. Estimates suggest that, 'the Baka, who are the largest group, number between 70,000 and 100,000 persons. They live in the eastern and southern parts of the country (Departments of Boumba-et-Ngoko, Haut-Nyong and Kadey). The Bakola or Bagyéli account for between 10,000 and 30,000 persons, and they live in the south of the country – more specifically in Akom II, Bipindi, Kribi, Campo, Ma'an and Lolodorf. There are fewer Bedzang, who number less than a thousand people, and they live in the northwest of the Mbam-et-Kim Division, on the Tikar Plain and also in Messondo in the Centre region. The Baka, Bagyéli and Bedzang are traditionally nomadic peoples, living from hunting and gathering.' Ibid.

11 E.M. Nkoué, *La protection des écosystèmes forestiers d'Afrique centrale à l'épreuve des nécessités de développement socio-économique: cas du Cameroun*, Doctoral thesis in international law, University of Grenoble Alpes, 2019, p. 138.

has advanced, in particular with the arrival of the Convention on the Rights of the Child, which Cameroon signed on 25 September 1990 and ratified on 11 January 1993. The African Charter on the Rights and Welfare of the Child was ratified by Cameroon on 5 September 1997, with a view of improving the conditions of Cameroon children. Law No. 2005/007 of 27 July 2005, laying down the Criminal Procedure Code, provides a framework for the prosecution and trial of minors[12] in Cameroon. In accordance with Article 709(1) of the Criminal Procedure Code, the court of first instance rules with regard to young offenders.

In Cameroon, access to the justice system, 'leaves much to be desired'.[13] There are numerous impediments that might stall, block, or even curtail access to the justice system[14] and thus leave the right flowing from it without effect. In view of these considerations, do indigenous children, due to their special status, face specific impediments hamstringing their access to the Cameroonian courts of law?

The present contribution provides insight on the problems of good governance in the justice sector in Cameroon. Through probing with analytical tools specific to law, combined with those of social sciences, the finding emerges that these impediments have to do with the judicial system or with the socio-cultural context.

2. THE IMPEDIMENTS INVOLVING CAMEROON'S JUDICIAL SYSTEM

The barriers to accessing the justice system for children of the indigenous peoples have to do simultaneously with the organization and functioning of Cameroon's judicial system.

---

12 See Articles 700 ff.

13 New Human Rights Cameroon, 'Pour une justice pénale plus accessible au Cameroun. Étude nationale sur les engagements du Cameroun en matière de justice pénale et d'effectivité des droits de le homme' (2019), p. 41, According to the NGO New Human Rights Cameroon, 'more than 48.3 per cent of the citizens surveyed are of the view that Cameroonian justice is very poor.' <http://ndhcam.org/wp-content/uploads/2019/06/NDH_2019_Pour-Une-Justice-pe%CC%81nale-Plus-accessible-au-Cameroun.pdf>.

14 Ibid., p. 41, according to the NGO New Human Rights Cameroon, '69 per cent of the persons questioned state that citizens lack ready access to the justice system in Cameroon'.

2.1. THE JUDICIAL SYSTEM'S ORGANIZATIONAL IMPEDIMENTS

The barriers linked to access to the justice system by indigenous children are due to the organizational shortcomings of Cameroon's judicial system. It should be noted that the latter are not the preserve of Africa, but they 'are particularly difficult to overcome'.[15] These obstacles translate into the distancing of persons subject to law, insufficient personnel, lack of territorial and material organization, etc.

Judicial proceedings are open to the public, but access to the justice system on the part of indigenous children is dependent of the geographical proximity of the courts of law to their place of residence. In general, the indigenous peoples of Cameroon live in enclaves or camps far from towns and villages. Efforts have been made by public authorities to bring the law closer. According to Article 13 of Law No. 2006/015 of 29 December 2006 bearing on judicial organization, amended and supplemented by Law No. 2011/027 of 14 December 2011, one court of first instance is created per district *[arrondissement]*. Nevertheless, following the demands of service, the jurisdiction of the courts may include several districts. However, these efforts on the part of the public authorities are still very limited and insufficient. Several districts are without a court of first degree. Mobile court hearings are often organized in the district; however, accessibility to the judicial administration from the indigenous peoples' camps is difficult if not virtually impossible. This further reinforces the distance between the modern judicial apparatus and children of the indigenous peoples.

In addition, the traditional courts of Cameroon are the courts of first degree and the customary courts (in the Francophone part of the State); the Alkali courts and the customary courts (in the Anglophone part of the State). The courts of first degree and the customary courts consist of a presiding judge and two non-presiding judges with voting rights.[16] The presiding judge of the court of first degree is appointed by decree of

[15] R. Degni-Ségui, 'L'accès à la justice et ses obstacles' in *L'effectivité des droits fondamentaux dans la communauté francophone*, Montréal, Aupelf-Uref, 1994, p. 242.

[16] Article 8 of Decree No. 69/DF/544 of 19.12.1969, establishing the judicial system and proceedings before the traditional courts of the former East Cameroon. However, the reading of Article 10 of this decree shows that each customary court includes two titular and four alternate non-presiding judges.

the Minister of Justice, from among the staff in service within the court's jurisdiction. In the event of the absence or incapacity of the presiding judge, they are automatically replaced by the sub-prefect of the district where the court holds its sessions, or by a district deputy named by this official. The presiding judge of the customary court is appointed by decree of the Minister of Justice, from among the notables with satisfactory knowledge of the tradition. The Minister of Justice also appoints by order the non-presiding judges for these courts, on the joint proposal of the prefect and of the presiding judge of the court of first instance of the jurisdictional territory. The list adopted is made up in such a way as to assure equitable representation of the traditions.[17] Several obstacles to access the justice system for children of indigenous peoples emerge from the foregoing. A problem arises of specialization of the judges of the traditional courts, who are not professional judges. In the traditional courts there is no section specialized in disputes involving juvenile offenders or at-risk children. These courts are responsible for disputes under general traditional law. In addition, the judges who are appointed to these courts do not have solid experience on issues linked with children's rights in general, and those of indigenous children in particular. With regard to young offenders, the judicial authorities are seldom trained to deal with cases of indigenous children in conflict with the law.

The impoverishment of some officials of the judicial system considerably worsens their working conditions, as well as the service rendered to users. The qualitative and quantitative inadequacy of staff is evident in the Cameroonian judicial administration. The workload is often very high in proportion to the staff in particular localities. This human resource shortfall inevitably leads to inappropriate treatment of the complaints brought to their attention. As a consequence, 'those persons subject to the law wishing to benefit from a professional and objective handling of their case must sometimes employ illicit means',[18] by paying for the service of public officials.

The poor jurisdictional coverage of the country, along with the shortage of human and financial resources, have repercussions on the performance of the judiciary.

17 Ibid., Article 10.
18 Above n. 13, p. 21.

2.2. THE FUNCTIONAL CONSTRAINTS ON THE JUDICIAL SYSTEM

Cameroon's indigenous face hurdles in accessing the justice system, due to problems involving the functioning of the judicial system, notably the slowness and costs of the court proceedings.

The slowness of the court proceedings constitutes a recurring concern in Africa in general and in Cameroon in particular. Judicial proceedings are relatively short and simplified before the lower courts, but they continue to be slow and long as one traverses the levels of the justice system. Even so, this shortcoming is not particular to indigenous children. The fact remains that the delays in judicial proceedings are simply a denial of justice leading children from the indigenous peoples to withdraw from it.

The principle in Cameroonian law is, 'justice being free of charge. This means the person subject to the law does not pay their judge, who is an official funded out of the central government budget'.[19] According to the NGO New Human Rights Cameroon, '87% of citizens believe the principle of justice being free of charge is not observed in Cameroon'.[20] The cost of legal proceedings limits accessibility to justice on the part of children of the indigenous peoples. This is the case of subpoenas and deposit with the court clerk of the monies necessary for payment of court costs. What is appalling for indigenous children is not only the high costs, but that the charge for the trial is difficult to assess. It is important to highlight that in most cases the indigenous peoples have meagre incomes, with some making a living from fishing, hunting, and gathering. Even if it is established that access to the justice system is a right recognized for every citizen by the Constitution, the fact that it is not free of charge, ipso facto condemns the communities living below the poverty line to being precluded. Thus, 'the various successive documents that entail charges may correspondingly dissuade them from engaging in or pursuing legal action'.[21] The same applies to the retaining of a lawyer. While the presence of a lawyer is not mandatory, except in the case of a crime, it would appear necessary due to the intricacies of the law and the procedures of modern law courts. The possibilities for indigenous children to access Cameroonian justice through a lawyer are weak and unequal, depending on their region. In the

19 G. Kenfack, 'L'accès à la justice au Cameroun' (1996) *Cahiers de l'UCAC*, p. 205.

20 Above n. 13, p. 41.

21 Above n. 15, p. 246.

Far North of Cameroon, for example, 'the rate of accessibility to a lawyer is of 1 per 837,000 inhabitants, while in the Centre and Coast it is 1 per 53,000. Persons subject to the law who are disadvantaged [like children of the indigenous peoples] are pushed out of the judicial system'.[22]

Fortunately, legal aid facilitates access to the justice system for a certain category of persons. In effect, legal aid is an assistance mechanism making it possible for certain individuals[23] – and on an exceptional basis legal entities[24] – to be excused from paying certain charges for legal proceedings, because of resource constraints. As laid down by Cameroonian legislation, this legal aid is expected to facilitate the effective exercise of legal action on the part of these children. Nevertheless, 'legal aid is confined to representation in court to the exclusion of assistance in access to the law, as has been the case in France since 1992'.[25] This institution is far from having yielded positive results on a practical level in Cameroonian society, since very few individuals have been informed of it. According to the report of the NGO New Human Rights Cameroon, 'around 50.5% of citizens are unaware of the law for legal aid in Cameroon'.[26] Also in the same report, 'around 80% of citizens are unacquainted with both the categories of persons able to benefit from legal aid, and with the benefits that this law provides'.[27] Implementation of this mechanism is highly limited to certain destitute persons in the large towns, to the exclusion of the majority of persons subject to the law living in villages. Since children of the indigenous peoples live in camps far removed from the villages and towns, it goes without saying that they do not request this aid and are automatically precluded from it. The appointment of public defenders in legal disputes involving indigenous minors poses a certain problem, as in all legal disputes. There is justification for 'fearing that the lawyer is unmotivated, preferring to devote all of their craft to the high-profile paying cases, to the detriment of those of the destitute [like a child from of the indigenous peoples], and/or abandon them outright into the hands of inexperienced trainees'.[28]

Access to the justice system on the part of these children is quite limited. Among the contributing factors to this structural and functional

22 Above n. 13, p. 21.
23 Article 5(2) of Law No. 2009/004 of 14.04.2009 providing legal aid in Cameroon.
24 Ibid., Article 5(5).
25 Above n. 15, p. 247.
26 Above n. 13, p. 41.
27 Ibid.
28 Above n. 15, p. 248.

failure, we must not omit the considerable influence the socio-cultural context exerts.

3. IMPEDIMENTS INVOLVING THE SOCIO-CULTURAL CONTEXT OF THE INDIGENOUS PEOPLES OF CAMEROON

The barriers of access for these children involving the socio-cultural context are linked to the specificities of these populations. We will emphasize the adverse socio-cultural situation and the resistance to relying on modern courts.

3.1. THE ADVERSE SOCIO-CULTURAL SITUATION

One of the major obstacles to access to justice is being unaware of one's rights. Among indigenous peoples there are a significant number of illiterate people or of individuals with low educational attainment.

In Cameroon, it is apparent most legal standards issued by the public authorities are disregarded by the large proportion of those from the indigenous peoples who remain illiterate. Although efforts have been undertaken for some years by the public authorities to school these groups, many are still illiterate. Following adoption of legislative instruments, public authorities often do not bother to disseminate them among all sections of Cameroonian society. As for popularization of the laws, it is noted that, 'there is always an asymmetry between the level of information possessed by [the public authorities and] that in the communities'.[29]

Most of these communities are unaware of the existence of the legislation and regulations organizing life under the rule of law. On this subject, Professor Dégni-Ségui states that, 'one of the major obstacles to access the courtroom in Africa is citizens' ignorance of the law in general, and of their rights in particular. Nevertheless, they are supposed not to disregard them, in accordance with the adage that ignorance of the law is no defence'.[30] Resistant illiteracy within these groups in the population produces consequences on children's access to the justice system, which becomes seriously compromised or even curtailed.

---

29 Above n. 11, p. 153.

30 Above n. 15, p. 252.

Moreover, the Pygmies and M'bororo prefer to live in the forests, given their way of life, and are constantly on the move. Unfortunately, a large number of children of the indigenous peoples continue to be without birth certificates, making it difficult to accurately determine their age.

Furthermore, in Cameroonian society, free access to the justice system is constantly hampered by the excessive reverence that indigenous persons subject to the law display towards 'the administration',[31] judges or, 'other Cameroonians'.[32] The mere mention of a court or of the name of a judge raises anxiety and fear. It is exceedingly rare for these groups to refer violations committed against their children to the courts. In light of the experience of discrimination practiced by the other residents of Cameroon, the indigenous communities 'often tend to be resigned to the injustices and to accept experiencing certain violations of their rights, without thinking about holding onto material or documented evidence of them (...) that could be used in their defence'.[33]

In the Cameroonian society, access to the justice system and the law is at times subject to bargaining. 'Consequently, only those who have the power of money manage; those who are impoverished [like children from the indigenous peoples] sink, in spite of the multitude of legal instruments affirming otherwise'.[34] Sometimes it is necessary to pay in order to have access to the service you are entitled to under the law, since, 'corruption has made its nest within the justice system, and as a consequence judges have lost their purity'.[35] The trading in services in the judicial administration constitutes a severe weight on access to the justice system, 'for the poor person who – instead of being reassured – finds themselves bullied. If you

31 Above n. 11, p. 158, According to E.M. Nkoué, 'the villagers living in the forest areas harbour a morbid fear of the local administrative authorities, who are known as "ngomna"'.

32 *Les Pygmées Baka et la gestion participative des aires protégées au Sud-est Cameroun: Une étude des zones d'Intérêt Cynégétique à gestion communautaire à la périphérie Nord du Parc de Lobéké*, University of Yaoundé I, Report at End of Internship, 2004, p. 20. According to O. Tegemo, '[t]he dependence of the Baka pygmy on the Bantu results from the development of inferiority complexes'.

33 C. Cheumani, 'Cadre de Planification en faveur des Populations Pygmées' (2012), p 27, <http://documents1.worldbank.org/curated/en/357521468227701262/pdf/IPP6410Cameroo00210201300Box377347B.pdf>.

34 Above n. 13, p. 20.

35 I.B.R. Njupouen, *Dynamiques alternatives pour l'accès au droit et à la justice dans un contexte de pauvreté: enjeux de l'état de droit, de la gouvernance et du développement durable*, Doctoral thesis in Sociology, University of Paris Dauphine – Paris IX, 2013, p. 166 <https://basepub.dauphine.fr/handle/123456789/13670>.

hope to obtain anything, you need to be able to afford a price that is beyond the reach of poor people'.[36]

The low level of recourse to the courts is also explained by the fact that the indigenous peoples, in general, live beyond the bounds of the modern courts.

3.2. RESISTANCE TO RELIANCE ON THE MODERN COURTS

Certain situations in a State may create an ongoing or temporary climate not conducive to respect for human rights. The encampments of indigenous peoples constitute this kind of place, which we may refer to as 'areas of resistance to the law'.[37] In fact, there is a certain wariness from individuals of indigenous communities in respect of modern justice. This is due in part to the fact that the law applied in Cameroon is essentially a law inherited from Franco-British colonialism. Justice in Cameroon took root on a base that had already been shaped by other cultures. Quite frankly, this modern law is in large measure foreign to the way of life of the Cameroonian population, and in particular to the members of the indigenous peoples. It is important to note that, 'behind the harmonious façade of a borrowed modernity, there exists a plurality of ethnic entities with their world-views, their forms of social and political organization and their value systems, ultimately making up a corresponding number of legal sub-orders within the space of the state'.[38]

The areas of resistance to certain fundamental rights are often consensual.[39] Even in the absence of a consensual foundation in a given community, it has been possible to observe that, 'the creation of enclaves where certain fundamental rights are suspended is justified in the name of established tradition, or further of a collective right to difference'.[40] Indeed, by 'superimposing dissimilar foreign cultures on African societies, colonization has sown confusion in them'.[41] One of the major obstacles to

---

36 Above n. 13, p. 21.

37 Y.-M. Morissette, 'L'accès à la justice et les droits fondamentaux comme moyen et fin' in *L'effectivité des droits fondamentaux dans la communauté francophone*, Montréal, Aupelf-Uref, 1994, p. 271.

38 M. Kamto, 'Une justice entre tradition et modernité' (1990) 156 *Afrique Contemporaine*, p. 60.

39 Above n. 37.

40 Ibid.

41 Above n. 38.

access to the justice system on the part of these children lies in the conflictual situation between modern law and traditional law. In the indigenous people's culture, a concern prevails to safeguard 'the group's cohesion and harmony',[42] by internalizing collective values – in contradiction to Western culture, which revolves around 'safeguarding individual values'.[43] Dean Maurice Kamto underlines that, 'indeed, in traditional Africa justice was a moment of reconciliation rather than one of division, because every dispute constitutes a disturbance of social cohesion'.[44] It is for this reason Professor Sawadogo points out that, 'the undertaking of legal proceedings is considered an act of hostility against the respondent, who will not lack opportunities to get even. It is thus unsurprising that a great many debtors are not brought to court'.[45]

Furthermore, access to the justice system for indigenous children is compromised since the modern justice system constitutes an unknown that elicits rejection, due to its procedures and its object, which are unfamiliar to them. According to Jacques Vergès, the modern justice system is designed as 'an arena fight in which the adversaries embrace as enemies, where the relentless cut and thrust of the arguments and procedural trickery must come to a conclusion in a dramatic end, with a winner and a loser, who turn their backs on each other on leaving the courtroom'.[46]

When the rights of an indigenous child are infringed, it is difficult for them to take legal action. Certainly, this is a fundamental judicial right, but this involves the 'judicial law, which is most restricted when the person claiming their rights is a child'.[47] Children may not undertake direct appeal before the Cameroonian courts. A child may litigate through their legal representative.[48] The latter must have the will, ability, and knowledge

42 Above n. 35, p. 48.

43 Ibid.

44 Above n. 38, p. 58.

45 F.M. Sawadogo, 'L'accès à la justice en Afrique francophone : problèmes et perspectives. Le cas du Burkina Faso', in *L'effectivité des droits fondamentaux dans la communauté francophone*, Montréal, Aupelf-Uref, 1994, p. 308.

46 J. Vergès, *Pour en finir avec Ponce Pilate, Paris, Le pré aux clercs*, 1983, p. 89.

47 M. Paré, 'L'accès des enfants à la justice et leur droit de participation devant les tribunaux : quelques réflexions' (2014) 44(1) *Revue générale de droit*, p. 92.

48 In civil and commercial matters, children lack capacity of execution, but have a right of action. However, an emancipated minor has capacity, except for engaging in trade. This representation of the child needs to be distinguished from representation *ad litem*. The power of representation does not dispense with the need to refer to the name of the child represented in the proceedings, in accordance with the maxim that, 'no one can litigate by proxy'. Indeed, this involves preventing the person who has the right of action from concealing their name.

required to institute proceedings in court with regard to the rights of their aggrieved child. Unfortunately, many of them seem to dread this excessively formalized modern justice. Indeed, modern jurisdictional complexity, of which 'the structuring into tiers, which is to say into levels of jurisdiction and power, complicates the proceedings, in the intricacies of which the persons subject to the law [coming from the indigenous peoples] get lost, and interminably drags out proceedings the outcome of which remains uncertain'.[49] In response to this atypical and complex situation, we readily grasp 'the disillusionment or disaffection experienced by persons subject to the law [from the indigenous peoples], who remain rooted in the traditional culture, or are of limited means, when faced with this marketable or cash-convertible justice, which substantiates so often this maxim of the French fabulist, 'Thus human courts acquit the strong, and doom the weak, as therefore wrong.'[50] We readily understand why most of these individuals believe the judgments of the modern courts are not well rendered, and consequently seldom send their children to them.

4. CONCLUSION

Access to the justice system by children from the indigenous peoples is a concern in Cameroon, with several impediments marring its efficacy. Accessibility to the Cameroonian legal system is subject to organization and functional dysfunctions. In addition, some socio-cultural problems (poverty, ignorance, illiteracy, lack of adequate government communication, and, at times, lack of confidence in modern justice) constrain access to the justice system on the part of these children. In the face of the indifference towards modern justice on the part of the members of indigenous peoples, alternative procedures emerge, such as recourse to out-of-court dispute settlement, in line with customary procedures. These customary procedures put into perspective the importance of modern legal formalities, and also embody the advantage of being uttered in 'the language of the litigants, following a law in the standards and principles of which they are knowledgeable'.[51]

---

49 Above n. 38, p. 63.

50 Ibid.

51 Ibid.

THE TRANSITION TOWARDS CHILD-FRIENDLY COMMUNICATION IN THE JUSTICE SYSTEM

'And You, Are You Listening to Me?'

Marine Braun

'Grown-ups never understand anything by themselves, and it is tiresome for children to be always and forever explaining things to them ....'[1]

1. INTRODUCTION

When children face the judicial system as witnesses, victims, suspects, or parties to the proceedings, they often encounter the different professionals

---

[1] Passage from the book *The Little Prince* by A. de Saint-Exupéry.

in this system for the first time.[2] No matter the kind of proceedings, whether civil, criminal, or administrative, the child must invariably repeat their side of the story, understand the role of the professionals, and try to situate themselves within the judicial system. This requires that they be provided with adequate information, that they understand this information, and that they are able to make themselves understood.[3] Furthermore, children must be certain that their opinions will be taken into account while participating in the proceedings, and that their opinions and concerns will have an impact on the decision being made on their behalf.[4] How can one avoid becoming overwhelmed when faced with such complexity?

> A child-friendly justice system is on the side of children, offering help provided by competent professionals.[5]

In order to provide children with guidance, the professionals involved must inform them in a language that is adapted to them, make sure they have understood their situation, their rights, their journey through the justice system, and the role of each actor involved in their journey.[6] The professionals must also give them support and answer all their questions, especially in situations as delicate as those encountered in the pre-trial phases, in court, or following the trial.[7] Children will in this way truly be able to have access to justice and benefit from informed and meaningful participation throughout the proceedings, in accordance with Article 12 of the Convention on the Rights of the Child (CRC).

This contribution addresses the professionals working with children who find themselves in the justice system. These professionals include police officers (or members of another law enforcement authority), interpreters, social workers, lawyers or statutory representatives, prosecutors, judges, educators, psychologists, psychiatrists, members of

---

2 European Union Agency for Fundamental Rights, *Child-friendly justice. Perspectives and experiences of children involved in judicial proceedings as victims, witnesses or parties in nine EU Member States*. Luxembourg: Publications Office of the European Union, 2017, p. 6, <https://fra.europa.eu/sites/default/files/fra_uploads/fra-2017-child-friendly-justice-children-s-perspective_en.pdf>.

3 Ibid., pp. 35 ff.

4 Ibid.

5 Council of Europe, *Guidelines of the Committee of Ministers of the Council of Europe on child-friendly justice*, 2010, p. 9, <https://rm.coe.int/16807000f1>.

6 Ibid.

7 Committee on the Rights of the Child, General Comment No. 12: The Right of the Child to be Heard, 2009, UN Doc. CRC/C/GC/12, §§25, 41, 45, 60, 82.

medical staff, probation officers, child protection officers, staff members of the asylum and immigration services, or any other person who interacts with children in the justice system.[8]

Moreover, this contribution seeks to emphasize the importance of communicating in a suitable way with children, and to restate or provide certain keys for professionals to be able to communicate in this way. While most actors involved in the justice system believe that communicating appropriately with children is something evident, experience and studies[9] show that this is not always the case. These are skills that are acquired through training. As an example, the Guidelines of the Committee of Ministers of the Council of Europe on Child-friendly Justice set out that professionals should receive training on the needs and rights of children and child-friendly communication techniques and procedures, with due regard for age differences and for the personal circumstances of the children.[10] As stated by a German family court judge:

> A lot of things […] where I had the feeling that I've done it somehow intuitively right before, maybe, but of course it's good once to hear how to do that right from a psychological view, and then be able to correct mistakes, and see to it that you also keep up with these guidelines a little bit. I wish there were many more training [courses], because there are absolutely none in judicial education.[11]

In addition to the observation of a lack of training, the question also arises of access to the tools that the professionals are able to use on a daily basis for communicating with children in the justice system. Our research tells us that numerous sources provide techniques for

---

8 Council of Europe, above n. 5; UN General Assembly, *Global study of Children Deprived of Liberty*, 2019, UN Doc. A/74/136, p. 67.

9 See for example: A. Daly and S. Rap, 'Children's Participation in Youth Justice and Civil Court Proceedings' in U. Kilkelly and T. Liefaard (Eds.), *International Human Rights of Children*, Singapore, Springer, 2018, p. 299; European Union Agency for Fundamental Rights, above n. 2; European Commission, *Children's involvement in criminal, civil and administrative judicial proceedings in the 28 Member States of the EU*. Policy Brief. Luxembourg, Publications Office of the European Union, 2017, <https://op.europa.eu/en/publication-detail/-/publication/c3cd307f-ff03-4010-b322-dcf7063403c5>.

10 Council of Europe, above n. 5, Section IV A 4, 5.

11 European Union Agency for Fundamental Rights, *Perspectives and experiences of professionals on children's participation in civil and criminal judicial proceedings in 10 EU Member States*, Luxembourg: Publications Office of the European Union, 2015, p. 105.

listening to children during an interrogation, interview or hearing.[12] Other sources are focused on groups of children, as is the case with the Council of Europe's Handbook For Frontline Professionals Working With Children in Migration,[13] or of the Practical Guide for Lawyers for Children in Conflict With the Law.[14] In carrying out the research, we realized that beyond this type of material – which is not always well-known, nor readily accessible – too few studies and publications address techniques for child-friendly communication in the justice system, considering them a cross-cutting skill of professionals. In this contribution, we will take up a number of techniques that constitute necessary preconditions for good communication. These techniques are undertaken through various exercises in listening, discussion, and dialogue. The following points are drawn from the literature, from my practice as an expert in children's rights and former lawyer and from various workshops on communication with children in the justice system,[15] training modules providing 'tools for developing motivation

---

12 See for example: C. Wilson and M. Powell, 'A Guide to Interviewing Children: Essential Skills for Counsellors, Police Lawyers and Social Workers' (2002) 7(4) *Child & Family Social Work*; F. Verkamp, 'Comment entendre un enfant témoin lors d'une audition judiciaire?' (2013) *Journal droits des jeunes*; H. Price and K. Roberts, 'A practical guide to interviewing child witnesses' (2007) 5(3/4) *Canadian Journal of Police & Security Services*.

13 Council of Europe, How to convey child-friendly information to children in migration: Handbook for frontline professionals, 2018, <https://rm.coe.int/how-to-convey-child-friendly-information-to-children-in-migration-a-ha/1680902f91>.

14 Défense des Enfants International (DEI) – Belgique, *Guide pratique pour les avocats: Comment assister un enfant en conflit avec la loi?* (2018), <https://lachild.eu/wp-content/uploads/2016/05/Guide_Avocats_FR-web.pdf>.

15 The first workshop, entitled 'Youth Justice Training for Solicitors', was organized in London in June 2017 by the Youth Justice Legal Centre <http://www.yjlc.uk/>. More information on communication techniques may be found on their website <https://yjlc.uk/resources/legal-updates/new-sra-toolkit-youth-court-advocacy> and on that of the Solicitors Regulation Authority, with a toolkit to aid lawyers practicing at the Youth Court <http://www.sra.org.uk/solicitors/cpd/youth-court-advocacy/communicating-effectively.page>. This toolkit was developed with support from Just for Kids Law (http://www.justforkidslaw.org/) and from the Association of Youth Offending Team Managers <http://aym.org.uk/>. The second workshop was organized by Fair Trials <https://www.fairtrials.org/>, in the context of the project for 'Advancing the Defence Rights of Children', in London in July 2017. The workshop on 'communicating with child suspects and accused persons' was led by Mai van Dijk-Fleetwood-Bird, a language therapist. For more information: <https://www.fairtrials.org/the-abcs-of-fair-trials-language-in-the-juvenile-justice-system/>.

and self-esteem and managing anxiety on the part of both the little ones and of grown-ups',[16] and training in 'non-violent communication'.[17]

2. CHILD-FRIENDLY JUSTICE REQUIRES CHILD-FRIENDLY COMMUNICATION

2.1. THE NEED FOR A CHILD-FRIENDLY JUSTICE SYSTEM

In its guidelines on children in contact with the justice system, the International Association of Youth and Family Judges and Magistrates (AIMJF) lists the various reasons that may lead children to come into contact with the justice system.[18] These include:

> [s]eparation of parents, custody, protection, adoption, children in conflict with the law, child victims of physical or psychological violence, sexual abuse or other crimes, health care, social security, unaccompanied children, displaced children, asylum-seeking and refugee children and so forth. They may appear before various types of courts, be they civil, criminal or administrative – including, in some countries, traditional or religious courts. They may appear as a party or as a witness.[19]

The so-called 'child-friendly justice' under discussion in this book, to which several authors have contributed, is accessible[20] to all children – 'irrespective of the child's or his or her parent's or legal guardian's race, colour, sex, language, religion, political or other opinion, national, ethnic or social origin, property, disability, birth or other status', pursuant to Article 2 of the CRC, recognized by the Committee on the Rights of the

---

16 The tools are accessible on the Pyschoeducation.be platform which provides training for adults and children. For more information, see: <https://www.psychoeducation.be/>.

17 Training in 'non-violent communication' is provided by Martine Marenne, certified trainer with the Association for Non-Violent Communication of French-speaking Belgium. For more information, see: <https://cnvbelgique.be/author/martinemarenne/>.

18 International Association of Youth and Family Judges and Magistrates, *Guidelines on Children in Contact with the Law*, 2017, <http://www.aimjf.org/storage/www.aimjf.org/Documentation_EN/AIMJF/Guidelines_-_ENG_-_Ratified_17.04.26.pdf>.

19 Ibid., p. 8.

20 Council of Europe, above n. 5, p. 17.

Child as the general principle of non-discrimination, as adapted to the (specific and individualized) needs of children.[21]

In looking to meet the demands for accessibility and adaptation of a child-friendly justice system, many tools must be implemented for children to understand how things work when they are faced with the judicial system, be it as witnesses, victims, suspects, or parties to the proceedings. The professionals are there to fulfil this duty of ensuring the children's preparation.

2.2. CHILD-FRIENDLY COMMUNICATION FOSTERS THEIR PARTICIPATION

Communication is among the professionals' core competencies (of knowledge, know-how, and interpersonal skills) with regard to children's rights.[22] Communication improves not only the professionals' practice, but also considerably improves children's experience within the justice system, as well as the outcomes of the proceedings in which they participate, especially those with an impact on the decisions affecting their lives.[23]

The concept of participation does not appear as such in Article 12 of the CRC. However, according to the Committee on the Rights of the Child, the notion is linked to this article, as well as to Article 17 (right to information) and to Articles 13 and 15 (freedoms of expression, religion, conscience, assembly, and association) of the CRC.[24] This notion encompasses, 'children's right to involvement in decisions and actions that affect them and to have their views taken into account by decision makers'.[25] This term is widely used in the justice field, 'to describe ongoing processes, which include information-sharing and dialogue between children and adults based on mutual respect, and in which children can learn how their views

21 Ibid.

22 Bureau international des Droits de le Enfants (IBCR), *Les compétences clefs en matière des droits de l'enfant, Pour une adaptation des pratiques du secteur de la justice, du travail social et des forces de sécurité en matière de droits de l'enfant*, 2020, <https://www.ibcr.org/wp-content/uploads/2020/06/Referentiel_competences_clefs.pdf>.

23 A. Daly and S. Rap, above n. 9, p. 299.

24 Council of Europe, *Listen – Act – Change; Handbook on children's participation for professionals working for and with children*, 2020, p. 15, <https://edoc.coe.int/en/children-s-rights/9288-listen-act-change-council-of-europe-handbook-on-childrens-participation.html>.

25 Ibid.

and those of adults are taken into account and shape the outcome of such processes.'[26]

3. SOME CHILD-FRIENDLY COMMUNICATION TECHNIQUES

It is important to emphasize that the communication techniques that are described below are general, developed from my experience, and do not specifically take into account the particularities of the different groups of children among those in contact with the justice system, or of their specific and individualized needs. It is, nevertheless, one would think, a fundamental element and we align ourselves with this view. All children are different, and their needs differ with regard to communication. This is the case in particular for those children who are said to be vulnerable, including those from minority groups, children with disabilities, migrant children and children who are in prisons, detention centres or other places that deprive them of their liberty.[27]

For instance, the Committee on the Rights of the Child calls for children with disabilities to have 'accommodations made by providing them with assistance with communication and the reading of documents'[28] and draws attention to the fact that 'proceedings should be conducted in a language the child fully understands or an interpreter is to be provided free of charge'.[29] This is the case, for example, when dealing with foreign children, or citizens who are not proficient in the language(s) of the country. For example, in Belgium a Flemish-speaking child will benefit from the assistance of an interpreter when the proceedings are in French or in German.

3.1. SUPPORTIVE LISTENING

The first stage in the establishment of good communication between the child and the adult consists of listening to the child for as long as necessary

26 International Association of Youth and Family Judges and Magistrates, above n. 18, p. 18.

27 See UNICEF, 'Justice for Children', online: <https://www.unicef.org/protection/justice-for-children>.

28 Committee on the Rights of the Child, General Comment No. 24 on children's rights in the child justice system, 2019, UN Doc. CRC/C/GC/24, §40.

29 Ibid., §46.

and accepting periods of silence.[30] It is expected of the adult that they listen actively to what the child has to say, without seeking to over-interpret their words.[31] In this regard, they could choose to be silent or respond to the child's words with the expression, 'oh?'. If we wish to initiate an exchange on an equal footing with the child, as is the case with an interview or a professional conversation, it is to be hoped that the adult places themselves at the same level as the child[32] (when the latter is smaller), that they let them speak, and that they observe them.

Non-verbal signals are good indicators of the child's motivation to engage in conversation. If the child's face and shoulders are closed and they are reluctant to speak, this is a signal of a lack of motivation.[33] They are entitled to remain silent and decline to give their opinion if they are involved in legal proceedings. Conversely, if the child stands up straight, turns towards their interlocutor, wants to tell what they have experienced, and looks their interlocutor in the eyes, this is indicative of good motivation for communicating. Taking into consideration the motivational state of the child must take centre stage among the concerns of the professional.[34]

The professional's body language is just as important: physical behaviour, tone of voice, posture, and eye contact.[35] With the aim of practicing supportive listening, the professional should seek to establish and maintain appropriate eye contact with the child. A positive and non-judgemental gaze will make it easier for the interlocutor to appear open to the child and this helps the latter to concentrate. If the child speaks, they cannot be interrupted. The use of encouraging words and gestures, such as a smile, a nod of approval, a thumbs-up, or any other non-verbal signal, encourages them to carry on telling their story.[36]

These techniques will make it possible for the professional to reassure the child and to establish a relationship of trust with them. It is only when the child has concluded their comments that the professional will speak.[37]

30 DEI – Belgique, above n. 14, p. 57.

31 L. Yéme, 'Faber et Mazlish, des outils pour soigner le dialogue', 2016, Les Pros de la Petite Enfance, updated 09.2020, <https://lesprosdelapetiteenfance.fr/bebes-enfants/psycho-pedagogie/education-bienveillante-etre-lecoute-des-tout-petits-et-de-leurs-emotions/faber-et-mazlish-des-outils-pour-soigner-le-dialogue>.

32 M. Delfos, *De l'écoute au respect, communiquer avec les enfants*, Toulouse, Éditions Érès, 2007, p. 68.

33 Ibid., p. 70.

34 Ibid.

35 Council of Europe, above n. 13.

36 DEI – Belgique, above n. 14, p. 57.

37 Ibid., p. 66.

3.2. OPEN CONVERSATION

The role of the adult is to inform the child, using a language that is straightforward, accessible, and suitable for the situation.

By adapting their language to the child, the professional must be capable of simplifying their vocabulary, of avoiding jargon and legal terms as much as possible, and of preferring the use of specific tools, such as visual aids, videos, Post-It notes, and games, over verbal language. Likewise, they must understand that the vocabulary used by children is often different, or has differing meanings, from that used among adults. For example, for children the term '*parquet*' (a French term) does not seem to refer to the prosecutor's office, but rather to wooden flooring. Although it is important for the professional to understand the slang words used by the child, they must ensure not to use this terminology with other professionals. One can hardly imagine the judge using the term, '*askip*' to the child's lawyer, as a slang phonetic abbreviation used in France or in Belgium for '*à ce qu'il paraît*' [apparently], or using the expression, 'you were there with the *keufs*' which is French and Belgian slang for police officers, to refer to the fact that the child was represented by their lawyer when interviewed by the police. Moreover, it is recommended that one avoid closed and leading questions. For example, it is important not to ask questions such as, 'do you understand?', since children are often impressionable and pliable, and this kind of question may prompt them to automatically reply 'yes'.[38]

The conversation with the child is made easier when the professional employs short sentences and a simple vocabulary, and when they use drawings, photos, or images. It is better to avoid the use of chronological concepts, such as two weeks ago, last year, at the time of the next court session or hearing, which children have trouble understanding. As well, it is recommended to frequently repeat the statements made by the child. An effective way to do this is by using phrases such as, 'you said xxxx, so did you mean that yyyy?'. This is very important because it makes it possible for the child to stop and go back to what they have said, and thus for the professional to check that they have understood correctly.[39]

The professional must not hesitate to keep informing the child by repeating the information several times if necessary to make sure that it has been well understood. It is likewise important to answer all of the

---

38 Ibid., p. 59.

39 DEI – Belgique, above n. 14, p. 58.

child's questions and to make sure that they indeed understand the answer, something which is not always the case.[40]

Lastly, it is helpful to summarize what the child says. This is a key competence for structuring the interaction. This tool may be used to confirm a clear understanding of the subject and the file, to collate different aspects brought up by the child into a coherent sentence, and then go beyond what the child has already presented or guide the interview towards a new subject.[41]

3.3. FLUID INTERACTION

3.3.1. A Dynamic

This dynamic operates within a logic of reciprocity. If we seek to keep the conversation with the child 'open', as one that, 'aims to be attentive to the child and not impose one's own ideas on them',[42] it is necessary to have an interaction undertaken with sincerity. Such sincerity, which is an 'important component of a fruitful exchange, is shown in the congruence between the verbal and the non-verbal communication'[43] referred to above. Such sincerity should encourage the professional to show vulnerability. By displaying some of their faults and/or by sharing one or more challenging times that they have gone through, the adult opens up to the child, draws their attention, and portrays themselves as their equal. This, in turn, boosts the child's confidence.[44]

In addition to sincerity and vulnerability, demonstrating empathy towards the child also fosters a horizontal relationship. An empathetic adult recognizes and understands their own needs, as well as the child's emotions and feelings.[45] This is an exercise that is not easy to master and also one that implies that the professional is knowledgeable in child psychology and development. We found from our interactions with numerous actors in the justice system that they complain of the lack of

40 Ibid., p. 48.
41 Ibid., p. 59.
42 M. Delfos, above n. 32, p. 64.
43 Ibid., p. 71.
44 Conclusions drawn from the exercises during workshops on communicating with children in the justice system, described above n. 15.
45 C. Boutillier, 'La place des besoins et des émotions de l'adulte dans sa relation avec l'enfant' in *La Bientraitance éducative* (2015), pp. 115–46.

access to a unit of this kind in their training, and this, irrespective of their role within the system and of the country where they work. Nevertheless, by talking about emotions and feelings, one learns. A professional who comes to take up these notions with the child and to reassure them about the emotions that they are revealing – while also revealing their own – will be able to actively undertake a reciprocated form of communication with the child. The use of humour is another technique that makes it possible to put the child at ease. However, it is important not to resort to sarcasm and not to use idioms or dialects that the child does not understand.[46]

3.3.2. Means for Interaction and Adaptation

The professional also needs to be able to identify the appropriate communication channel for the interaction. 'It was by going out to the playground that I was able to have an exchange with a little girl of four years of age, a victim of violence – even though at the hearing she had remained silent.'[47]

As a consequence, face-to-face meetings are highly recommended for applying the language techniques mentioned above. Depending on the professional's role and the type or stage of the proceedings, the meeting site will need to be considered so as to be as pleasant and appropriate as possible for the exchange to take place. According to the Guidelines on Child-Friendly Justice, '[a]s far as appropriate and possible, interviewing and waiting rooms should be arranged for children in a child-friendly environment.'[48] Moreover, social networks have established themselves as a favoured channel of communication among children and young people. They may, as a consequence, be used to ensure a relatively regular communication. Nevertheless, it is necessary to explain to the child that not all of these channels guarantee the same level of confidentiality. For example, the police could analyze the contents of a telephone (WhatsApp, messaging, or other applications) that had been seized during the investigation, which could for example adversely affect the exchanges between the child and their lawyer.[49] It is therefore essential to establish clear rules concerning the contents of the exchanges and the times during which the child may contact and/or expect a reply from the professional.

---

46 DEI – Belgique, above n. 14, p. 59.
47 Interview with a children's magistrate with the family court, Lisbon, 05.2019.
48 Council of Europe, above n. 5, p. 31.
49 DEI – Belgique, above n. 14, p. 60.

Even if these means appear to be effective, using the telephone and social networks may have as consequence the child contacting the professional at arbitrary times, and the latter replying to them immediately.[50] The objective is not to create frustration, but rather a smooth exchange between the professional and the child.

4. CONCLUSION

The techniques briefly set out within the framework of this contribution are not the only ones that may be implemented to ensure a horizontal and respectful relationship between the professional and the child within the justice system. A variety of other techniques and tools exist, above and beyond the non-exhaustive selection illustrated in this contribution. Mainly based on my own experience, I have tried to identify the communication techniques that are common to the parties involved in the justice system as a whole. Of course, these will need to be further developed, qualified, and tested, by taking into account the age, specific needs, and status of the child, but also the type or stage of the proceedings in which they find themselves, and above all to the role of the professional wishing to implement this advice in their practice.

Generally, the techniques of supportive listening and of open-ended discussion aim to foster a dialogue between the professional and the child. It is only when they feel safe, listened to, and understood, that children truly possess a right to participate. They therefore become a party to the proceedings that they are confronted with. If they wish, they can express their thoughts and have their opinions heard. Lastly, they realize that their opinions are taken into account, and they feel supported.

In order to have all parties intervening in the system be acquainted with and use the tools of child-friendly communication, it is vital to include, within the programme of basic and ongoing training[51] for the various parties involved, units on the way the professional may combine their role and their interpersonal skills with the child. These units will

---

50 Ibid.

51 Professionals working within the justice system must be trained as prescribed in the international and regional instruments and standards, in particular in: General Comments No. 12 and No. 24 of the Committee on the Rights of the Child, above n. 7 and 28; the European directives related to human trafficking, to the right to a fair trial in criminal proceedings, to migration or mediation; and the *Guidelines of the Committee of Ministers of the Council of Europe on child-friendly justice*, above n. 5.

need to be articulated mainly around child pedagogy, psychology and development, 'active' listening and 'open-ended' discussions with the child, respect and horizontal relationships, management of their own emotions and those of the child, the use of language and vocabulary that are adapted and accessible, and interactions with the other professionals around these communications issues.

Ideally, the key techniques for child-friendly communication should be included in the international and regional instruments and standards relating to the issues of justice for and with children, such as the above-mentioned General Comment No. 12 of the Committee on the Rights of the Child on the right of the child to be heard, General Comment No. 24 on children's rights in the child justice system, in the Guidelines of the Committee of Ministers of the Council of Europe on Child-Friendly Justice, and the Guidelines of the AIMJF on children in contact with the justice system.

LEGAL REPRESENTATION AS A NECESSARY ELEMENT OF CHILDREN'S ACCESS TO AND PARTICIPATION IN FAMILY JUSTICE

Caterina TEMPESTA*

1. INTRODUCTION

With the adoption of the Convention on the Rights of the Child (CRC), children were specifically recognized in international law as holders of a broad range of rights. While some of these rights overlap with those applicable to all persons under other international and regional human

* Caterina Tempesta is senior counsel at the Office of the Children's Lawyer (OCL) in Ontario. The opinions reflected in this contribution are her own and do not necessarily reflect the opinions of the OCL.

rights instruments, a number are specific to children. Article 12 is considered the 'linchpin' of the CRC,[1] elevating children from objects of charity to independent rights-holders with entitlements to participate in all decisions affecting their lives, including those arising in judicial processes.[2]

This contribution focuses on the issue of legal representation as a necessary element of children's access to, and meaningful participation in, family justice processes. It also considers the significance of participation for children's interests and contribution towards more sustainable outcomes, and critically analyzes legal methods by which children's views may be placed before family courts, including guardians *ad litem*, *amicus curiae*, and instructional advocates.[3] This contribution concludes that the child advocate model of representation aligns most closely with human rights principles, empowering children to participate in fundamental decisions about their own lives, achieving not only effective realization of Article 12 of the CRC, but substantive and procedural access to justice.

2. THE RIGHT TO LEGAL REPRESENTATION: INTERNATIONAL AND REGIONAL HUMAN RIGHTS STANDARDS

2.1. INTERNATIONAL INSTRUMENTS

2.1.1. CRC and General Comments

As a general principle of the CRC, Article 12 is of 'fundamental importance', integral to both the interpretation of all other rights and the implementation of the Convention as a whole.[4] Although the CRC does

---

1 M. Freeman, 'Whither Children: Protection Participation, Autonomy?' (1994) 22 *Manitoba Law Journal* 307, p. 319; UN Committee on the Rights of the Child, General Comment No. 12 [2009]: The right of the child to be heard, CRC/C/GC/12, para. 86.

2 J. Tobin (Ed.), *The UN Convention on the Rights of the Child: A Commentary* (2019), p. 398; M. Freeman, 'The Future of Children's Rights' (2000) 14 *Children & Society* 277, p. 288; A. Daly, *Children, Autonomy and the Courts: Beyond the Right to Be Heard* (2018), p. 11; A. Parkes, *Children and International Human Rights Law: The Right of the Child to be Heard* (2013), p. 5.

3 References to international jurisprudence are provided with a focus on Canadian case law.

4 R. Hodgkin and P. Newell, *Implementation Handbook for the Convention on the Rights of the Child (UNICEF)*, 3rd ed. (2007), p. 149; above n. 1, para. 2.

not make explicit reference to a right to legal representation for children in civil court processes, a purposive reading of the Convention[5] supports such an interpretation, starting from the preamble which recognizes that children, by reason of their physical and mental immaturity, require special safeguards and care, including appropriate legal protection.

In addition to Article 12, Articles 9(2), 21(a), and 25 indirectly contemplate children's participation in decision-making in the child protection, parental separation, and adoption contexts.[6] To the extent that these decisions are made in judicial or administrative proceedings, the child may require legal representation to ensure their views are heard and interests protected. Article 4 reinforces this interpretation by requiring States Parties to undertake all appropriate legislative, administrative, and other measures for the implementation of the rights recognized in the Convention.

The General Comments of the UN Committee on the Rights of the Child provide more explicit support for the procedural safeguards necessary for children to 'access justice'. General Comment No. 5 states that for 'rights to have meaning, effective remedies must be available to redress violations'.[7] The Committee references the need for 'effective, child-sensitive procedures', including the provision of child-friendly information, advice, advocacy, access to independent complaints procedures and the courts with necessary legal and other assistance.[8]

This is consistent with General Comment No. 14 which outlines eight necessary procedural safeguards to ensure the correct implementation of the best interests principle in decision-making, including the need for 'all appropriate legal representation' when the child's best interests are to be formally assessed and determined by courts and equivalent bodies.[9]

General Comment No. 12 suggests that the 'representative' in Article 12(2) can be 'the parent(s), a lawyer or another person (inter alia, a social worker)'. However, the Committee recognizes the 'risks of a

---

5 Article 31(1), United Nations, Vienna Convention on the Law of Treaties, Treaty Series, vol. 1155, p. 331 (1969).

6 See also, above n. 1, para. 33.

7 Committee on the Rights of the Child, General Comment No. 5 [2003]: General measures of implementation of the Convention on the Rights of the Child (Articles 4, 42-4, para. 6), CRC/GC/2003/5 (2003), para. 24.

8 Ibid.

9 Committee on the Rights of the Child, General Comment No. 14 (2013) on the right of the child to have his or her best interests taken as a primary consideration (Article 3, para. 1), CRC/C/GC/14 (2013), paras. 6, 85–99.

conflict of interest between a child and their most obvious representative, parent(s)',[10] a risk inherent in family law proceedings.

The Committee also indicates States are expected to 'comply with the basic rules of fair proceedings'.[11] Given the direct impact of family law proceedings on children's interests, the right to a fair hearing must be seen to encompass the right to legal representation.

The Committee also emphasizes that implementation of the general principles of the Convention cannot be dependent on resources.[12] Civil and political rights, including the child's rights under Article 12, are not subject to the progressive implementation afforded to economic, social and cultural rights under Article 4. Failure to adequately fund a legal aid system allowing children to have consistent access to legal representation in matters where their best interests are being assessed, runs contrary to the interpretive principles articulated by the Committee in its General Comments and Article 4 of the Convention.

2.1.2. Other International Standards

The need for effective remedies to redress rights violations is implicit in the CRC[13] and referred to in other major international human rights treaties. Children are encompassed by the human rights guarantees afforded to all persons in the International Bill of Rights and interpretation of the CRC may have regard to the provisions of these other treaties.[14]

Both the Universal Declaration of Human Rights (UDHR) and the International Covenant on Civil and Political Rights (ICCPR) recognize the right to 'legal personality' and equality before the law without discrimination, including the right to a fair hearing.[15] This offers potential for children to access remedies for rights violations separate from the mechanisms in place under the CRC and its optional protocols. This is significant given the relatively low rate of ratification of the Optional Protocol on a communications procedure.[16]

---

10 Above n. 1, para. 36.

11 Ibid., para. 38.

12 Article 4 of the CRC; above n. 7, para. 6; above n. 4, p. 160.

13 Above n. 7, para. 24.

14 Above n. 5, Article 31(3)(c). See also Article 41 of the CRC.

15 Articles 6, 7, 8, 10 of the UDHR; Articles 2.3, 14, 16, 26 of the ICCPR. See also Human Rights Committee, General Comment No. 32, Article 14: Right to equality before courts and tribunals and to a fair trial, UN Doc. CCPR/C/GC/32 (2007), paras. 3, 10, and 13.

16 Only 46 countries have ratified the Third Optional Protocol (as of 26.10.2020).

In 2013, the UN High Commissioner for Human Rights issued a Report devoted to access to justice for children, emphasizing that '[t]he concept of access to justice for children requires the legal empowerment of all children'.[17] The Report highlights children's 'acute' need for legal assistance given their disadvantage when engaging with complex legal systems generally designed for adults.[18] Legal assistance is seen as 'essential' for the protection of children's rights and States are called upon to provide such assistance to children free of charge in all matters affecting them.[19]

A 2014 Human Rights Council Resolution on children's rights/access to justice identifies barriers and makes recommendations regarding due process guarantees, including the child's right to their own lawyer in proceedings where there is a potential conflict between the child and a parent.[20] Other key recommendations include the same legal guarantees accorded to adults, including all fair trial guarantees with concurrent special protections because of their status as children, the right to privacy, the guarantee of legal aid under the same or more lenient conditions as adults, and the right to challenge decisions with a higher judicial authority.[21]

In addition to UN-based institutions, the International Association of Youth and Family Judges and Magistrates (AIMJF) ratified Guidelines on Children in Contact with the Justice System in 2017.[22] The Guidelines highlight the child's 'right to legal or other appropriate assistance for the preparation and presentation of their case' not only in criminal, but civil, child protection, and administrative law procedures.[23] They recommend State-funded legal representation in children's contacts with the justice system, with the lawyer expressing and defending exclusively the views of the child.[24] Lawyers have the same obligations towards children as adult clients while the execution of such obligations must occur in a manner consistent with the level of understanding and communication of the child.[25] The AIMJF Guidelines recognize the legal status of children as

17 Human Rights Council, Report of the United Nations High Commissioner for Human Rights: Access to justice for children, UN Doc. A/HRC/25/35 (2013), paras. 4 and 5.

18 Ibid., paras. 15, 40, and 58.

19 Ibid., para. 42.

20 Human Rights Council, Right of the child: access to justice, UN Doc. A/HRC/25/L.10 (2014), para. 11.

21 Ibid, paras. 3 and 9.

22 International Association of Youth and Family Judges and Magistrates, *Guidelines on Children in Contact with the Justice System* (2017), <http://www.aimjf.org/download//Documentation_EN/AIMJF/Guidelines_-_ENG_-_Ratified_17.04.26.pdf>.

23 Ibid., pp. 23, 27, and 29.

24 Ibid., pp. 27 and 28.

25 Ibid., pp. 27–29.

rights-bearers, consistent with the procedural protections afforded by the CRC.

2.2. REGIONAL INSTRUMENTS

Notable among regional instruments which address barriers faced by children in accessing justice processes, including the issue of legal representation, are the European Convention on the Exercise of Children's Rights,[26] the Charter of Fundamental Rights of the European Union,[27] and the African Charter on the Rights and Welfare of Children.[28]

Further, in 2010, the Council of Europe adopted broad-ranging Guidelines on Child-Friendly Justice addressing children's due process rights in all proceedings.[29] The Guidelines articulate that the rule of law should apply fully to children as it does to adults, emphasizing that the right to a fair trial, the right to legal advice and representation, the right to access to courts, and the right to appeal should be guaranteed for children as they are for adults and should not be minimized or denied under the pretext of the child's best interests.[30]

3. CHILD PARTICIPATION IN JUDICIAL PROCESSES

The philosophical underpinning of the CRC reflects a construction of childhood recognizing children as competent social actors. Meaningful participation by children in judicial decision-making not only results in better process experiences but leads to more sustainable outcomes.[31]

---

26 European Convention on the Exercise of Children's Rights, Strasbourg, ETS No. 160, 25.01.1996. See Articles 2–6 and 9.

27 European Union, Charter of Fundamental Rights of the European Union, 26.10.2012, 2012/C 326/02. See Articles 24(1) and 47.

28 African Charter on the Rights and Welfare of Children, Organization of African Unity, 11.07.1990, CAB/LEG/24.9/49 (1990). See Article 4(2). For an interpretation of the combined effect of the African Charter and the CRC, see *Centre for Child Law v. Governing Body of Hoerskool Fochville*, (156/2015) [2015] ZASCA 155 (08.10.2015), para. 20.

29 Council of Europe, *Guidelines of the Committee of Ministers of the Council of Europe on child friendly justice and their explanatory memorandum*, 17.11.2010.

30 Ibid., para. III(A)(2) and pp. 37–42.

31 J. Cashmore, 'Promoting the participation of children and young people in care' (2002) 26 *Child Abuse and Neglect*, p. 837; R. Birnbaum and N. Bala, 'The Child's Perspective on Legal Representation: Young Adults Report on Their Experiences

The harm of denial of autonomy and exclusion was recognized by the Yukon Supreme Court in *B.J.G. v. D.L.G.*, identifying both immediate and long-term adverse effects of not consulting children.[32]

Participation is a right which can improve children's skills and self-esteem, inform decision-making, and promote children's safety and short- and long-term well-being.[33] It can also be a protective factor for children who experience domestic or other forms of violence.[34] The CRC Committee emphasizes that children must be provided with the space to freely express their views and have them given due weight in all aspects of prevention, reporting, and monitoring of violence against them.[35]

---

with Child Lawyers' (2009) 25 *Canadian Journal of Family Law* 11, p. 24; K. Hollingsworth and H. Stalford, 'Judging Parental Abduction: What Does it Mean to Adopt a Children's Rights-Based Approach?', in G. Douglas, M. Murch and V. Stephens (Eds.), *International and National Perspectives on Child and Family Law: Essays in Honour of Nigel Lowe*, 2018, p. 135. See also *B.J.G. v. D.L.G.*, 2010 YKSC 44, para. 21.

32 *B.J.G. v. D.L.G.*, 2010 YKSC 44, paras. 18, 23–24; see also, N. Taylor, 'What do we know about involving children and young people in family law decision making? A Research update' (2006) 20 *Australian Journal of Family Law* 154, p. 164; and above n. 2, A. Daly, pp. 35–36.

33 R. Birnbaum and M. Saini, 'A Qualitative Synthesis of Children's Participation in Custody Disputes' (2012) 22(4) *Research on Social Work Practice*, p. 400; R. Birnbaum and M. Saini, 'A scoping review of qualitative studies about children experiencing parental separation' (2012) 20(2) *Childhood*, p. 260; S. Holt, 'A voice or a choice? Children's views on participating in decisions about post-separation contact with domestically abusive fathers' (2018) 40 *Journal of Social Welfare and Family Law* 459, p. 460. See also *A.C. v. Manitoba (Director of Child and Family Services)*, 2009 SCC 30, paras. 92–93; and *Ontario (Children's Lawyer) v. Ontario (Information and Privacy Commissioner)*, 2018 ONCA 559, para. 62.

34 D. Martinson and M. Jackson, *Family Violence and Parenting Assessments: Law, Skills and Social Context*, Simon Fraser University FREDA Centre for Research on Violence Against Women and Children (2019), pp. 20–22, <https://fredacentre.com/wp-content/uploads/D.-Martinson-and-M.-Jackson-Report-Family-Violence-and-Parenting-Assessments-Law-Skills-and-Social-Context-1.pdf>; J. Cossar, M. Brandon, and P. Jordan, 'You've got to trust her and she's got to trust you: Children's views on participation in the child protection system' (2016) 21 *Child & Family Social Work* 103, p. 104; above n. 33, S. Holt, p. 460; D. Martinson and C. Tempesta, 'Young People as Humans in Family Court Processes: A Child Rights Approach to Legal Representation' (2018) 31 *Canadian Journal of Family Law* 151, p. 168; F. Morrison, E.K.M. Tisdall, and J.E.M. Callaghan, 'Manipulation and Domestic Abuse in Contested Contact – Threats to Children's Participation Rights' (2020) 58 *Family Court Review* 403, p. 413.

35 Above n. 1, para. 119; Committee on the Rights of the Child, General Comment No. 13 (2011), The right of the child to freedom from all forms of violence, Doc. CRC/C/GC/13 (2011), para. 63.

Despite the legal obligations created by the CRC and a broadening consensus recognizing children as competent actors in their own lives, there remains an implementation gap, with concerns that participation will unduly burden children and harm them by placing them in the middle of adult conflicts.[36] In particular, children's susceptibility to undue pressure or 'parental alienation' is an often-cited concern in the context of family law proceedings and may be used as justification for failing to hear from the child or according minimal weight to their views.[37]

Although separating parents do sometimes engage in this behaviour, these allegations have the potential to minimize and even silence the voice of the child.[38] Daly describes the 'corrosive suffering' of children feeling powerless to influence decisions affecting them and the 'trajectory of suffering' which research indicates many children experience in such circumstances.[39] Moreover, the therapeutic interventions forced on children in some cases to address alleged alienation are concerning, arguably violating their rights to personal and psychological integrity.[40]

Raising the specter of alienation serves to diminish the perspectives of children and a more nuanced examination of the complexities of child-parent relationships. Frequently, there are various factors contributing to the issue, ranging from a child's natural affinity for one parent to realistic estrangement from the other parent due to abusive or other less-than-ideal

---

36 *Re L.C.* [2014] UKSC 1, para. 48. See also: above n. 31, R. Birnbaum and N. Bala, pp. 24–25; above n. 33, S. Holt, p. 460; above n. 2, A. Daly, pp. 35–36; Daly and Rap, p. 12; M. Henaghan, 'What Does a Child's Right to Be Heard in Legal Proceedings Really Mean? ABA Standards Do No Go Far Enough' (2008) 42 *Family Law Quarterly* 117, p. 118.

37 Above n. 34, F. Morrison, E.K.M. Tisdall, and J.E.M. Callaghan; B.J. Fidler and N. Bala, 'Concepts, Controversies and Conundrums of "Alienation": Lessons Learned in a Decade and Reflections on Challenges Ahead' (2020) 58 *Family Court Review* 576, p. 591; *Justice for Children and Youth v. J.G.*, 2020 ONSC 4716, paras. 49 and 74.

38 Above n. 2, A. Daly, p. 358; above n. 34, F. Morrison, E.K.M. Tisdall, and J.E.M. Callaghan.

39 Above n. 2, A. Daly p. 358; J. Johnston, 'Children of Divorce who Reject a Parent and Refuse Visitation: Recent Research and Social Policy Implications for the Alienated Child' (2005) 38 *Family Law Quarterly*, p. 757. For case examples, see *Office of the Children's Lawyer v. Balev*, 2018 SCC 16, Factum of the Appellant dated 14.08.2017, para. 30, <https://www.scc-csc.ca/WebDocuments-DocumentsWeb/37250/FM010_Appellant_Office-of-the-Children's-Lawyer.pdf>; *A.M. v. C.H.*, 2019 ONCA 764, paras. 81, 84, 86–91; *V.L. v. M.L.*, 2019 ONSC 7367, para. 124; *Re M. (A Minor) (Child Abduction)* [1994] 1 FLR 390 (EWCA), p. 2; *Re M. (Republic of Ireland) (Child's Objections) (Joinder of Children as Parties to Appeal)* [2015] EWCA Civ. 26, para. 124.

40 See, for example, *Children's Aid Society of Peel Region v. F.(K.J.)*, 2009 ONCJ 198, para. 16; *A.M. v. C.H.*, 2019 ONCA 764, paras. 81, 84, 86–91; *V.L. v. M.L.*, 2019 ONSC 7367, at para. 124. See also above n. 37, B. Fidler and N. Bala, p. 588.

parenting behaviours.[41] Johnston (and others) confirm the multi-factoral nature of the phenomena.[42] Fortin's research does not support the contention that children are unduly influenced by the resident parent,[43] and the work of May and Smart suggests children are often aware of parents' attempts to manipulate them.[44] The research further indicates the number of cases of genuine 'alienation' are rare.[45]

The popular preoccupation with this issue is reflected in research[46] and case law, a phenomenon particularly apparent in the latter when judges disagree with children's views.[47] Decision-makers must be cautious not to automatically discount a child's views when concerns about parental manipulation are raised. As Daly notes, '[t]o divide children's views into "manipulated" and "their own" fails to recognize the relational nature of experiences and decision-making'.[48] An approach which considers the extent to which the child's views are rooted in reality, or might reasonably be perceived as such by the child, is preferable, as it considers the situation from the child's perspective, consistent with the child's right to have due weight attached to their views.[49]

---

41 R. Warshak, 'When Evaluators Get it Wrong: False Positive IDs and Parental Alienation' (2020) 26 *Psychology, Public Policy and Law* 54, pp. 58–60; Concerned family law academics, family violence experts, family violence research institutes, child development and child abuse experts, children's rights networks and associations, 'Collective Memo of Concern to: World Health Organization RE: Inclusion of "Parental Alienation" as a "Caregiver-child relationship problem Code QE52.0 in the International Classification of Diseases 11th Revision (ICD-11), (17-06-2019)', <https://www.learningtoendabuse.ca/collective-memo-of-concern-to-WHO-about-parental-alienation.html>.

42 J. Kelly and J. Johnston, 'The alienated child: A reformulation of parental alienation syndrome' (2001) 39(3) *Family Court Review*, p. 249; above n. 36, M. Henaghan, p. 129.

43 J. Fortin, J. Hunt, and L. Scanlan, *Taking a Longer View of Contact: The Perspectives of Young Adults who Experienced Parental Separation in their Youth* (2012), p. 246.

44 V. May and C. Smart, 'Silence in Court?: Hearing Children in Residence and Contact Disputes' (2004) 16 *Child & Family Law Quarterly*, p. 305.

45 J. Cashmore and P. Parkinson, 'Children's Participation in Family Law Disputes: The Views of Children, Parents, Lawyers, Counsellors' (2009) 82 *Family Matters* 15, p. 20.

46 See special issue of the AFCC Family Court Review, Volume 58, No. 2, focusing on Parent-Child Contact Problems.

47 *K. (Children)* [2016] EWCA 99, para. 5; and *H (Children)* [2014] EWCA Civ. 733, paras. 72 and 75; *A.M. v. C.H.*, 2019 ONCA 764; *Justice for Children and Youth v. J.G.*, 2020 ONSC 4716, paras. 24–25; *Jewish Family and Child Service of Greater Toronto v. L.R.*, 2017 ONCJ 472.

48 Above n. 2, A. Daly, p. 376; above n. 31, K. Hollingsworth and H. Stalford, pp. 137–38.

49 R. Schuz, *The Hague Child Abduction Convention: A Critical Analysis* (2013), pp. 330, 332, and 334; above n. 34, D. Martinson and C. Tempesta, p. 168; above n. 34,

4. NOT ALL METHODS OF HEARING FROM THE CHILD ARE CREATED EQUALLY

There is a lack of consensus on the ideal method by which children should be heard in family court processes. This section considers the most common methods of legal representation, having regard to their relative compliance with Article 12 of the CRC and the goal of empowered child participation.[50]

4.1. LEGAL REPRESENTATION: ADULT-DIRECTED MODELS

4.1.1. Guardian ad litem

Article 12(2) of the CRC contemplates the possibility of the child being heard through a representative in judicial proceedings. A guardian *ad litem* (GAL) is one such option. The CRC Committee, however, provides no guidance on the functions of a GAL and there is no consistent definition or uniform practice internationally.[51] The GAL's primary role is to determine and report to the court what they consider to be in the child's best interests, which may include eliciting and advising the court on the child's views.

An inherent tension exists when the views of the child and the GAL's perception of what is in the child's best interests do not align. This has the potential to undermine the child's effective participation, replacing the child's voice with that of the GAL.[52] As noted by Liefaard, an assessment of the child's best interests does not equate to legal representation.[53]

F. Morrison, E.K.M. Tisdall, and J.E.M. Callaghan, pp. 406 and 412. See also *F.(M.) v. L(J.)*, 2002 CanLII 63106 (QueCA), para. 52.

50 Non-legal representational methods of placing a child's views before the court include assessments, Voice of the Child Reports and judicial interviews. An examination of these modalities is beyond the scope of this contribution but there are limitations to each with respect to achieving meaningful child participation.

51 Above n. 2, A. Parkes, p. 99; above n. 2, A. Daly, p. 239.

52 Similar to the GAL, Bala and Birnbaum's proposed lawyer models risk undermining both the child's voice and their confidence in the legal system: N. Bala and R. Birnbaum, 'Rethinking the Role of Lawyers for Children: Child Representation in Canadian Family Relationship Cases' (2018) 59 *Les Cahiers de Droit*, p. 787.

53 T. Liefaard, 'Access to Justice for Children: Toward a Specific Research and Implementation Agenda' (2019) 27 *International Journal of Children's Rights* 1, p. 14.

The 'essential paternalism' of the role of the GAL was recognized by the UK Court of Appeal in *Mabon v. Mabon*,[54] while the Ontario Divisional Court in *C.M.M. v. D.G.C.* found that a requirement for a litigation guardian creates an access to justice issue for children in family law matters.[55]

4.1.2. Amicus curiae

In some jurisdictions, courts may appoint a lawyer to act as an *amicus curiae*. Like the GAL, there is no fixed definition of the role of *amicus*,[56] although it generally entails ensuring that relevant evidence and argument is before the court to assist the judge in making a decision. The specific parameters of the role are defined by the court in a given case.[57] The *amicus* lawyer may investigate the child's circumstances and/or interview the child and place evidence before the court but does not advocate from the perspective of the child, nor provide advice to the child. No confidentiality attaches to the communications between them. Apart from serving as a possible vehicle for the transmission of the child's views to the court, use of an *amicus* inadequately protects the rights of children in court processes.[58]

4.2. LEGAL EMPOWERMENT: THE CHILD ADVOCATE

The CRC Committee has identified legal representation as one of the 'strict' procedural safeguards when the child's best interests are being assessed in formal decision-making processes.[59] The six other safeguards relevant to family court processes are: ensuring the right of the child to express their own views; establishing relevant facts; avoiding delays in decision-making; using qualified professionals; ensuring appropriate 'legal reasoning' by the courts; and facilitating mechanisms to review or revise decisions.[60]

---

54 *Mabon v. Mabon* [2005] EWCA Civ 634, para. 28.

55 *C.M.M. v. D.G.C.*, 2015 ONSC 2447 (SCJ – Divisional Court), para. 24.

56 *R. v. Russel*, 2011 ONCA 303, para. 44.

57 *Morwald-Benevides v. Benevides*, 2019 ONCA 1023, paras. 39–40; *R. v. Russel*, 2011 ONCA 303, paras. 41–46; *Catholic Children's Aid Society of Toronto v. M.C.*, 2018 ONCJ 619, paras. 388–94; *Coates v. Watson*, 2017 ONCJ 454, para. 2(d).

58 Above n. 34, D. Martinson and C. Tempesta, p. 187. See also R. Bessner, *The Voice of the Child in Divorce, Custody and Access Proceedings*, report presented to the Family, Children and Youth Section, Department of Justice Canada (2002), <https://www.justice.gc.ca/eng/rp-pr/fl-lf/famil/2002_1/index.html>; *Strobridge v. Strobridge* (1992) 10 O.R. (3d) 540 (G.D.), p. II.

59 Above n. 9, para. 96.

60 Ibid., paras. 85–99.

The child advocate is uniquely positioned to ensure compliance with each of these safeguards.

Having regard to maximizing the child's empowered participation, distinct attributes of the advocate model of legal representation compared to other legal and non-legal means of placing the child's views before the court include:

- The child's lawyer is able to offer the highest degree of confidentiality to the child-client, a factor which is crucial to engendering the child's trust[61] and to the exchange of information, including the provision of legal advice regarding the viability of potential legal options.[62]
- The child advocate is the only representative who protects the child's legal interests; all other representatives either lack this expertise or do not have this primary mandate.[63] In adversarial legal systems, only the child advocate gathers and tests evidence relevant to the child's position and makes legal arguments in support of the child's desired outcome.[64] This is critical to ensuring the child's views are not merely heard but given due consideration by decision-makers, as required by Article 12.
- The child advocate's involvement throughout the legal proceedings ensures the child's participation is a process rather than 'a momentary act'.[65] This can facilitate settlement consistent with the child's interests,[66] as well as the provision of up-to-date information about the child's views and circumstances, particularly when proceedings do not resolve quickly.
- The child advocate is the only representative able to directly assess, advise on, and access review or appeal mechanisms. This is significant if the child's views have been inadequately considered or explained in the judgment.[67]

---

61 Above n. 1, para. 43. See also *Ontario (Children's Lawyer) v. Ontario (Information and Privacy Commissioner)*, 2018 ONCA 559, paras. 70–76, 87–88, and 128.

62 Above n. 1, para. 25.

63 Above n. 34, F. Morrison, E.K.M. Tisdall, and J.E.M. Callaghan, p. 405.

64 Ibid., paras. 66 and 79. See also, *Ludwig v. Ludwig*, 2019 ONCA 680, para. 69; *Strobridge v. Strobridge*, (1984) 18 O.R. (3d) 753, 4 R.F.L. (4th) 169 (OCA), p. 764; *Re W.*, [1979], 27 O.R. (2d) 314, 13 R.F.L. (2d) (Ont. Prov. Ct.), para. 6; above n. 34, D. Martinson and C. Tempesta, pp. 189–190; above n. 58.

65 Above n. 1, para. 13; above n. 34, F. Morrison, E.K.M. Tisdall, and J.E.M. Callaghan, p. 413.

66 Above n. 58.

67 Above n. 9, para. 98.

As Tobin observes, representation under Article 12(2) of the CRC does not mean it is appropriate for *anyone* to represent the child.[68] The representative must be 'independent and competent' if the child's right to representation is to be effective.[69] Legal competency is critical when the forum is the courtroom. Competency further requires that the child's views be 'transmitted correctly to the decision-maker'.[70] This favours a child advocate model rather than a best interests model of legal representation and is consistent with what children want. Empirical research demonstrates that, '[m]any children feel marginalised by "best interests" advocacy'[71] and the adoption of a child-directed advocacy approach 'will leave children more satisfied with the process'.[72]

5. CONCLUSION

Article 12 of the CRC embodies the principle that participation is a fundamental human right. As such, '[i]t enables us to demand rights'.[73] In judicial processes where a child's interests are directly affected, the child requires a qualified legal representative to assist in asserting their rights. It is insufficient to have the assistance of a non-legally trained support person when the setting is the courtroom.

States parties must allocate resources to ensure children have access to legal representation in family court processes. Reductions in legal aid funding in many countries have negatively impacted children's access to legal support.[74] This is inconsistent with implementation obligations under

68 Above n. 2, J. Tobin, p. 427.
69 Ibid. See also above n. 1, para. 36.
70 Above n. 2, J. Tobin, p. 428; Above n. 1, para. 36.
71 Fernando, p. 49, citing Australian Law Reform Commission and Human Rights and Equal Opportunity Commission, *Seen and Heard: Priority for Children in the Legal Process*, Report no. 84 (1997), p. 13.56.
72 Above n. 31, R. Birnbaum and N. Bala, pp. 22 and 60. See also A. Bilson and S. White, 'Representing Children's Views and Best-Interests in Court: An International Comparison' (2005) 14 *Child Abuse Review* 220, p. 236; and D. Kennan, B. Brady, and C. Forkan, 'Supporting Children's Participation in Decision Making: A Systematic Literature Review Exploring the Effectiveness of Participatory Processes' (2018) 48 *British Journal of Social Work* 1985, pp. 1993–95 and 1997.
73 M. Freeman, 'Why It Remains Important to Take Children's Rights Seriously' (2007) 15 *International Journal of Children's Rights* 5, p. 5.
74 CRIN, *Rights Remedies & Representation: Global Report on Access to Justice for Children*, (2016), <https://archive.crin.org/sites/default/files/crin_a2j_global_report_final_1.pdf>, p. 29. In Canada, the unmet need for legal services has been widely acknowledged (Family Justice Working Group of the Action Committee on Access

Article 4 of the CRC.[75] Care must also be taken not to burden courts with concerns regarding available resources when exercising their discretion to appoint lawyers for children: 'it is the function of judges to apply the law, not to serve as a gatekeeper for public resources'.[76]

Decision-makers must also guard against protectionist tendencies aimed at keeping children out of adult conflicts, failing to recognize that children have lived these conflicts and are keenly aware of what is at stake for them,[77] as well as the significant body of research that confirms the benefits of children's participation and the harms of not participating in matters which directly affect them.

Extensive support for children's empowered legal participation as an access to justice issue is found in the many international and regional human rights standards discussed. This includes ensuring the child-lawyer relationship is not compromised by the dilution of the lawyer's role. Research indicates that children want assurances of confidentiality in their communications with their representatives in the context of court processes[78] and want their legal representatives to advocate for their views. Respect for children and their autonomy interests, as well as their expertise in their own lives, must guide the model of representation afforded to them rather than adult perceptions of what is best for them. Children need to know they have trusted, skilled allies in court processes where their best interests are being determined. Only in this way can children truly have access to, and meaningful participation in, family justice processes.

---

to Justice in Civil and Family Matters, Final Report: *Meaningful Change for Family Justice: Beyond Wise Words* (2013), <https://www.cfcj-fcjc.org/sites/default/files/docs/2013/Report%20of%20the%20Family%20Law%20WG%20Meaningful%20Change%20April%202013.pdf>, pp. 16 and 19); above n. 2, A. Daly, p. 229; K. Goldthorpe, *Access to justice without access to funding: legal aid cuts*, The Lawyer's Daily, 06.05.2019. For similar concerns in the U.K, see Bach Commission, *The Right to Justice: The Final Report of the Bach Commission* (2017), pp. 5–7 and 31.

75 Above n. 7, para. 24.

76 Above n. 2, A. Daly, p. 233.

77 Above n. 34, F. Morrison, E.K.M. Tisdall, and J.E.M. Callaghan, pp. 412 and 413; above n. 58.

78 *Ontario (Children's Lawyer) v. Ontario (Information and Privacy Commissioner)*, 2018 ONCA 559, paras. 70, 71, 73–75.

ACCESS TO JUSTICE IN PROTECTION OF YOUNG PEOPLE IN QUEBEC

The Current Status and Recommendations from those Primarily Concerned – The Children

Malika SAHER

'For me, having access to justice means being heard'

– Sarah, 14 years of age, interviewed for this research

1. INTRODUCTION

Access to justice is a substantial issue, bringing up numerous ramifications and interpretations. Here is what children think about it:

> It's for upholding our rights – our right to participate, the right to express ourselves, to be listened to. For the judge to really listen and notice, and take that into account, more than anything. (Anthony, 13 years of age.)

> It's having access to the court. It's not right for there to be a court and you aren't there. You have to be there, speaking to the judge. You're obliged to be there, they're talking about you, about your future. (Pavel, 13 years of age.)

Children associate access to justice with being heard. This contribution is therefore a qualitative analysis of the effective application of the right to participate of the nine children queried on the legal proceedings concerning them.

Pursuant to the Youth Protection Act (YPA), children have a right to participate in decision-making and in the choice of any measures concerning them,[1] and to be advised and represented by a lawyer.[2] Nevertheless, in practice, some children believe their right to participate has not been implemented.

When questioned about the role of the office of the Director of Youth Protection (DYP), the children responded as follows. Allisson, 10 years of age, said, 'The role of the [DYP] is to help us, the children – and also the adults – to change, to do better.' Pavel, 13 years of age, said, 'It's true that basically they [the DYP] want to help children, but they do not take what they say into account.'

Is Pavel's perception shared by his peers? What factors could contribute to such a perception? In concrete terms, to what extent and in what way has the right of these children to participate in proceedings concerning them been implemented or is being implemented? The children's responses are fundamental, inasmuch as they tell us their perception of the implementation of their right to participate, of their access to justice, and of how real their status is as subjects of law.

We met with nine children between the ages of 10 and 15 years, who are followed at the Community Social Pediatrics Centre (CSPC) in Montreal. The project of writing the present contribution was presented to the caseworkers, who in turn informed the children having previously taken part in child protection proceedings. The interested children were contacted by telephone to inform them of the project and the process of seeking their opinions and recommendations, to confirm their interest in participating, and to choose the location.[3] Four children were already informed of their rights, as part of the Children's Rights Committee of the CSPC, and are mobilized in defence of these rights. The aim of this

---

1 Youth Protection Act, CQLR c P-34. 1, Article 2.3(b).

2 Ibid., Article 80.

3 The children were able to choose whether they preferred to be met with in small groups or individually. Five children were met with in groups and four individually.

contribution is not to draw generalizations based on the opinions of the children queried, but rather have their voices heard and put into context.

We will analyze the scope of the right to participation of the children queried, pursuant to the YPA – in theory and in practice – from their perspective. We will then share the recommendations brought forth by the children for effective implementation of their right to participate.

2. CURRENT STATUS

The YPA, adopted in 1977, came into force in 1979.[4] Prior to the adoption of the Convention on the Rights of the Child (CRC), the YPA had already attributed the status of subject of law[5] to children whose safety or development is deemed to be or potentially be compromised,[6] acknowledging in theory their right to participate in the proceedings pertaining to them.[7]

In 1991, Quebec declared itself bound by the CRC.[8] The DYP is attached to the Ministry of Health and Social Services of Quebec, and as such is a Quebec government institution. The YPA should – in principle – be in step with the CRC.

Article 12 of the CRC formulates that the State party 'assures' the child of the right to express their opinions in proceedings pertaining to them, with these being 'given due weight'. As stressed by Paré and Bé, States parties are required to put in place the resources to enable children to benefit from this right.[9] In what way and to what extent has children's participation been fostered?

Our discussion with them concentrated on four topics: the principle of the best interests of the child; the right to information; testifying; and representation by a lawyer. We will thus limit our analysis to these topics, given their importance to children.

---

4 Comité de la protection de la jeunesse, 'Les droits des jeunes et le droit d'être jeune' [01.17.1979] *Le Devoir*, p. 5; <http://numerique.banq.qc.ca/patrimoine/details/52327/2776180>.

5 Above n. 1, Article 3.

6 Ibid., Articles 2 and 38.

7 Ibid., Articles 2.4(1), (2), and (4).

8 D 1676-91, (1992) GOQ II, 51.

9 M. Paré and D. Bé, 'La participation des enfants aux procédures de protection de la jeunesse à travers le prisme de la vulnérabilité' (2020) 61(1) *Les Cahiers de droit*, pp. 223, 245.

2.1. THE CHILD'S BEST INTERESTS

In Quebec, the Youth Division of the Quebec Court has jurisdiction in the first instance to hear applications related to the YPA.[10] We asked the children to explain to us, in their own words, the role of this court. They unanimously associate it with decision-making in the child's interests.

Lena, 12 years of age stated, 'It's making decisions for the child, good decisions, for the child to be happy.' Allisson, 10 years of age stated, 'The judge is there to issue the judgment as to whether it's better that you be placed in care or not.' The children's perspective is in line with that of the YPA, with the latter setting out that all decisions taken pursuant to this law, 'must be in the interest of the child and respect his rights'.[11] It allows them to have their opinions and concerns heard.[12]

In sharing their visions of the role of the court, the children made reference tacitly or expressly to the principle of the best interests of the child. We subsequently confirmed their remarks by informing them of the existence of Article 3 of the YPA, which embodies the best interests principle, as does Article 3.1 of the CRC. Upon reading this provision Lena, 12 years of age, stated:

> If they don't listen to what the child has to say, how do they propose to find out what their best interests are? They should listen a little to the children, or even a lot! And take them seriously. They should stop saying that 'they're just children and we know what's best for them' – when no, they don't know.

Danny, 12 years of age, said, 'The judge didn't ask me. I think that I know what's best for me, because I'm living it.' Elena, 14 years of age, stated:

> It's necessary for the child to understand what their interest is. It's necessary to explain to them what is good for them – the advantages and disadvantages, and the difference between their needs and their desires.

Some of the children addressed the best interests of the child and the right to participation as having a complementary role.[13] According to them, one

10 Courts of Justice Act, CQLR c T-16, Articles 83(2), 79, and 80.
11 Above n. 1, Article 3.
12 Ibid., Articles 2(4)(4) and 6.
13 Committee on the Rights of the Child, General Comment No. 12 [2009]: The right of the child to be heard, [07.20.2009], CRC/C/GC/12 para. 74. See also paras. 70–74. <https://www.refworld.org/docid/4ae562c52.html>.

can only define the best interests of a child by allowing them to express themselves in this regard, and by taking their opinions into account. Moreover, the Youth Division has reiterated the importance of hearing the children in order to determine their best interests.[14]

In this regard, Article 2.3(b) of the YPA sets out that all interventions must prioritize the means allowing the child to take an active part. These means are not specified, and the very concept of participation remains dim for some children, parents, and caseworkers. Danny, 12 years of age, was refused access to the review process[15] by the caseworker responsible for application of protective measures in his case. 'I went with my dad, but the caseworker told me to leave or to wait outside.'

While evaluating the impacts of the YPA, amended in 2006,[16] Turcotte et al. assessed the perception of the amendments aimed at the active participation of parents and children, and the difficulties in their application.[17] While the majority of the department heads and of the caseworkers believe the amendments to be useful or very useful, and found little or no difficulties in applying them,[18] 24.7% of the caseworkers consider them either not very useful, unnecessary, or inapplicable.[19]

In light of the opinions of the children, of this assessment, and of our practical experience, it appears involving children in the decision-making process is not anchored in youth protection practices.

---

14 *Québec (Directeur de la protection de la jeunesse) v. L. (J.)*, 2001 QCCQ 24383, para. 124; *Protection de la jeunesse – 112512*, 2011 QCCQ 10730, para. 45; *Protection de la jeunesse – 119444*, 2011 QCCQ 20736, para. 313, 320–22; *Protection de la jeunesse – 129559*, 2012 QCCQ 20628, paras. 36, 39, 40; *Protection de la jeunesse – 1223*, 2012 QCCQ 675, paras. 34, 35, 41–44; *Protection de la jeunesse – 145331*, 2014 QCCQ 16946, para. 8.

15 Above n. 1, Articles 32(d), 57, and 57.2. See also *Regulation respecting the review of the situation of a child Youth Protection Act*, CQLR c. P-34.1, r. 8.

16 D. Turcotte, et al., *Évaluation des impacts de la nouvelle Loi sur la protection de la jeunesse au Québec*, [2011], Rapport de recherche (Ed.), Programme Actions concertées, Québec, Fonds de recherche sur la société et la culture (FQRSC).

17 Ibid., Annexes, Table 21 – Perception of the amendments aimed at the participation of parents and children, p. 55.

18 Ibid., Annexes, Table 22 – Difficulties in the application of the amendments aimed at the participation of parents and children, p. 56. Department heads believe 89.6% and caseworkers 75.2% that the amendments aimed at encouraging the active participation of the child and their parents are useful or very useful. Of the caseworkers, 14.3% considered this amendment non-applicable. 88% of department heads and 83.1% of the caseworkers find that there is no difficulty or little difficulty in applying the amendments aimed at the participation by the child and their parents.

19 Ibid., 7.9% consider the amendment to be not very useful, 2.5% consider that it is unnecessary and 14.3% are of the view that it does not apply. Of the caseworkers, 16.9% consider that it involves difficulties, 15.1% think that it involves some difficulties, and 1.8% think that it involves multiple difficulties.

2.2. THE RIGHT TO BE INFORMED

The YPA grants children the right to be provided with the information and explanations they need, while adapting them to their age and level of understanding.[20] The right to information and the right to participation are intrinsically linked. Anthony, 13 years of age, offered the following parallel, 'It's like having the right to vote in a country, but you don't speak the language. You can't really vote if people don't explain things to you.'

Access to information is a prerequisite for the right to participate. To the extent that a child will share their opinions, needs, and desires if they are informed of their right to do so, failing to properly inform them of this right is likely to violate their right to participate in court proceedings.

For children to express themselves in an informed manner, they must be equipped with their rights, informed of the goal of hearing them, and of the way their opinions will be handled. It must also be made sure that by taking the child's opinion into consideration, the child benefits from accountability.

In practice, only three children out of nine consider that they know their rights under the YPA.[21] According to Allisson, 10 years of age, 'They didn't really tell me my rights. I didn't feel that I had rights.' Alex, 15 years of age, stated, 'I don't even know if my case has concluded … My case file gets closed and concludes when I turn 18 – that's all I know.' Lena, 12 years of age, stated:

> The caseworker showed me a report, but only the bits that she wanted to. And sometimes I didn't even understand what she was saying – I am nine years old. That stressed me, I said to myself, 'hmm, what is it that they are going to choose?'. No one told me anything, they didn't tell me how it was going to work. I felt sad.

2.3. TESTIFYING

The children emphasized the importance of making oneself heard 'directly' by the judge. Tara, 13 years of age, stated, 'The judge should speak to the

20 Above n. 1, Articles 2.4(2) and 5.

21 These three children gave ratings of 5/10, 8/10, and 10/10 to their knowledge of their rights under the YPA, and stated they were informed of these rights thanks to their 'family', to 'a book at the youth centre that explained our rights to us' or to the 'children's rights committee of the CSPC'. The six other children gave a score of 0/10.

child, and the child should express their opinions; the judge should find solutions for that to get resolved.'

In order to be able to make an informed decision, it is the court that carries out the entire enquiry.[22]

The YPA stipulates that the child must have the opportunity to be heard,[23] and provides for a presumption that children under 14 years of age are fit to testify.[24] The YPA also provides, 'by way of exception', and if, 'warranted in the circumstances', for testimony from the child without the presence of the parties, but in the presence of the lawyers.[25] Therefore, the general rule would have a child testify, unless doing so would be detrimental to them.[26] Out of the nine children questioned, five stated they had never testified. Three of these five children had nevertheless explicitly requested to do so.

> I wanted to speak to the judge, but they didn't let me. My lawyer told me 'I'll see what I can do', but in the end I was unable to speak because I already had a lawyer to speak for me. (Anthony, 13 years of age.)

> When I was supposed to go to court, my caseworker told me: 'don't appear, that achieves nothing'. But if you don't appear, who is there in the court? The [DYP]. You don't tell your side of the story – because you're not there. (Pavel, 13 years of age.)

Elena, 14 years of age, shared with us that over seven years she has had between seven and 10 hearings in court, and added:

> I don't know what was said before the judge, and I didn't have the right to talk to him. I was never in the room, I don't even know what it looks like in there. That same day the lawyer would ask us what we think, she tells it to the judge, she returns and tells us what she said, and that's it.

Pavel explained:

> What I have seen is that the judge reads the file aloud. But the problem is that he doesn't ask the child whether it's true, or what they think about it. And since the lawyer ... you speak to them on the same day ... well you don't have the

22 Above n. 1, Article 77.
23 Ibid., Article 6.
24 Ibid., Article 85.1.
25 Ibid., Article 85.4.
26 Ibid., Article 85.2.

time to explain everything to them – the details. They're details … but they're important.

The children who indicated their desire to speak directly to the court were unable to do so, with their opinion being deemed to have already been passed on via their attorney and/or an assessment report issued by the DYP.

In that regard, under the YPA, when a child is excused from testifying,[27] their prior statements will be admissible.[28] Statements may be collected by the caseworker, who is the DYP's representative in court proceedings. The child is a party to the proceedings,[29] and some of their statements may be collected and passed on to the court by another party in adversarial proceedings.[30] It is thus possible these statements do not reflect the child's views.

2.4. REPRESENTATION

The YPA sets out that the court ensure that a lawyer advise and represent the child when their interest is opposed to their parents.[31] In practice, the child is always represented.[32] There are two types of mandates: conventional, when the child is able to express their will, and legal, when they are not able to do so.[33] It is the child's lawyer who will assess which mandate applies, basing themselves on the capacity of their client to instruct them.[34] According to what the children told us, and considering their age at the time of the launching of the proceedings, all were represented in accordance with a conventional mandate, meaning they were able to instruct their lawyer.

Case law informs us that the lawyer must be able to discuss the evidence with their client, compare the latter's version to the known evidence, prepare testimony, and lead their own evidence.[35] Six children reported

---

27 Ibid.

28 Above n. 1, Article 85.5.

29 Above n. 1, Article 81.

30 *Youth protection – 202580*, 2020 QCCS 2007, para. 8; *Youth protection – 121978*, 2012 QCCQ 8312, para. 4.

31 Above n. 1, Article 80.

32 *Youth protection – 112512*, 2011 QCCQ 10730, para. 25; *Youth protection – 083*, 2008 QCCQ 757, paras. 59 and 63.

33 Barreau du Québec, *Mémoire sur la représentation des enfants par avocat – dix ans plus tard*, Montreal, Barreau du Québec, 2006, p. 22. <https://collections.banq.qc.ca/ark:/52327/bs61009>; *M.F v. J.L. et F.L.*, [2002] R.J.Q. 676 (C.A.), para. 39.

34 Ibid., p. 9; *Youth protection – 1811300*, 2018 QCCQ 13373 para. 36.

35 *Youth protection – 083*, 2008 QCCQ 757 para. 68.

that meeting their lawyer on the same day as the hearing adversely affected their right to participation, due to the absence of a bond of trust. Five children considered that the fact that an intermediary reports their comments is an obstacle to this right. They favour addressing the court directly, orally, or in writing. Here are their observations:

> They let the lawyer come back [into the courtroom], who technically I am not acquainted with, while the family caseworker, they don't want to hear them. (Anthony, 13 years of age.)
>
> That's true, we speak to the lawyer on the same day. (Allisson, 10 years old.)
>
> I haven't spoken once in court – it's the lawyer who has said everything on my behalf. I don't call that taking into account what the young person concerned says. It's all well and good to speak for their client, but the client needs to speak for themselves. (Pavel, 13 years of age.)
>
> It's not really participating if you make everything go through an adult. Once more it's a way of minimizing children and not taking into account what they say. Honestly, I no longer recall how many lawyers I have had. The last one said things, but she didn't let me speak. When X was testifying, I wanted her to tell the judge that what X was saying wasn't true – but she didn't want to. So I didn't feel that that lawyer was there for me. (Lena, 12 years of age.)

The Committee on the Rights of the Child considers that with regard to youth protection, children's right to participation is not always taken into account by the States parties.[36] It therefore advises them to see the implementation of this right, by means of laws, regulations, and directives.[37] The provisions of the YPA and of Article 12 of the CRC converge towards taking into consideration the views of children in the legal proceedings concerning them.[38] In theory, children can rest assured that they will be able to participate in these proceedings, and the Committee would declare itself satisfied with the Quebec legislation. Nevertheless, eight children out of nine consider they have not been heard, or at least that they lack the information allowing them to conclude that their opinions – when shared – have been duly considered.

The passing of laws, regulations, and directives does not suffice. In this case, despite the adoption of the YPA, soliciting and considering the opinions of children appear to remain optional. As is illustrated,

36 Above n. 13, para. 54.
37 Ibid., para. 12.
38 Above n. 9, p. 249.

impediments remain for the implementation of children's right to participation. Several States parties are conscious of the existence of these obstacles and devote time and energy to seeking solutions. However, few tend to search for these solutions among the interested parties and the experts in their situation – the children.

3. RECOMMENDATIONS FOR EFFECTIVE IMPLEMENTATION OF CHILDREN'S RIGHT TO PARTICIPATION

The children were asked the following question: 'Twenty years from now, you have become a judge in the Youth Division; what do you do to ensure children's participation in their cases?' Here are their recommendations:

Active listening to the children, within a safe environment that is adapted to their circumstances

- 'Be "all ears" for them, which means listening attentively to what the child is going to say.'
- 'Instead of the judge being up high and the child down low, go into a room and speak face-to-face, and note exactly what the child says, in order to be able to undertake a better assessment and be able to take into account what the child wants and what is best for them.'
- 'The fact that the judge is up high. You're supposed to listen to what I tell you. Except that you need to feel superior to me. You need to be higher than me. I find that egotistical and demeaning. It's a pity that people perceive children as inferior to them.'
- 'Have them talk to me; I'm going to tell them: give me your opinion, I'm here to decide what's best for you, and I need your opinion.'
- 'Make sure the child speaks more. Ask them questions so they share their views and participate. Ask them questions on the situation, on how they feel.'
- 'Maybe speak to them in a room, alone.'
- 'How the judge dresses depends on the child's age – in a black robe for children over 10 years of age, and when they are under 10 years old, dressing normally so that they're less afraid.'
- 'I'm going to listen a lot and try to make every effort for the child to be able to say what they want to say … but it has never occurred to me to be a judge!'

- 'Let the child be like they are, because like technically you can't be what other people want you to be – you are who you are, that's all there is to it.'

A fluid and easy chance to get access to speak directly to the courts

- 'I would listen to them and I would apply what is best for them. I wouldn't listen to the lawyer – I would listen to the child first.'
- 'That the judge take into consideration the child's point of view as much as that of the DYP – that would be real justice. The DYP wants to protect us, OK, but we want what's good for us – it's still our life.'
- 'That the children be able to speak directly to the judges. It's not really children's views that are voiced to the judges – it's what the lawyers have to say. We don't know if they are going to change our words. If they change our words, it's not the truth. If you tell the truth, and you send someone to say it on your behalf, the judge won't believe you. You have to say it yourself – that's worth more.'
- 'If you'd like, to tell the judge what you'd like to have.'

Children's right to accountability from the courts

- 'I'll know that the judge has really taken into account what I say when I see the report [the ruling].'
- 'Listen to the child, to get their opinion, and show them that they are being listened to, so they trust us the next time. We can make changes and say that the changes were made after having listened to the child, and say to them: "you see, look at my ruling, I have listened to you".'
- 'You speak to the children, you tell them: "you will be placed into care because blah, blah, blah" – everything that has happened during the hearing. You explain the ruling. If it's the lawyer who tells the young people, sometimes it's not really the judge's words.'
- 'It's important that the judges directly address the children, to explain the ruling to them, using words that they understand.'

Development of a bond of trust with their lawyer

- 'Meet the lawyers before [the child is heard]. The majority of lawyers, you meet them for the first time on the same day. You'd have to meet the lawyer at least one month beforehand, precisely to speak with them, develop trust between the two and learn more about each other.

> We need to create a bond, to talk about these more personal things: what's happening at home, how you feel. Sometimes children do not really like to express themselves with people that they don't know that well. They're not comfortable. That's normal, right?'

We support the children's recommendations. We are convinced awareness-raising and training on the fundamental rights of children are crucial for the children, the adults, and the caseworkers. Without these, children's status as the subjects of rights is liable to remain nothing more than theoretical.

When informed of their fundamental rights, and thus, conscious of their right to participation, children are in a position to put these rights into action, to develop a critical awareness towards situations they experience, and to play an active role in their lives. During the group discussions, the positive effect of informing the children was considerable. Some children said they realized they had experienced injustices and that they had not been heard. They were involved in the development of this contribution, and we hope their contribution will lead to other children having implementation of their right to be heard as mandatory.

4. CONCLUSION

On 17 January 1979, on the occasion of the entry into force of the YPA and of the beginning of the International Year of the Child, the Youth Protection Committee wrote:

> Despite having the best laws and having good resources available, the application of these laws and the use of these resources remain largely dependent on the mental and psycho-social attitudes of those who use them. How do we view young people?[39]

More than 40 years later, these comments are still relevant, and obstacles continue to block the implementation of children's right to participation in their proceedings.

Children's fundamental rights must be understood as an inseparable package. Every action, intervention, or ruling in relation to a child, must be guided by the implementation of all rights in the CRC. And yet, it sometimes happens that we invoke implementation of one right in order

39 Above n. 4.

to justify infringement of another. In practice, according to the children's comments in these discussions, it appears that the right to protection is perceived in isolation, impervious to their other fundamental rights – including participation. Considering children solely through the prism of their vulnerability results in the erosion of their status as subjects of law.[40] This erosion is experienced by the people most directly concerned. The message conveyed is their inability to have an influence on the decisions concerning them, their environment, and their life.

In community social paediatrics, the child is the primary ally of the clinical team. They take the resources and time to create a trust-based relationship with the child and their family, for a better sharing of information on the sources of stress affecting them. This is done in order to understand their needs and learn about their strengths and interests. It is starting from these factors that the child guides the drawing up of the comprehensive action plan. The participation by the children and their families in the development of the action plan, and in its implementation, makes it possible to re-empower them to act, to have a positive influence on their life – a power of which they are often deprived.

The adults' perception – that they are responsible for assessment of a child's situation, for application of protection measures, or for decision-making in their best interests – has a major impact on the implementation of their right to participate. As a society, it is necessary to step back and take a new look at children, at the legitimacy attributed to their opinions, and at our role in making their status as subjects of law a reality. 'We have opinions, and they need to be listened to and taken it into account. Justice needs to be done for children.' (Anthony, 13 years of age.)

---

40 Above n. 9; J. Tobin, 'Understanding Children's Rights: A Vision beyond Vulnerability' (2015) 84 *Nordic J. Intl L.* 155, p. 166.

PHOTOVOICE AS A TOOL FOR INDIGENOUS CHILDREN'S PARTICIPATION IN THE JUSTICE SYSTEM

Fanny JOLICOEUR

1. INTRODUCTION

Over the past 50 years, social research has been interested in children's expression and participation.[1] A large number of child-centered research

---

1 I. CÔTÉ, K. LAVOIE, and R-P. TROTTIER-CYR, *La recherche centrée sur l'enfant. Défis éthiques et innovations méthodologiques*, Presses de l'Université Laval, Québec 2020, p. 2.

projects bear witness to their life experience and reality in various areas of their lives.[2]

But what about research in law? While social research has developed several methods for collecting children's views, the latter still remains to be developed in the field of law. This is particularly so when it involves offering a path to indigenous children for accessing the justice system.

Article 12 of the Convention on the Rights of the Child stipulates children must be able to express themselves freely on matters that concern them.[3] Beyond this principle, however, some challenges remain to putting this into practice.[4] In this sense, children's participation in the development of public policy poses methodological challenges, in particular, in an indigenous context. In the context of research efforts with indigenous children, how does one meet the imperatives of the research, while also ensuring that the approach is culturally safe? Ensuring that the approach is culturally safe means that the culture, values, and identity of the participants are valued and respected.[5]

This contribution presents a participatory research method that would appear to be particularly well adapted to this objective: *Photovoice*. Using photography and narration as a tool for expression,[6] this data-collection method might allow indigenous children to grasp legal concepts by meaningfully participating in their development, in order to articulate in their own way how they wish to be treated and heard.

2. *PHOTOVOICE*

2.1. ORIGIN AND PROCESS OF IMPLEMENTATION

First, the origin of *Photovoice* should be presented, along with the ways of implementing the various steps in this method. We will then see the principal means of undertaking data collection and analysis, based on

2 M. Dembele and I. Traoré, 'Enquêter avec et auprès des jeunes en difficulté en contexte africain: une démarche méthodologique par le bas' (2017) *Open Editions Journals*, p. 4. <journals.openedition.org/sejed/8443#text>.

3 United Nations Convention of the Rights of the Child, 20.11.1989, 1577 UNTS 3, Article 12.

4 Above n. 1, p. 5.

5 C. Lévesque, 'Promouvoir la sécurisation culturelle' (2015) 34(2) *R Droits et libertés*, p. 16.

6 C. Wang and M.A. Burris, 'Photovoice: Concept, Methodology and Use for Participatory Needs Assessment' (1997) 24(3) *Health Education & Behavior*, p. 369.

photographs taken by the participants. Following this, we look at the ethical challenges to bear in mind, both on the part of the researchers and also among the participants, who, through their engagement in a participatory community initiative, are also themselves co-investigators.

Photovoice is a qualitative and participatory research method for which photography constitutes the primary medium and basis for participants to express themselves. This method makes it possible to spark the empowerment of the participants and to bring about social change within their group or community.[7]

The *Photovoice* method is deployed starting from an identified problematic, lived, and recognized by a particular population. One part of this group is led to voluntarily capture images that they consider meaningful and that will contribute to bringing to light the elements that best depict that problematic and the means to be deployed in order to rectify it. After the photographs are taken, the participants are encouraged to express themselves orally or in writing, based on their images. The fruit of this collective work is subsequently disseminated throughout the community and among decision-makers, with a view to bringing about changes to the problem situation.

The *Photovoice* method includes data collection throughout the entire process, the central step of which is the group discussion that occurs following the selection of the photos by the participants.[8] Since the objective of the approach is to change the initial problematic situation, this discussion leads to another one, involving determination of the means that the group seeks to foster for making the work public.[9] Dissemination may be undertaken in a variety of ways, such as by means of an exhibition, a book, a video, or online distribution.[10]

There are a number of challenges for using *Photovoice* in respect of ethical implications. Indeed, the visual aspect that is central to this technique requires sound knowledge of the rules of ethics on the part of the researchers, but likewise by those participants who will be asked to take photos, some of which will have human beings as their subjects.[11]

---

7 L. Douville, et al., 'La démarche *Photovoice* à titre de outil de changement social auprès des jeunes de la rue' (2017) *Revue Intervention*, p. 45. <revueintervention.org/wp-content/uploads/2017/05/ri_145_2017.1_douville_et_al.pdf>.

8 Above n. 6, p. 369.

9 L.M. Gant, et al., 'Effects of Photovoice: Civic Engagement Among Older Youth in Urban Communities' (2009) 17(4) *Journal of Community Practice*, pp. 358, 361.

10 Ibid.

11 C. Mitchell, *Doing Visual Research*, SAGE Publications, London (UK) 2011, p. 21.

2.2. FROM AWARENESS-RAISING TO PARTICIPATION: THE OBJECTIVES GUIDING *PHOTOVOICE*

The group of researchers who practice *Photovoice* base themselves, closely or loosely, on the works of Caroline Wang and Mary Ann Burris. Their article '*Photovoice*: Concept, Methodology and Use for Participatory Needs Assessment', published in 1997, dealt with the health needs of Chinese women in the Yunnan region. Aiming to improve the social conditions 'by and for' the most directly concerned, Wang and Burris developed the *Photovoice* method, drawing on the principles of consciousness-raising pedagogy and action developed by the Brazilian educator, Paulo Freire.

In order to put together a narrative and visual tool enabling marginalized communities to express themselves through the medium of photography, the researchers articulate the following three principles:

> (1) capture and reveal – by means of photos – the strengths and concerns of individuals and communities; (2) by means of discussion groups among the participating photographers, spark a dialogue and critical knowledge concerning the issues, and personal community problems; and (3) connect with the authorities responsible for developing public policies.[12]

As with the works of Freire, the *Photovoice* approach, as proposed by Wang and Burris, is situated within a perspective of community-based participatory research, and is aimed at effecting changes based on the concerns of members of a given community.[13] In the final analysis, in addition to bringing about change for the collective community, the *Photovoice* approach seeks to increase the personal confidence of the participants, while making them keen to become engaged in their communities.[14]

While there is no question that the works of Wang and Burris continue to be a source of inspiration for *Photovoice* enthusiasts, researchers have been able to adapt this method as a function of the study population, the duration of the projects, the technological progress, the financial resources, and other contingencies particular to each research project.

---

12 Above n. 6; above n. 7.

13 E.D. Carlson, J. Engebretson, and R.M. Chamberlain, 'Photovoice as a Social Process of Critical Consciousness' (2006) 16(6) *Qualitative Health Research*, pp. 836, 841.

14 J. Hannay, et al., 'Combining Photovoice and Focus Groups' (2013) 44(3) *American J Preventive Medicine*, p. S215, DOI: <10.1016/j.amepre.2012.11.011>.

This also applies for the influence of the works of Freire in the implementation of *Photovoice*, onto which, over time, other schools of thoughts have been grafted. Indeed, while the objective of social transformation remains at the heart of the *Photovoice* approach, these days, implementation of these projects is undertaken in practice in a more horizontal way, and is more and more focused towards the principle of agency:[15] the role of the researcher or of 'the intellectual' tends to be more diffuse, and more egalitarian power relations are sought between the researcher and the participants.[16] In other words, marginalized people are no longer perceived solely as being victims of social structures, since increasingly, their capability to act on the world is acknowledged, independently of 'learned' persons to guide them in their steps toward better living conditions. The participants are perceived as co-investigators possessing a legitimate expertise.[17]

From among the examples of adaptation and development in the *Photovoice* method, we shall see in the following section that *Photovoice* makes it possible to create tools able to lead to social change, while being undertaken within the context of culturally safe research.

3. THE USE OF *PHOTOVOICE* WITH INDIGENOUS COMMUNITIES TO FOSTER A CULTURALLY SAFE RESEARCH APPROACH

Following this general overview of the *Photovoice* methodological process and of its origin and development, it is interesting to note that this method is particularly appropriate in the context of research projects bearing on legal issues directly affecting indigenous peoples.[18] Since it makes

---

15 L. Bachmann and S. Rodari, 'Analyser le travail social. Une approche intégrant l'agentivité et les rapports sociaux' (2014) 36(2) *R Pensée plurielle*, pp. 121, 130.

16 C. Guay and M. Thibault, 'Libérer les mots: pour une utilisation éthique de l'approche biographique en contexte autochtone' (2012) *Open Edition Journals* <journals.openedition.org/ethiquepublique/956>.

17 Ibid.

18 J.M. Shea, et al., 'Reflections from a Creative Community-Based Participatory Research Project Exploring Health and Body Image with First Nations Girls' (2013) 12(1) *Intl J Qualitative Methods*, p. 272; B. Bennett, et al., 'The Gaataae aabing Visual Research Method: A Culturally Safe Anishinaabek Transformation of Photovoice' (2019) 18 *Intl J Qualitative Methods*, p. 1; A. Goodman, M. Snyder, and K. Wilson, 'Exploring Indigenous youth perspectives of mobility and social relationships: A Photovoice approach' (2018) 62(3) *Géographe Can*, p. 314; H. Castleden,

egalitarian relations possible between the researcher and the participants and encourages the active participation of the latter at all stages of the project, we will see that when it is used to this end, *Photovoice* establishes favourable conditions for culturally safe research projects.[19] Lastly, we will highlight the advantages that *Photovoice* embodies with indigenous children, as well as the conditions for success to be able to facilitate the process with them.

3.1. PARTICIPATORY ACTION RESEARCH: A QUALITATIVE APPROACH FOR ELICITING THE VIEWPOINTS OF THE PERSONS PRIMARILY CONCERNED ON ISSUES RELATED TO THE LAW

As mentioned above, *Photovoice* falls within the lineage of community-based participatory research, aimed at development among marginalized population groups of the power to act, in an equal partnership with researchers.[20] The participants are invited to take part in all stages of the research (data collection, analysis, and dissemination), by collectively attempting to effect positive change, both for themselves and for the members of their community.[21] In her publication on participatory research, Marta Anadón summarizes the definition of participatory research in its various forms as follows:

> These types of research projects – participatory research, action research, collaborative research, research and training – are characterized by a process of knowledge production carried out in concert with the actors on the ground.

T. Garvin, and Huu-ay-aht First Nation, 'Modifying Photovoice for community-based participatory Indigenous research' (2008) 66(6) *Soc Science & Medicine*, p. 1393; L. Douville and M-P. Sylvestre, 'Saisir le regard de futures éducatrices autochtones sur la santé mentale à le aide de Photovoice' (2019) *Recherche qualitative*, <www.recherche-qualitative.qc.ca/documents/files/revue/hors_serie/HS-23/rq-hs23-douville-sylvestre.pdf>; G. Perrault-Sullivan, *Étude qualitative de la vision et des besoins des jeunes Inuit du Nunavik en matière de santé mentale et aperçu de la réponse fournie par les organismes du milieu, mémoire de maitrise en psychoéducation* (2015) Université du Québec à Trois-Rivières [unpublished].

19 Above n. 18.

20 B.A. Israel, et al., 'Review of Community-Based Research: Assessing Partnership Approaches to Improve Public Health' (1998) 19 *Annual Rev Public Health*, p. 173, DOI: <10.1146/annurev.publhealth.19.1.173>.

21 K. Charlebois, et al., 'The involvement of vulnerable people in participatory research in primary care: a literature review' (2014) 21(3) *Global Health Promotion*, p. 38, DOI: <10.1177/1757975913517123>.

> It has as a corollary the valuing of the knowledge of citizens, the highlighting of the potentials of the participants, and the strengthening among those involved of an awareness of their own abilities to spark and to oversee the action.[22]

Concerning participatory action research, *Photovoice* makes it possible, through images and narration, to delve deeper into social issues, including those that are linked to the law. Indeed, the techniques for the collection of qualitative data – more often used in social sciences – may be very fruitful for grasping the participants' opinions on legal issues that concern them. This idea is raised by Bernheim, who is of the view that the borrowing of qualitative methods brings benefits as much for the researchers as for the study population – inasmuch as, above and beyond its contribution in legal terms, the research becomes socially useful.[23] It is in this spirit of usefulness, of contributing to the debate within society, and of improvement in community life, that the *Photovoice* method may be mobilized by legal researchers. It therefore becomes possible to make use of this lever to raise issues directly impacting the rights of individuals, including the rights of indigenous children. The endeavours flowing from *Photovoice* may also culminate in changes in the law or in the administration of justice, making access to it easier. In view of its potential for social transformation, *Photovoice* constitutes in this sense a research method that tangibly offers improved access to justice for the individuals who participate in the methodology, as well as for the groups represented by these participants.

3.2. USE OF *PHOTOVOICE* WITH INDIGENOUS PEOPLE: ADVANTAGES AND ADAPTATIONS

As it recognizes the power, expertise, and indigenous knowledge in relationships that are meant to be egalitarian between the partners,[24]

---

22 M. Anadón, 'La recherche participative, une préoccupation toujours vivace' in Marta Anadón (Ed.), *La recherche participative: Multiples regards*, Presses de l'Université du Québec, Québec 2007, p. 1.

23 E. Bernheim, 'Prendre le droit comme un "fait social" – la sociologie du droit par et pour elle-même' in *Les cadres théoriques et le droit. Actes de la journée d'étude sur la méthodologie et l'épistémologie juridiques held in May 2012 in Cowansville, Québec*, Yvon Blais, QC 2012, p. 99.

24 N. Wallerstein and B. Duran, 'Community-Based Participatory Research Contributions to Intervention Research: The Intersection of Science and Practice to Improve Health Equity' (2010) 100(1) *American J Public Health*, p. S40.

community-based participatory research takes on its full applicability in decolonizing research.[25]

In addition to making culturally safe approaches possible, maintaining horizontal relationships, arousing the power to act, and to bring about social change,[26] visual research methodologies – including that of *Photovoice* – are particularly characterized by being 'respectful of orality as a traditional mode of transmission of indigenous knowledge'.[27] Indeed, the use of photography as a medium of expression has the benefit of giving the participants the opportunity to give oral expression to their ideas and concerns, starting from visual tools.[28] Like other creative and visual tools, the use of photography constitutes an interesting strategy for collecting the views of children and youth. Less intimidating than the standard semi-directive interview, the visual point of departure will foster the participants' reflexivity and contribute favourably to oral expression.[29]

The *Photovoice* method nevertheless requires some adaptations in order to be appropriate and to respect the principles of cultural safety in research with indigenous people.[30]

Developed over the course of the 1980s in New Zealand around care provided to the Maori,[31] the concept of cultural safety consists in being mindful of the culture, values, history, identity, and oppressions experienced by a people.[32] Cultural safety is aimed at strengthening and fostering cultural identity, while ensuring the safeguarding and protection of the culture and language.[33] One will say for example that

---

25 Above n. 18, J. M Shea, et al.

26 Above n. 18, G. Perrault-Sullivan, p. 30.

27 C. Guay, 'The legitimacy of Indigenous narrative in the development of social work knowledge' (2015) 45(2/3) *Recherches amérindiennes au Québec*, p. 15.

28 Above, n. 18, L. Douville and M-P. Sylvestre.

29 M. Braizaz, 'Proposer un photoreportage alimentaire à des préadolescentes: Montre-moi ce que tu manges', in I. Côté, K. Lavoie and R-P. Trottier-Cyr (Eds.), *La recherche centrée sur l'Enfant: défis éthiques et innovations méthodologiques*, Presses de l'Université Laval, Québec 2020, p. 278.

30 Above n. 18, L. Douville and M-P. Sylvestre, p. 275.

31 C. Lévesque, 'La sécurisation culturelle: moteur de changement social' (19.06.2017) *Commission d'enquête sur les relations entre les Autochtones et certains services publics* <www.cerp.gouv.qc.ca/fileadmin/Fichiers_clients/Documents_deposes_a_la_Commission/P-038.pdf>.

32 Above n. 5.

33 C. Guay, F. Jolicoeur, and L. Ellington (accepted for publication), 'Une gouvernance innue de protection de la jeunesse pour préserver et développer l'identité des enfants innus'. Actes du Colloque international, *La jeunesse au carrefour: entre famille, communauté, État et société*. Organized by ADAJ (Access to the Law and to Justice) in collaboration with the Partnership for research on parental separation and family reunification, held on 23.05.2019 and 24.05.2019 at the University of Montreal.

there is cultural safety 'when the indigenous people feel that they can have confidence in their care providers'[34] and that the latter value and respect their cultural identity. Better knowledge of these particularities on the part of social workers or researchers in an indigenous context contributes to simultaneous improvement of indigenous people's living conditions, as well as of the relationships between non-indigenous and indigenous people.[35] Moreover, engagement in community-based participatory research with indigenous people that includes the use of *Photovoice* poses its own ethical challenges.[36] Among these are the specific ways of conceiving the research and the role of each of the people involved. Clarification of the role of the researcher is fundamental in this regard, particularly when they are non-indigenous.[37] Therefore, the researcher must first acknowledge their origins, their own history, their cultural biases, and their standpoint. Donald describes this groundwork as follows:

> [E]thical relationality is an ecological understanding of human relationality that does not deny difference, but rather seeks to understand more deeply how our different histories and experiences position us in relation to each other.[38]

By way of example, Castelden and her colleagues, who undertook a research project with members of a First Nation in British Columbia, noted that the 'classic' *Photovoice* method as suggested by Wang and Burris was unsuitable for this population group, particularly with respect to the duration of the immersion in the field that was necessary for the building of a relationship of trust between the researchers and the participants:

> Wang's approach to Photovoice was initially planned for the Huu-ay-aht study. However, it quickly became apparent that the 'classic' Photovoice approach

34 First Nations of Quebec and Labrador Health and Social Services Commission, *Another Step Toward Self-Determination and Upholding the Rights of First Nations Children and Families: Protocol for Reforming First Nations Child and Family Services (CFSIC): Final Report*, Québec 2017, p. 24.

35 Above n. 32.

36 Assembly of First Nations Quebec-Labrador, 'First Nations in Quebec and Labrador's Research Protocol' (2014), *Comité d'éthique de la recherche pour les projets étudiants impliquant des êtres humains* <https://achh.ca/wp-content/uploads/2018/07/Protocol_FN-Research-Protocol-in-Labrador-and-Quebec.pdf>.

37 C. Guay, *Le savoir autochtone dans tous ses états: Regards sur la pratique singulière des intervenants sociaux innus de Uashat mak Mani-Utenam*, Presses de l'Université du Québec, Québec 2017, p. 22.

38 D. Donald, 'Indigenous Métissage: a decolonizing research sensibility' (2012) 25(5) *Intl J Qualitative Studies in Education*, p. 535, DOI: <10.1080/09518398.2011.554449>.

> was similar to the academic trend of doing 'parachute' research in Indigenous communities. In previous Photovoice studies, data were often collected in a few short weeks, whereas the data collection for this study extended for six months. This prolonged immersion in the field served to establish rapport and build trust.[39]

For research purposes with indigenous people, it thus becomes necessary to adapt the 'original' *Photovoice* method so that it may meet the requirements of cultural safety in research,[40] in particular by significantly investing in the creation of links with the participants and the members of the community. Establishment of these relationships will, among other things, mean taking the time that is needed during research fieldwork visits.

3.3. *PHOTOVOICE* WITH INDIGENOUS CHILDREN

Researchers are increasingly interested in the views of children and youth, so as to better understand their perspectives and the social phenomena that concern them. These young social actors would be in the best position to express, in their own words, their reality and that of their peers.[41] Indeed, 'many researchers who have directly investigated children and young people need to have high-level reflective skills'.[42] In this regard, Danic and her colleagues address the importance that should be given to the voices of youth and to the unique skills they have to account for their own reality as social actors, 'capable of acting and reacting to the situations that they encounter'.[43]

It is in this perspective that it is appropriate to implement concrete ways of understanding the opinions and aspirations of children and young people on the legal issues that concern them – provided that certain parameters are respected to ensure their well-being throughout the entire research process. Côté, Lavoie, and Trottier-Cyr highlight three

---

39 Above n. 18, H. Castleden, T. Garvin, and Huu-ay-aht First Nation, p. 1401.

40 L.R. Thomas, et al., 'Community-based participatory research in Indian country: Definitions, theory, rationale, examples, and principles' in *American Indian and Alaska Native Children and Mental Health: Development, Context, Prevention and Treatment*, ABC-CLIO, Santa Barbara 2011, p. 166.

41 Above n. 2.

42 Ibid.

43 I. Danic, J. Delalande, and P. Rayou, *Enquêter auprès d'enfants et de jeunes: objets, méthodes et terrains de recherche en sciences sociales*, Presses Universitaires de Rennes, Rennes 2006, p. 11.

considerations during research with children, 'namely recognition of the legitimacy of the child's point of view in knowledge construction, the empathy of the adults for the well-being of the young people, and respect for their agency'.[44]

Once again, those visual collection tools, the principles of which are associated with the conditions to be respected in research with children, will be of relevance for collecting the viewpoints of minors, particularly those of indigenous children. In this regard, Armagnague-Roucher and Rigoni attest to the ease with which visual methods can be developed with young people from more vulnerable groups, in the context of research undertaken by adults:

> [T]hey function as media for exchange adapted to the purpose of apprehending the reality of the children and (pre-)adolescents in a more empirical fashion, one that is less intimidating and less adult-centred. In certain areas, in particular among (pre-)adolescents who at times are doubtful if not critical towards the presence of the researcher, the role of the photographer makes it possible for the latter to occupy a role as witness, one that the young people accept more readily, since the researcher/photographer proposes a relationship of 'give-and-take'.[45]

The age difference between the researcher and the participants, and the flexibility in adapting to the needs and fears of the young people, would also have to be taken into consideration, in order to alleviate the power relations.[46]

A study conducted by Goodman, Snyder, and Wilson, interested in the point of view of young indigenous people, made it possible to cast some light on the most suitable means for collaborating with minors in a *Photovoice* approach.[47] The results identified by the research of Goodman and her collaborators underline how important it is to develop authentic relationships and the trust that the young people need to have in the researchers and the resource persons in order to foster their participation in *Photovoice*.[48] Thus, the importance of establishing bonds of trust is a

---

44 Above n. 1, p. 3.

45 M. Armagnague and I. Rigoni, 'Saisir le point de vue de l'enfant. Enquêter sur la participation socioscolaire des élèves migrants' (2016) *Recherche qualitative*, pp. 311–29 <www.recherche-qualitative.qc.ca/documents/files/revue/hors_serie/HS-20/rq-hs-20-armagnague-rigoni.pdf>.

46 Above n. 2, p. 8.

47 Above n. 18, A. Goodman, M. Snyder, and K. Wilson.

48 Ibid., p. 317.

key component for young people, even more so for indigenous children participating in *Photovoice*, whose viewpoint is under-represented.[49] This trust is won with time invested in the research process, but even more so through the quality of the relationship and the transparency with which information is passed on to the children.[50]

In short, the importance of developing a relationship of trust, of taking the time that needs to be invested on the ground in the research, respecting the views of the participants, establishing egalitarian relationships, and remaining flexible, are all considerations brought to the fore in the community action research that *Photovoice* is part of. The principles to be respected in research with children appear to be particularly in line with those of *Photovoice*, provided that the approach is adapted to the principles of cultural safety in research.

4. CONCLUSION

Use of the *Photovoice* method, while recent in the history of research, has many enthusiasts in the studies undertaken in collaboration with marginalized population groups from a variety of backgrounds. Despite this diversity, we have been able to identify the broad stages that, in general, mark the process around this method.

This contribution has also set out the participatory and visual dimension under which the *Photovoice* research method is pursued. This holds interesting potential for undertaking research projects in an indigenous context, provided that the adaptations necessary for cultural safety and the decolonization of research are made.

We have set out the compatibility of the *Photovoice* method within a context of research with indigenous children, whose perspectives will be expressed more easily through creativity and in relationships that are intended to be egalitarian with the adult researchers.

Finally, we have demonstrated the relevance of gathering the viewpoint of the people concerned when it comes to conducting research with indigenous children on issues that directly affect their rights. Indeed, children's rights would undoubtedly benefit from being imbued with the

49 Ibid.

50 S. Euillet, 'Enjeux psychologiques des supports utilisés en recherche auprès d'enfants accueillis en protection de l'enfance' (2017) 18 *Sociétés et jeunesses en difficulté*, p. 14 <http://journals.openedition.org/sejed/8287>.

vision that they have of them, as social actors 'bearers of a life experience that only they are able to express, having lived it, in words that are their own, but also words that are close to the lived reality'.[51] Indigenous children's perspectives can certainly enrich thinking about how to understand and build policies and institutions that care about their well-being. In this sense – due to its accessible, egalitarian, and democratic aspect, and its potential for ensuring cultural safety – the *Photovoice* method is seen to be an ideal research methodology for fostering better access to justice on the part of indigenous children.

51 Above n. 43, p. 7.

PART IV

CRITICAL REFLECTIONS ON CHILDREN'S ACCESS TO JUSTICE

THE RISKS OF UNANTICIPATED CONSEQUENCES FROM CHILDREN'S PARTICIPATION IN THE JUSTICE SYSTEM

Thierry MOREAU

1. INTRODUCTION

More than 30 years have passed since the signing of the Convention on the Rights of the Child (CRC). It has served as a basis for numerous demands and initiatives, among which several have to do with children's access to justice in cases concerning them.

The purpose of this contribution is to question the risks of seeing children's access to justice turn against them in order to better understand how to avoid these risks.[1]

---

[1] The French expression '*effet pervers*' (literally 'perverse effect') which is used in the French version of this text is difficult to translate into English. It means 'unanticipated consequences', 'pernicious effect', 'negative effect', 'undesirable effect' and 'counter-productive

The subject is vast and the question difficult. The following thoughts are necessarily fragmentary, in light of the space allotted to this contribution. They draw their inspiration principally from observation of the Belgian legal system, and to a lesser extent, of some other Western systems. They are built on both my practice as a lawyer and my research. The present contribution is by no means the last word on the topic. Its sole purpose is to contribute to the debate and analysis.

2. CHILDREN AT THE HEART OF A DIALECTICAL TENSION

The child is both *similar* and *different* from the adult. They are similar because they are a thinking and speaking human being. However, they are different because of their physical and mental characteristics, their lack of experience, their relationship to the world, the use of codes specific to them, etc. These factual differences change over the life of the child. In the first years of life, children find themselves in a position of weakness due to their dependence on adults, who need to cover many of their needs. Subsequently, the difference embodied in older teenagers may take on 'a negative image, one that is a little monstrous: too old to be cajoled, too young to be treated as an adult, they embarrass, provoke and frighten'.[2] Rousseau already stressed that childhood was the condition of humanity: we cannot be adults without having been children.[3] Childhood thus does not take the form of a succession of thresholds to be crossed in order to attain the perfect stage, that of adulthood. The (age-specific) stages through which children pass are just as perfect as adulthood, but different. The child 'is our fellow human – not only in the "becoming human" that they contain within themselves, but in their childhood as such'.[4] Just like adults, children have the right to be what they are. Their way of being in the world and their opinion are of the same value as those of the adult.

effect'. In French, *effet pervers* is where an agent, who intends to do their best, actually ends up achieving the worst, i.e. the opposite effect. It also refers to the effect obtained by one who consciously manipulates a system or a concept to seek the opposite of what he or she must achieve. In this contribution we will use the expression 'unanticipated consequences' but ask the reader to read this in the context of the French meaning.

2 A. Garapon, 'Les ambiguïtés du débat actuel sur les droits de l'enfant' in J. Rubellin-Devichi and M. Andrieux (Eds.), *Enfance et violence*, P.U.L., Lyon 1992, p. 165.

3 J.-J. Rousseau, *Emile: or, On Education*, Basic Books, New York 1979.

4 D. Youf, *Penser les droits de l'enfant*, P.U.F., Paris 2002, p. 22.

Nevertheless, from a legal point of view, up to the end of the 20th century, this approach was not the one that prevailed. Children were considered a different kind of being. The incapacity to exercise their rights and take legal action was the rule. Recognition of the rights of children overturned this perspective. The child is no longer confined within this difference, but nor are they considered in legal terms as the adult they are not.[5] On the one hand, by virtue of their common humanity, children and adults are equal before the law. Thus, minors and adults are subjects of fundamental rights, and the exercise of these rights must be recognized in an equivalent manner. On the other hand, common humanity is the basis of respect for the differences between the two categories, which may take several forms from a legal point of view: sometimes to strengthen, for the benefit of the child, the fundamental rights recognized to adults, sometimes to make them more flexible, sometimes to institute particular rights specific to the child. Common humanity is also the limit of the field of differences. Indeed, shutting a child into a judicial system that is so different, that their guaranteed rights are no longer respected is as much a failure to recognise their rights as a failure to respect their differences.

From this perspective, the dialectical tension is at its height between the child who is both the same and different from an adult. The assertion of children's rights continually puts to the test the fragile balance that is built between the two poles of the tension: not to let them take on excessive burdens, but neither prevent them from being an actor in their life; not leave them with no authority, but likewise not require them to remain silent; not crush them under responsibility, but not take them as someone who is totally incapable; not let them do everything, but not dash any and all initiative, etc. However, many parents and field practitioners did not wait for the signing of the Convention to broach and deal with children by taking them as human beings who have the same worth as adults. With the CRC, the novelty is that this approach, respectful of the tension, has become a legal requirement.

3. THE RISKS OF UNANTICIPATED CONSEQUENCES OF CHILDREN'S ACCESS TO THE JUSTICE SYSTEM

Children's rights are of a *sui generis* character since they have been designed and recognized by the democracy of adults, in which they do

5 See J. Korczak, *Comment aimer un enfant*, R. Laffont, 2006, p. 159.

not participate. Yet it is indisputable that – because of their position – adults have a perspective oriented towards the needs of youth, towards the problems that youth encounter, and towards the solutions to bring to them. They thus do not necessarily address these issues like young people would. For the latter, the priorities are not always those adopted by adults.[6] From a legal point of view, children's rights appear conferred by the adult world onto children. For this reason, they appear above all as a program aimed at adults, rather than as an instrument entrusted to children. Children's rights are thus primarily a prohibition on adults to educate and intervene with regard to children in any way, to pursue any end.

As discussed above, recognizing children's rights rests on a willingness to give them a role as actors, respecting their particularities. However, as the following demonstrates, formal recognition alone is not sufficient to eliminate the unanticipated consequences and the phenomena of instrumentalization by which children's access to justice might become the means for pursuing purposes other than improvement of the condition of children and their development. Particular diligence and commitment on the part of adults is necessary to ensure that they benefit children.

The conferred nature of children's rights raises an initial provocative question with regard to the relationship between children and justice. When looking to respect children's specificities, are legal proceedings the most appropriate process when children's rights are called into question, threatened, or violated? Might respecting children have the corollary of inventing new methods of conflict resolution, or favouring some that are too neglected today? Holding to a traditional approach to justice is perhaps the first perverse effect present in the relations between children and justice. Indeed, justice is an adult construction; it may well be an illusion to believe that it can truly become child-friendly. Would it be better to adapt a mechanism for the child that has not been conceived for them, or to create a new one that really focuses on the child? There is a certain urgency to reflect on this issue.

Currently, the issue of the unanticipated consequences of children's access to justice is reflected mainly in the context of legal proceedings around two fundamental requirements. On the one hand, the child must be in a position to enforce their rights, both substantive and procedural. On the other hand, they must be able to occupy a place as an actor on the

---

6 On this point see C. Moreau and Th. Moreau, 'Children's Voices on Their Right to be Heard in the Field of Child Protection in Belgium (*Communauté française*): Highlighting of Blind Spots Regarding the Place and Role of the Parents', in this volume.

legal scene, where they are an equivalent to an adult, without having to be treated like a mini-adult to be a full litigant.

These questions are particularly complex because of the different forms that the place of a child in the justice system can take. Thus, depending on the case, they may be the object at stake in the proceeding; the witness to an event; the victim of an act; or the author of the latter, whether this act constitutes an infraction or not. They can access the proceeding in different capacities: taking legal action as a complainant; being sued as a respondent or defendant; being heard in order to give their opinion in proceedings concerning them; being called as a witness to report on what they saw and heard, etc. It is therefore not possible to fully and exhaustively address the unanticipated consequences that threaten each of these forms of access to justice for children. Only a few specific questions will be addressed.

3.1. THE CHILD'S VOICE IN THE JUSTICE SYSTEM

The idea that a judicial decision concerning a child may only be made if they have been heard, is increasingly taken as a given. If, however, like all human beings, children have the right to access justice in order to make their voice known, the justice system must still be able to fully respect their specificities. However, it is not certain that, to date, children's access to justice allows them to bring their own rationality and differing relationship to the world into the courtroom. Justice mechanisms have primarily undergone procedural transformations to organize the gathering of children's voices. In terms of substantive rights, little change has been observed. It follows that the collection of the child's view does not guarantee that the object of the debates and the judgment will ultimately be the respect of their rights. It is not uncommon for the child's word to serve other interests. This is the case, for example, when in a parental conflict, the hearing of the child is used by the judge as a means of investigation to discover hidden aspects relating to the family, rather than to seek to understand the specific sentiments and rationality with which the child perceives their situation in this conflict, in order to take them into account in the decision.

There is also a danger in taking the child's word literally and interpreting it as an adult's word. A child's language is unique to them, in particular because they are in a period of learning and discovery of both its content and its functions. Moreover, the relationship of the interpreter to the world is not that of the child. Judicial authorities have an obligation to take children's voices seriously, which means going beyond the words spoken. They have a responsibility to question the meaning of children's views, at the risk of not hearing what they really mean. Thus, 'I no longer want to see my father' may have multiple meanings when coming from a child, some of which may paradoxically indicate a need to see him again or a call for him to take action. A similar phenomenon can be observed in the field of juvenile delinquency. Extrajudicial measures, such as mediation, often rest on contracts entered into between the child and adult victims. This contractualization process can lead to a failure to take into account the weak position of the child if specific provisions are not implemented to restore the balance and respect the differences that, in civil law, the minor is not able to enter into a contract.

The child's voice can also be instrumentalized by being used by the legal system for purposes that it was not intended to be used for. This concerns, in particular, the problem of using their voice as evidence in court when it is based on the belief that the truth would come from the mouths of children. Bensoussan and Rault recall that:

> If the child is telling 'their' truth, that does not mean that they are telling 'the' truth. And we have had to examine a great many children whose stories have been induced and suggested, either by the anxious solicitude of those around them, or by the large number of extraordinarily badly conducted and suggestive domestic interrogations. This child is obviously convinced that they experienced what they recounted (translated by the author).[7]

This raises the question of the use of expert opinions about the credibility of the child's view as a means of evidence in criminal proceedings in matters of sexual abuse of minors. The developers of these methods recalled that they were designed to assess the validity of certain tests used by psychologists and not to determine whether, in legal proceedings, the word of the child victim was more believable than that of the perpetrator. They also recalled their limited reliability, with the error rate typically ranging between 15% and 35%. The risk is thus to bring the child to a place where they do not want to be, as reflected in these words of a young girl that I heard a few years after she was the subject of such an expertise: 'I sent my father to prison. They didn't get it. I was speaking for mom not against him'.

Another risk of an undesirable effect that the collection of the child's voice in court can produce is that of transforming it into a decision. This

---

[7] P. Bensoussan and F. Rault, *La dictature de l'émotion. La protection de l'enfant et ses dérives*, Belfond, Paris 2002, pp. 233 ff. Along the same lines, see the contributions of Y.-H. Haesevoets and P.-H. Mambourg, in M. Sereno, *Comment priver un enfant de son père*, Editions Jeunesse et Droit, Liège 2009, p. 380.

process is like asking the child for solutions that responsible adults are unable to find, or do not dare to take. It is obviously difficult to assess, depending on the case, if it is necessary to follow the opinion expressed by the child, or whether, as adults, it is necessary to distance oneself from this opinion in order to allow better respect for their rights. The *Hokkanen v. Finland* judgment of the European Court of Human Rights illustrates the complexity of the issue. A father had entrusted his child to the maternal grandparents after the death of his wife because he was not well. Later, when he wanted to get the child back, the grandparents objected and even disappeared with her for several years. A majority of the judges of the European Court of Human Rights 'reached the conclusion that the 10-year-old child had become sufficiently mature to have her opinion taken into account and that as a consequence visits against her will should not be allowed'.[8] The child's view was thus held to be the sole criterion determining her best interest. Other judges of the Court nevertheless underlined that the child's word should have been put into perspective with her right to live with her father, taking into account the influence of the grandparents and the fact that they had deprived her of contact for several years with the one who had, through the action of time, become a stranger to her.[9] In such a situation, the authority is faced with two options, each of which has legitimacy. On the one hand, the fact that the child alone will bear the burden of the decision in the future may justify following the path that the child says they prefer. On the other hand, the child is in a particular situation where they must both exercise their rights with regard to what they are experiencing *hic* et *nunc* and, at the same time, discover all the substance of these rights while ignoring the unknown of what the respect of these rights can reveal.

3.2. A CREDIBLE JUSTICE

Currently, the courtroom is made more accessible to children in some areas than in others that concern them just as much. For a long time now, children have had a place within proceedings where they are prosecuted for having breached the criminal law, or because they are the object of a protective intervention. Since the end of the 20th century, children may

---

8 *Hokkanen v. Finland*, No. 19823/92, §61, ECHR 1994, <https://hudoc.echr.coe.int/eng#{%22itemid%22:[%22001-57911%22]}>.

9 Ibid., partly dissenting opinion of Judge De Meyer, joined by Judges Russo and Jungwiert.

be a party or heard in proceedings addressing their parentage, housing, emancipation, health, schooling, access to the territory of the country, employment, and so on. However, it is not enough for the child to be able to express their opinion in court; their opinion must also be taken into account. From the right to speak comes a right to a response which must be effective, comprehensive and accessible, which is not always the case. For example, in family matters the child is often heard by the judge, but the latter addresses the judgment only to the parents, who are the sole parties in the case. The child receives no personal response and does not know what has been done with their word. They will only know what their parents tell them. The obligation to institute the most child-friendly option, one that implies researching the best interest of the minor, is thus far from being encountered. Quite different would be the formula which would consist, for example, in seeing the judge write to the young person, in parallel with the judgment, a document explaining the points of the decision which concerns them by explaining to them, in understandable language, how they took their word into consideration. Another problem is the lack of recourse available to the child if they discover that their word has been misinterpreted or has been used for a purpose other than that for which they entrusted it.

It is also much more difficult for children to make their voice heard in court if they ask uncomfortable questions. They are then confronted with certain principles of law, such as the inability to take legal action, which confines them to a different status. Yet these questions are often of great relevance. This is the case for certain violations of their fundamental rights which find their sources in poverty and inequalities, in their poor educational conditions, in discrimination, in flawed social policies, etc. Quite often, either the judge declares themselves not competent to rule on these questions and refers them to politics, or they decide that the children do not have the capacity to address the judge in this regard. Under these conditions, is it really credible in the eyes of children to claim that they all have the same rights if it is not possible for them to ask the courts to guarantee them in practice? Young people are likewise more sensitive to certain realities, and envisage them from a whole new angle, the legitimacy of which adult justice is not always ready to acknowledge. The climate issue is an excellent example. For young people, this is a vital reality. More than adults, they sense that they might be living the end of the world. They see the problem with new approaches that challenge the traditional legal perspective. Even if the justice system often did not hear their appeals, it nevertheless seems to be starting a turnaround, of which the judgment of the Supreme Court of Colombia of 5 April 2018 is a good illustration.[10] Following the action of 25 children assisted by the NGO Dejusticia, the Court recognized the Amazon as a subject of law and obliged the authorities to create an intergenerational pact for the life of the Colombian Amazon. In Europe, on 7 September 2020, six young Portuguese people, including several minors, filed a complaint against 33 States before the European Court of Human Rights on the grounds that they do not respect their commitments relating to the climate and thus violate Articles 2 (right to life), 8 (respect for private and family life) and 14 (non-discrimination) of the European Convention on Human Rights. On November 13, 2020, the Court decided to treat the request as a priority, thus demonstrating to the children its willingness to take their requests seriously.[11]

3.3. THE RETURN TO CRIMINAL JUSTICE

If the recognition of the rights of the child has helped to develop forms of justice more adapted to children within the framework of the social reaction to juvenile delinquency (mediation, restorative justice, educational regime, etc.), paradoxically, they also serve to support a movement that considers it unrealistic to hold children as irresponsible people that need educating, which imputes greater criminal responsibility to the child and which establishes more severe penalties.[12]

In this approach, contrary to what has been observed in other fields, similarity takes precedence over difference and expropriates the minor of his or her specificities. It entails the following syllogism: everyone who exercises their rights is responsible for their actions; the minor exercises more and more rights; therefore the minor must be held responsible for his or her actions, and in particular for the acts of delinquency of which he or she is guilty. If they are responsible, they must therefore – like adults – be subject to a social reaction that is built on the incriminated action and around the concept of punishment. Recognition of minors' rights thus diminishes the distance that separates them from adults, which makes it possible to justify the recourse to sanctions comparable to those applied to adults.

---

10 The text of the decision, <https://cortesuprema.gov.co/corte/index.php/2018/04/05/corte-suprema-ordena-proteccion-inmediata-de-la-amazonia-colombiana/>.

11 *Duarte Agostinho and Others v. Portugal and 32 other States*, No. 39371/20, § IV, ECHR 2020, <http://hudoc.echr.coe.int/fre/?i=001-206535>.

12 See D. Kaminski, 'Juger le fait, juger la personne … ou échapper à ce dilemme?' (2001) 209 *J.D.J.*, pp. 8 ff.

The minor's place in the process is particularly illustrative of this potential for drift. Indeed, the minor has always had access to justice when he or she was prosecuted for having committed an offense but since the beginning of the twentieth century, in many States, he or she has reported to a special judge who applied a paternalistic and educational type of justice. Since this judge sought the best for the child, procedural safeguards were deemed not to be very necessary. The absence of these guarantees has been questioned by those who campaigned for the recognition of the rights of the child due to numerous abuses.[13] They argued that procedural guarantees were fundamental rights that should be recognized for minors, regardless of the model of justice, confirmed by Article 40, §2 of the CRC. At the same time, however, court decisions have emerged, justifying the use of security-oriented practices or the introduction of more severe sanctions on the grounds that the child has more guarantees to ensure the defense of their rights. Such use of guarantees is, however, improper in view of their nature. They are intended firstly to be a shield serving the individual who is the object of intervention. Here, they are used as a means of raising the tolerance threshold by admitting measures previously deemed unacceptable.[14] The paradox is that, in a way, minors would have a better fate if these guarantees were not given to them. The instrumentalization is all the greater since, without a massive investment to give them consistency, guarantees can be little more than ink on paper where the measures are real and very concrete. The recognition of guarantees therefore represents a lower cost in view of the considerable advances which benefit from security and punitive approaches.

4. THE BEST INTERESTS OF THE CHILD AS BULWARK AGAINST UNANTICIPATED CONSEQUENCES: FROM A VAGUE AND BLURRED CONCEPT TO THE REQUIREMENT OF METHODOLOGICAL RIGOR

The best interests of the child is a central concept when it comes to children and law. However, the recognition of the rights of the child has radically transformed it.

---

13 B.S. Alper, 'L'affaire Gault: une mise à l'épreuve du tribunal de la jeunesse' (1971–72) *Rev. dr. pén. crim.*, pp. 769–97; C.J.E.F., Le nouvel ordre protecteur, Brussels 1981; F. Tulkens and Th. Moreau, *Le droit de la jeunesse en Belgique. Aide, assistance et protection*, Larcier, Brussels 2000, pp. 279 ff.

14 J. Carbonnier, 'Effectivité et ineffectivité de la règle de droit' (1958) *Année sociologique*, p. 17.

Previously, the best interests of the minor was a notion that was characterized by its lack of precision, its ubiquity, and its flexibility.[15] This variable-content concept made it possible to correlate decisions to an average type of individual, behaviour, or situation.[16] The interest of the child was presented as a general principle of law which referred to normality without receiving any legal content. It was a simple container in which the magistrate placed the content they determined with a discretion that could border on arbitrariness. Based on a pure assessment of fact, this content could not be subject to any legality review. For this reason, the child's best interests could even be invoked in order to dismiss respect for the law or for the fundamental rights of the child.[17]

The recognition of the rights of the child marked the transition from a substantive to a functional concept. Far from being mutually exclusive, *children's rights* and the *child's best interests* present two sides of the same coin, reflecting the dialectical tension between the child as the same as and different to adults. The interests of the child are therefore no longer presented as hidden content that some would have, more than others, the capacity to discover, but as a concrete method to be implemented by those who are in charge of the child as part of a collective research process. For any problematic situation, there is therefore not only one solution that would correspond with the best interests of the child. The latter appears rather as a *way of thinking and acting* in accompanying a child on the uncertain path of their existence and their care.

Placed at the apex of the CRC, Article 3 makes of the primacy of the child's best interests a paramount consideration in all situations concerning them. It thus indicates that the first function of the best interests of the child is to be a *substantive right*. It is the right of the child to see their rights being respected.[18] The child's best interests can therefore no longer be the ground invoked to justify decisions which deviate from the respect of the children's rights. The interest of the child, understood as a substantive right is, on the one hand, the affirmation of the need for a different legal treatment of the child compared to the adult and, on the

---

15 F. Ost, *Entre droit et non-droit: l'intérêt*, Publications of Facultés Universitaires Saint-Louis, Brussels 1990, p. 185.

16 M. van de Kerchove, '*A propos d'une clôture*', *Dix ans ... devant soi*, Ed. du Jeune Barreau, Liège 1989, pp. 230–31.

17 See above n. 13, F. Tulkens and Th. Moreau, pp. 1006, 1021 ff.; above n. 15, p. 74.

18 See, Committee on the Rights of the Child, General Comment No. 14 [2013]: on the right of the child to have his or her best interests taken as a primary consideration (Art. 3, para. 1), UN Doc. CRC/C/GC/14, §4.

other hand, the obligation not to impose differential treatment on the child beyond what is necessary, at the risk of no longer treating them as a human being.

The second function of the best interests of the child is to be a *principle of interpretation* compelling the authorities to respect children's specificities and to take them into account in the implementation of children's rights. Both at the level of substantive rights and at the level of procedural rights, the interests of the child require appropriate implementation, which is perfectly reflected by the expression 'child friendly'.[19] For example, this principle may sometimes lead to removing or adjusting guarantees considered essential for adults, and sometimes lead to strengthening them. It must also guide the choices that have to be made in the event of conflicts of rights or in the situations to which the rights of the child do not provide a clear answer. This function reflects that the method still requires discretionary interpretation on the part of the adult. Nevertheless, this discretion is considerably reduced by the first function which invites one to retain an interpretation which, on the one hand, comes as close as possible to the spirit which is deduced from the rights of the child and, on the other, allows one to return as quickly as possible to a situation where all the rights of the child are respected. In addition, this interpretation function invites responsible adults to regularly question their interpretation when their intervention extends over a certain period of time and to respond to questions from the child, their parents or other stakeholders.

The third function is to be a multifaceted *rule of procedure*, underlining in this way the co-constructed aspect of the content given to the notion. First of all, it imposes on the person whose mission it is to make a decision concerning the child to explain their conception of what is most beneficial for the child, the assessment criteria selected and the articulation made between the interests of the child and the other primordial values with which the best interests of the child are balanced.[20] Then, this procedural dimension requires the participation of all parties involved, and in particular that of the child and the parents, in the decision-making process

19 See, Guidelines of the Committee of Ministers of the Council of Europe on Child-friendly Justice adopted by the Committee of Ministers of the Council of Europe on 17.11.2010, <www.coe.int>.

20 In this regard, it is important to note that in Article 3 of the CRC it is clearly specified that the best interests of the child shall be a primary consideration (and not the paramount consideration) in all decisions concerning children. The only instance where the best interests of the child are adopted as the paramount consideration, and not as one of several, is the adoption scenario referred to in Article 21 of the Convention.

and in the debate which will lead to the decision. Lastly, this procedural dimension requires the implementation of a maximum of investigations to fuel the debate and make the most informed decision possible. It also gives the various actors concerned the right to request investigations from the authorities.

Considered as a method, the best interests of the child appears as a juridical effective bulwark against the unanticipated consequences that may threaten the recognition of the rights of the child – for two reasons in particular. On the one hand, the obligation to respect the three functions makes a certain control of legality possible, because of the named character of the rights. Any decision or practice which, by formally invoking the child's best interests, violates their rights may be subject to censure. On the other hand, the primacy granted to the child's best interests refers the adults back to their responsibilities and highlights that the rights of the child cannot be fully guaranteed without their commitment. They must give themselves the time, energy, competence and human and material resources so that their intervention allows, with the greatest rigor, the implementation of the method which consists of, on the one hand, preventing an interpretation from being given to the interests of the minor that is incompatible with respect for their rights and, on the other hand, seeking the path that best optimizes the rights recognized to the child.

5. CONCLUSION

As may be seen, recognizing the right of the child to have access to justice raises certain questions and is not without risk. In order for it to be advantageous for the child, access to justice cannot be conceived without a concrete, massive and radical commitment on the part of adults to make of it an effective instrument for the protection of their rights. One of the forms that this commitment must make is less often highlighted. It is about methodological rigour in respect of rights. The latter constitutes, without doubt, the most evolved form of the child's best interests.

CONCLUDING REMARKS ON CHILDREN'S ACCESS TO AND PARTICIPATION IN JUSTICE

Adeline Gouttenoire

From all the rich contributions in this volume, it emerges first of all that the participatory rights of minors are now enshrined and firmly anchored on international as well as national foundations. The right of the child to participate in decisions that concern them is now implemented in most countries to varying degrees and in different ways. This diversity in the implementation of participatory rights, which sometimes borders on inequality, can be seen at various levels.

The child's right to be heard differs according to their age and, above all, according to whether or not they are capable of 'discernment' or capable of forming their own views. In my opinion, only discerning minors should participate because otherwise children risk being manipulated and making statements they do not understand, and which could be turned against them. In particular, in the context of child protection, when the minor is not capable of discernment, thought must be given to autonomous and independent representation of the child's interests because, in most cases, there is a conflict of loyalty between the child and their parents or between the child and their foster family or the structure that assumes their care.

Nor are the participatory rights of the child the same depending on the proceedings in which they are applied or the position of the child in the proceedings. The participation of the child is obviously different depending on whether they are a party or not, and therefore legally capable or not. In the latter case, the child's hearing is more important because it is their only means of participating in the proceedings.

When the child is the subject of criminal proceedings, it is no longer a question of mere participation, but of a charge that could lead to a conviction. Given the age of the child concerned, a specialized overall regime must be put in place, from the beginning to the end of the procedure, including the phase of implementing the sanction. However, this specialization remains fragmented and is even declining.

When the child is a victim of criminal offences, there is sometimes confusion between the child's testimony and their opinion, and this confusion is also found in relation to the child at risk in the context of child protection. The child victim must be protected from the procedure and measures aimed at discovering the truth, because this objective cannot override the best interests of the child, which do not always lie in knowing the truth and condemning the perpetrator at all costs. The minor should at least be able to give their opinion on certain aspects of the criminal procedure. Depending on the legal context, this may include the public nature of the proceedings or the question of damages. In the context of child protection, a distinction must be made between the participation of the minor, including silent participation if they so wish, and the hearing of the minor.

When the child is concerned by the separation of their parents, it is imperative that the child expresses only their opinion and does not serve as a witness. Manipulation of the child by the parents must be avoided, of course, but also by the judge, who might be tempted to use the child to gain insight into the family situation.

This diversity implies adapting the implementation of the child's participatory rights, which in turn explains the complexity and even the disparity of the practices.

There are, however, certain constant features. The first is the necessary specialization of the child's interlocutors at all stages and the need for personalized support for the child throughout the procedure. A certain unity in this support is imperative to avoid the child being lost in the face of a multitude of stakeholders.

For the right to participate in decisions that concern them to be effective, a balance must be sought in order to provide support to the child without lapsing into paternalism. Yet, it would be dangerous to consider the child as an active subject of law without nuance, at the risk of placing too much responsibility on them.

While the child's right to participate in decision-making is enshrined, the child is not a decision-maker. The opposite could be dangerous for them, even if it can be considered that on certain points and issues, they could be recognized as having the capacity to decide or at least to choose between several alternatives. If the child is not a decision-maker, they should be made aware of this, and it should be explained to them who is deciding and why. It is essential to be transparent to the child about the weight of their voice. They must be fully informed, because they cannot give a useful opinion if they do not know all the elements of the context of their hearing, but also of the measures that are possible or not, and of the people who will have access to what they have said.

In conclusion, it is fundamental that the exercise of the child's right to be heard should always be something positive and never negative. The presumption that the child's participation is in their best interests must be reversed; the minor must be given the right to remain silent. It is important to educate all children to exercise their rights, but also their parents and teachers. The right to be heard must be mastered by the child. It must also be harmonised, with common principles, even if adaptations must be possible. An important common principle consists of taking the time to listen to the child.

www.ingramcontent.com/pod-product-compliance
Ingram Content Group UK Ltd.
Pitfield, Milton Keynes, MK11 3LW, UK
UKHW021827100926
8556IPUK00003B/200

9 781839 701979